Published by:
Santa Monica Press LLC
P.O. Box 850
Solana Beach, CA 92075
1-800-784-9553
www.santamonicapress.com
books@santamonicapress.com

Printed in China

Santa Monica Press books are available at special quantity discounts
when purchased in bulk by corporations, organizations, or groups.
Please call our Special Sales department at 1-800-784-9553.

ISBN-13 978-1-59580-110-4

Publisher's Cataloging-in-Publication data

Names: Lawler, Ralph A., author. | Epting, Chris, 1961-, author. | Walton, Bill, 1952-,
foreword author. | Paul, Chris E., contributor. | Rivers, Glenn, contributor.
Title: Bingo ! Forty years in the NBA / Ralph Lawler; with Chris Epting; foreword by
Bill Walton; introduction by Chris Paul; afterword by Doc Rivers.
Description: Solana Beach, CA: Santa Monica Press, 2022.
Identifiers: ISBN: 978-1-59580-110-4 (paperback) | 978-1-59580-779-3 (ebook)
Subjects: LCSH Lawler, Ralph A. | Sportscasters--United States--Biography. | Sports-
-History--20th century. | Sports--History--21st century. | Los Angeles Clippers
(Basketball team) | National Basketball Association. | BISAC BIOGRAPHY &
AUTOBIOGRAPHY / Sports | SPORTS & RECREATION / Basketball
Classification: LCC GV742.42 .L39 2022 | DDC 070.4/49796092--dc23

Cover and interior design and production by Future Studio

Cover illustration by filipfoto

PHOTO CREDITS:
xviii (top): Photo by Nathaniel S. Butler/NBA via Getty Images
xviii (bottom), xxvii (bottom) , xxxii (top), xxxii (bottom), xxxiv (top), xxxv (bottom),
    xxxvi (bottom): Photos by Andrew D. Bernstein/NBA via Getty Images
xxx (top): Photo by Jeff Gross/Getty Images Sport via Getty Images
xxxvii (top): Photo by Juan Ocampo/NBA via Getty Images
xxxviii (bottom): Photo by Harry How/Getty Images Sport via Getty Images

DEDICATION

This book is dedicated to the folks
who have made my life worth living.

First, for my wife, Jo,
without whom there would have been no career worth a mention.

For all basketball fans and the fans of life.
We have all taken separate, yet fascinating journeys
to reach exactly where we are today.

And finally, to the Ralph W. Lawler who inspired me,
and to the Ralph W. Lawler II who I hope to have inspired.

CONTENTS

THIRD QUARTER: BANK SHOTS

FOURTH QUARTER: MY FAVORITE PICK-AND-ROLL DUO

The U.S. involvement in World War II started in 1941, stripping professional basketball of the majority of its players. Able-bodied athletes were drafted into the military, and virtually all sports teams were left severely short-handed.

Over the years, pro hoop teams played in the loosely structured National Basketball League, the Midwest Basketball Conference, and the American Basketball League. Black teams had played White teams over the years, but the teams had been either all White or all Black. About the only quality athletes to avoid the military draft were those exempted because they were working in essential jobs, such as building wartime equipment at the transformed automotive plants in Detroit. Those workers were a mixture of Blacks and Whites.

The 1942–1943 National Basketball League season brought about a remarkable change. Sid Goldberg, an innovative owner of the NBL team in Toledo, Ohio, raided the factories and brought Black athletes into the previously all-White National Basketball League. The team in Chicago did the same. The players would work in the factory by day and play basketball at night. This was eight years before the yet-to-be-born National Basketball Association would be integrated.

The end of the obscene NBA color line in 1950 was great for everyone except the Harlem Globetrotters. They no longer had the prime pipeline to the best Black players in the country. The NBA could simply out-bid the Globetrotters, and out-bid them they did. Team owner Saperstein adroitly re-molded the traveling Trotters, emphasizing their fun-filled antics over traditional basketball competition. They could still play the game at a high level, but realized they could sell more tickets around the world with their theatrics rather than just their athletics. Every now and then, though, they would play a foe a little more formidable than their barnstorming rivals, the purposefully inept Washington Generals.

On April 2, 1956, a basketball double-header was played at Madison Square Garden in New York City, featuring the Harlem Globetrotters against a team of legitimate college all-stars and Olympians-to-be. This was the first of an eighteen-game exhibition series between the two teams. The college stars were led by future Basketball Hall of Famer and NBA champion Tommy Heinsohn. In today's NBA, there is endless talk about "load management." But that day/

night double-header featured the same players on both teams competing twice in full-length games on the same day. Each team played only
nine players, and the Trotters won both games.

Dad and I were excited when the NBA had its first national television contract in 1953, on the long-defunct Dumont Network. The
games were on Saturday afternoons for thirteen straight weeks. TV
was new in our house, and these games were a must-watch for Pop
and me. My dad and I would huddle in front of the fifteen-inch black-
and-white screen and marvel with wide eyes at the skill and shooting

TIME OUT George Mikan

George Mikan was a giant of a man when he entered the pro league
in 1948 out of DePaul University in Chicago. He stood six foot ten
and weighed 245 pounds. His size was unmatched. He led the Lakers to repeated championships and was an unstoppable offensive
force in the early NBA.

During the 1950–1951 season, Minneapolis Laker coach John
Kundla would station the young Mikan just outside the six-foot-wide
foul lane near the basket. It was easy to lob the ball into him, and
he would then turn and score an unstoppable lay-up or a short hook
shot with either his right or left hand. Big George led the league in
scoring at 28 points a game, almost 7 points more than anyone else
in the league. He was absolutely dominating the sport at the offensive end. It was the third straight year that Mikan, by then known as
"Mr. Basketball," led the league in scoring. Think of it this way—when
Mikan was averaging 28 points a game, NBA teams of the day were
scoring only 84 points a game. That was 33 percent of the points
teams were scoring in a game in the day. That would compute to
something like 36 points a game in today's higher-scoring NBA.

The easy-score strategy and the Lakers' two titles in three years
led the league to seek out ways to keep teams from planting a big
man at the rim where he could score so simply. Prior to the 1951–
1952 season, the league widened the free throw lane, or "key,"
from six feet to twelve feet. The three-second rule in the lane would
keep the game's giants from simply taking office at the rim for the
easy scores.

The move was effective. Mikan would never again led the
league in scoring. The widened lane dropped his per-game scoring

prowess of George Yardley and Paul Arizin, the size of the gigantic George Mikan and Neil Johnston, and the passing and dribbling skills of Bob Cousy and Bob Davies. The great Marty Glickman described the action featuring Ed Macauley, Dolph Schayes, Ray Felix, and so many others. It was the beginning of the NBA's sometimes halting rise to relevance. We loved the pro game from first sight. Little did I know that, in less than twenty-five years, I would have my foot in the NBA door.

Television opened a whole new world for a now sports-starved

---

average by 5 points a game, and his field goal percentage plummeted from 43 percent to 38 percent. Until then, Big George was a never-before-seen force in the game, and was named the Greatest Basketball Player of the sport's first half-century. The six-foot lane had served him well.

The overall lack of scoring in the league had been boring to all but the most fervent members of the pro ball fan base. The game in the 1950-1951 season was all about Mikan's dominance. I would have to wait nearly fifty years to finally meet my first basketball idol.

Mikan continued to make his home in Minneapolis, and often took in a game involving the hometown Timberwolves. One night, before a game between the Clippers and the T-Wolves at the Target Center, I walked into the media dining room and saw a gray-haired man seated across the room. He was alone at a table, enjoying a pre-game meal. No question in my mind; it was George Mikan. I was as nervous as a young kid walking up to Shaquille O'Neal to ask for an autograph, but I screwed up all my courage and asked if he had a minute to talk. I told him I had seen him play at DePaul, and then for years with the Minneapolis Lakers. I was relieved to note that he actually seemed happy to talk to somebody who had seen him play the game. Some may have viewed him as an aging relic of days long past, but to me he was, well, "Mr. Basketball." I think we both really enjoyed talking about players, coaches, and changes in the game.

Sadly, diabetes would shrink this mountain of a man in his later years. It eventually cost him a leg and left him wheelchair-bound as he split his time between Minneapolis and the Arizona desert.

George Mikan passed in 2005 at the age of eighty. It is important today to appreciate his impact on the game of basketball. •

teen in Peoria, Illinois. I could see Ernie Banks playing for my dear
Chicago Cubs. I could see Mikan, Yardley, Shue, and Sharman in
their NBA primes. My early broadcast heroes were Glickman, Bill
Stern, Buddy Blattner, Dizzy Dean, Burt Wilson, and Harry Caray.
I loved watching games on television, but I was somehow especially
drawn to games on the radio. My path was being paved before I even
knew it.

I have loved the game of basketball since as early as I can remember.
My friends and I would play softball in the spring and flag football in
the fall, but I played basketball year-round. It was a passion for me,
from the first time I dribbled one of those old, slick rubber basketballs.

I will never forget the day that my dad and a neighbor friend attached a wooden backboard and metal hoop over our two-car garage. I
spent more time outside shooting hoops in that driveway than I did in
the house. I could shoot baskets whenever I wanted, and I wanted to
all the time. Neither snow nor ice could stop me. It was the only time
in my life that I was a willing snow shoveler. Nightfall was not a deter-
rent, either. We would illuminate the court with a floodlight mounted
from my upstairs bedroom window, or with the headlights of our car
in the driveway. It is just about all I wanted to do.

You cannot play baseball or football by yourself. That was the great
thing about basketball. I'd be there all afternoon, shooting alone while
awaiting a neighbor friend to join me. Dad and my brother-in-law,
Don Bell, would come home from work, rip off their ties, roll up their
sleeves, and join us for what we called a game of 20 and 4—first team
to 20 points, but you had to win by at least 4 points. God, it was fun.
My mother might disagree. She told me years later how the incessant
bouncing of the rubber ball on the cement driveway drove her nuts
as she was preparing dinner in the house. She thought it would never
stop. It seldom did. She never said a word at the time.

My first experience actually being on a team was representing
Columbia Grade School in Peoria, Illinois. I was an eight-year-old,
third-grade "student/athlete." I can clearly remember the thrill of putting on that gold jersey and those shiny green short shorts. No NBA

champion has ever worn their uniform more proudly. It was a transformative time in my life as a young boy.

Playing ball and following Bradley U basketball were the most important things in my young life. I was lucky enough to play at the newly opened Thomas Jefferson Grade School in Peoria, on one of the best K-8 teams in the city in the early '50s. We beat all comers and were especially excited when we would see high school coaches on the sidelines scouting for talent. It was the most fun I ever had playing basketball. I graduated grade school at thirteen, and I was on top of the world.

Several years ago, my wife and I stopped by my old grade school during a visit to my beloved hometown of Peoria. It was a hot, steamy summer day. I parked in front of the old grade school and noted that, surprisingly, the front doors of the building were wide open. We ventured into the aging yellow brick building, and the old gym where I had played my first formal basketball game was straight ahead.

We soon learned why the doors had been left open. They had just varnished the old wooden court, and the noxious fumes were wafting through the air. It smelled like expensive French perfume to me as we stood at the doorway to the gymnasium. It was as if time had stood still. I vividly remembered the thrill of playing a game there about sixty years earlier. It was a *Back to the Future* moment. I could almost feel the tears that had run down my cheeks after losing one of those schoolboy games. I suspect the final score was something like 12–8. I cannot recapture much about the game itself, but I certainly can recapture the pain of losing. Little did I know that I was taking the early steps on a basketball journey that would last a lifetime.

As a twelve-year-old in the eighth grade, I stood five foot seven. I desperately wanted to reach six four. I was a six-footer as a freshman, and six two as a fourteen-year-old sophomore. Mom was hardly able to keep up with my growth spurts; I would out-grow blue jeans and shoes month by month. I was well on my way to my desired height— or so I thought. Once I hit six two, I was done growing. Six two it was, and six two it still is.

High school ball was a challenge for me, but my first two years went well. Bruce Sauers was the assistant coach for the varsity team and head coach of the freshman and sophomore teams. He was very encouraging and supportive. I recall a game in my sophomore season when I scored 20 points on 9 of 11 shooting, and Coach Sauers told me I could be special—maybe all-state and certainly all-city. I was pumped, and it just made me work harder. I loved practice, and I just loved being in the gym.

I had a chance to go back to the old school gym in 2006 during the fifty-year reunion of the class of 1956, and I could almost hear varsity coach Dawdy Hawkins cursing at me. In Coach Hawkins' eyes, I was a rich kid because my parents owned the local drive-in movie theater, and he seemed to resent me for that. He rode me relentlessly: "Come on, Lawler, rich kids need to play hard, too." I did not handle it well and never came close to reaching my potential. It wasn't Coach Hawkins' fault; he challenged me, and I was not up to the challenge. It's a disappointment that I still feel to this day.

I loved the game so much. Other school buddies were preoccupied with girls, but I was all in with basketball. We had good teams at Peoria Central. We went to the state tournament's "Elite 8" three times in my four years. We were especially good in my senior season. We raced through the regionals and sectionals before going to Champaign, Illinois, for the eight-team state tournament.

We were one of the two favorites to win it all. Sadly, we were bounced by Oak Park-River Forest in the quarter finals at Huff Gym on the University of Illinois campus. It was devastating. After the game, I sat alone in the solemn locker room with tears welling up in my eyes. Coach Hawkins was going from player to player with what I assumed were some final consoling words. When he got to me, he said, "You got lucky on that late game call. Looked to me like you were guilty of a charge." Even at that moment, he had to have one final dig.

It seemed to be the bitter end of my basketball career. I made the team in my freshman year at DePauw University in Greencastle, Indiana, but a nagging groin injury kept me from playing.

Though I was a late bloomer when it came to dating, I had gotten the hang of it in my senior year of high school and fell head over heels for the magnificent Margy Olson. We wrote each other daily when I was at DePauw. Oh, how I missed my first girlfriend. She would come to DePauw for the homecoming dance and the like, but that only amplified the pain of being apart. I came home over Christmas to be reunited with Margy and all our high school friends. I knew then that I was a Peoria boy who belonged in Peoria.

I transferred to Bradley at the end of my first semester at DePauw, and never played organized basketball again. This allowed me to be back at the field house, watching the Braves play again. They continued to have great teams with stars like Bob Carney, Shelly McMillan, Barney Cable, and Chet Walker, all of whom went on to play in the NBA. Walker was a Hall of Fame Inductee in 2012. Then there was the colorful Bobby Joe Mason, who played for the Harlem Globetrotters for twelve seasons. Bradley basketball was in my blood.

Margy was the main reason I decided to transfer to Bradley, and she was the only reason that I discovered the route to broadcasting. Near the end of my first semester as a junior studying business administration, I was studying for a final exam in economics when I came across this sentence in one of my books: "There are 200,000 wholesale establishments in the United States." It sounded like a final exam question to me. It also made me realize that I did not give a damn. I slammed my book shut and stormed out of the study hall, realizing that my time in the School of Business was over. That was the easy part.

I was committed to finishing college and knew I had to find a new field of study, but I didn't have a clue what direction to take. Margy was in Theatre Arts, and she encouraged me to take some classes with her. I signed up for classes like Speech, The Speaking Voice, and Introduction to Radio, and even signed on to act in some university stage productions. It was a new world. My radio professor kept singling me out for my outstanding work in his class. It was music to my ears. I'd never heard much (or any) praise in my accounting class. I was hooked. This influential professor, Henry VanderHeyden, helped me get my first jobs in radio in the Peoria area. I am forever grateful.

Though I was no longer playing organized basketball, the game was never far away. I played intramural ball at Bradley, and even after I moved west in 1961, I always had hoops in the drive at our homes in Riverside. I was still playing rec league basketball during my years in San Diego. I never passed up a chance to play. An appearance against the Harlem Clowns in Riverside with Bill Cosby as a teammate was a memorable event. I played in a game in which we all rode donkeys on the court. I later played in an outdoor promotional event in downtown

Philadelphia.

My love for basketball would never waiver; but back then, I had no clue that it would be a central part of my life into my eighties. Little did I know that the best was yet to come.

Chapter 2

My First Brush with Basketball Greatness

SEVENTY YEARS AGO, THE NBA was not on anybody's radar in Peoria, Illinois, or anywhere in small-town USA. Today you may find Chicago Bulls fans in downstate Illinois, but back in the late 1940s, nobody there was attached to any pro basketball team. Bradley U basketball was the very heartbeat of this midwestern city in the center of the nation's corn belt.

In 1949, the university erected a bright new building on campus for the popular college team to call home. Robertson Memorial Field-house cost $400,000 to build and boasted a seating capacity of 8,200, and every game was a screaming sell-out. As a point of reference, the NBA New York Knicks averaged 4,200 fans a night that same year at Madison Square Garden. The Clippers never averaged 8,200 fans in any of their six seasons in San Diego, and attracted only a reported 7,711 a night in their third year in Los Angeles.

The school had repurposed a pair of World War II hangars to form the frame of the building, which housed a unique raised hardwood floor that served as a stage-like home court. It was truly a one-of-a-kind sports venue, and it gave the local school a significant home-court advantage.

This marked a special era in Bradley basketball history. You were envied in town if you could say you were at the game the night before to see the latest win by the Braves. And there were plenty of wins. Over the years, the school played 500 games at the Fieldhouse, and won 400 of them. Our family had three season seats for the games, and I was there for virtually every Bradley home game. I was such a fan that I kept scrapbooks with clippings of every high and low. I still have two of those musty old scrapbooks, and I wistfully thumb through them from time to time.

Bradley took on all comers of the era: Houston, DePaul, Georgia Tech, Ohio State, Georgetown, Pitt, St. Joseph's, TCU, Kentucky, Oklahoma State, UCLA, Kansas, Duke, Syracuse, and St. John's. The Braves were the toast of the town and helped put Peoria, a community of roughly 103,000 residents, on the national map.

I saw some of the game's greatest stars play Bradley during the 1940s and '50s: George Mikan of DePaul, Bob Kurland of Oklahoma A&M, Ed Macauley of St. Louis U, Elgin Baylor of Seattle U, and Oscar Robertson of Cincinnati. All became Hall of Fame players. It truly was a special time and place to be a young basketball fan.

There were no one-and-done players in college basketball in those early days. No player would jump straight from high school to the NBA, nor would they play just a single season of college ball before entering the pro draft. It was not a group of fuzzy-faced eighteen or nineteen-year-old kids who entered the embryonic professional league; it was twenty-two and twenty-three-year-old young men who were well-seasoned from four years of intercollegiate basketball. Even the very best college players of the era waited patiently for their NBA opportunity.

Some college stars in the early 1950s spurned the pro league to play in the National Industrial Basketball League. It was AAU basketball. Teams like the Peoria Caterpillars, the Akron Goodyears, and the Phillips 66ers could basically match the NBA salaries of the day, and provided the players with on-the-job training for their careers after basketball. Bob Boozer, Clyde Lovellette, and Bob Kurland were but a few of the many players who originally opted for the industrial league rather than the NBA. All three are now enshrined in the Naismith Memorial Basketball Hall of Fame. And, oh yes, we were also regulars at the Caterpillar games that were also played at the Bradley campus Fieldhouse. But by the end of the 1950s, the pro league salaries had grown to the point that the amateur league could no longer compete for players, and the NIBL disbanded in 1961.

At Bradley, the biggest post-season college basketball tournament of the day was without question the National Invitation Tournament (NIT), established in 1938. (The now-revered NCAA tournament—which has since spawned "March Madness" from coast to coast—came about a year later and played catch-up throughout the 1940s and into the '50s.) When the NIT opened at Madison Square Garden in New York City, it was a much bigger event than anything the NBA could offer. Only eight teams would be invited to the tournament, rather than the sixty-eight that currently entered the brackets for college basketball's championship.

My Bradley Braves were the top-ranked college basketball team in the country in 1950, and were favored to conquer all those who would dare to face them. Bradley raced past Syracuse, and then St. John's. That set up a title game against City College of New York, or CCNY as they were known. It was not a good night for Coach Fordy Anderson's Bradley team, who would fall to Coach Nat Holman's Beavers 69–61. But they soon learned they'd get a quick shot at redemption. It was offered by the NCAA tournament, which gave both NIT finalists an invite for a re-match at MSG in just six days.

Emboldened by their season-long success, the Braves did their due diligence and longed for another shot at CCNY. But they had work to do first. They easily dispatched John Wooden's UCLA Bruins in the opening round, but then were deftly challenged in a nail-biting 68–66 win over Baylor in the semi-finals. Meanwhile, CCNY needed a pair of challenging wins over Ohio State and North Carolina State to set up the dream finals re-match against Bradley. The big city school was led by Ed Roman, Irwin Dambrot, and Ed Warner. Each seemed destined for promising careers in the NBA and they were certainly intent on proving that their win over Bradley ten-nights earlier was no fluke.

The Braves wanted to validate their regular season ranking as the top college basketball team in the country, and to erase the stench of their recent loss to their big-city rivals. Though the Bradley stars were heroes in central Illinois, they were viewed as a bunch of small-town bumpkins in New York City. Paul Unruh, Gene Melchiorre, and Billy Mann confidently led the Braves onto the famed MSG court that night on March 28. The game was a classic. No national television. Fans were huddled around their radios, hoping for a big win by their favored team. It went down to the wire, with the Beavers scoring the remarkable National Title repeat: CCNY 71–Bradley 68.

The previously unheralded CCNY was on top of the college basketball world with twin championships in the NIT and NCAA hoop
tournaments. It had never happened before, and will never happen
again. Bradley was twice the bridesmaid but never put on the ring. I
was heartbroken twice in the course of two weeks. Still, two finals appearances in fourteen days was not bad. Each team was led by sure-fire
NBA stars of the future, and both clubs would bring back four of their
five starters from their great 1949–1950 rosters. What could possibly
go wrong for either team in the 1950–1951 season?

Well, here's a *Jeopardy* question to help you win bets at your favorite sports bar: The only number-one overall pick in the NBA draft
since 1950 to never play a game in the league. The winning response:
Who is Gene "Squeaky" Melchiorre?

Let me tell you a little about Squeaky. He was a pigeon-toed, five-
foot-eight-and-a-half guard from Highland Park, Illinois. He attended Bradley University on the GI Bill after serving two years in the U.S.
Army. The Braves would win between twenty-seven and thirty-two
games in each of his four seasons on the Bradley Hilltop. The twenty-
three-year-old senior dominated the sport as none his size had ever
done. If he had played in the NBA, there is every likelihood that he
would have gone down as one of the greatest small men to ever play in
the league. Today, he would be remembered right there with the five-
foot-nine Hall of Famer Calvin Murphy, the five-six Spud Webb, and
the five-three Muggsy Bogues in the list of the league's all-time great
"little men."

The 1950–1951 Bradley squad was obviously Melchiorre's team.
Paul Unruh had graduated the previous June. It was another very good
team. They would win thirty-two games and lose only six in the regular
season. Yet, they failed to win their conference title. Hank Iba's Oklahoma A&M topped them by one game in the MVC and thus denied
them the automatic invite to the NCAA Tournament.

That left the Peoria school in a quandary. There were rumblings of
a college basketball point-shaving scandal centered in New York City.
Long Island U, CCNY, and Kentucky were the first to be implicated.
In an effort to avoid a possibly contaminating spotlight that would
surely shine on them had they returned to the NIT, Bradley turned

down the invite.

The city remained unflinchingly proud of its local team, though this was the end of an era. They had loved the four magical years of Squeaky Melchiorre. It was an era that was cherished by young fans like me. It was also a vivid illustration of the pain brought on by losing.

The diminutive Melchiorre was a consensus first-team All-American. His future could not have been brighter. Or so we thought. In the NBA draft, staged on April 25, 1951, Squeaky was the number-one overall pick by the Baltimore Bullets, and our still-innocent eyes began to bring the young pro league into sharper focus.

We now know that Melchiorre, who died in September of 2019 at the age of ninety-two, was tortured by fear and guilt throughout his final two years at Bradley. The New York investigation into the college basketball scandal was expanding. It touched on the NBA as well.

A referee named Sol Levy was suspended by the league for "fixing" six NBA games in 1950. That would be a front-page story today, but in 1950 and 1951, the lightly covered league's problems were totally overshadowed by the mounting college scandal that would eventually taint seven schools and thirty-three players.

July 24, 1951, is a day that I will remember for as long as I live. It is seared in my mind as clearly as the end of WWII, the Kennedy and King assassinations, and even 9/11 or the recent coronavirus pandemic. This was before we had a television set at home. Most people received their news by reading the newspaper or listening to the radio. We counted on *Life* magazine for photos of the people we'd been hearing and reading about. We would also rely on the newsreels we watched at movie theaters; after the coming attractions and cartoons, the newsreels played before the feature films.

Radio was the messenger on the morning of this bright and shiny mid-summer day in Peoria. Bradley stars Melchiorre, Billy Mann, Mike Chianakas, Bud Grover, Aaron Preece, and Jim Kelly had admitted to taking bribes to hold down scores in at least two games during the 1950–1951 season. After hearing this, I was one stunned and disillusioned thirteen-year-old as I aimlessly rode my Schwinn bicycle up and down Peoria's North Biltmore Avenue with tears running down my cheeks. It is a pain that hurts to this day. These were my childhood heroes! I had idolized them.

The players faced up to three years in jail. However, in the end, Melchiorre, Mann, and Chianakas received suspended sentences while no charges were filed against their teammates.

The scandal cost the NBA dearly, as it led to a lifetime ban for all the thirty-three players implicated in the point-shaving ignominy. As a result, NBA history does not include any memorable contributions from likely stars such as Melchiorre, Sherman White, Ed Warner, Alex Groza, or Ralph Beard.

Sadly, we will never know what might have been.

In 1946, eleven teams quietly formed what was first called the Basketball Association of America (BAA). There remains a mild debate over whether this really marks the beginning of the present-day NBA (the league did not actually become known as the National Basketball Association until 1949), but the league certainly counts 1946 as its birth year while celebrating its seventy-fifth season in 2021–2022. The first-ever game is recognized as the New York Knicks against the Toronto Huskies in Canada on November 1, 1946. Maybe we can agree: born 1946, christened 1949.

The early pro game was little like the modern-day NBA. Joe Fulks of the champion Philadelphia Warriors led the league in scoring that first year. He averaged 23 points a game while making barely more than 30 percent of his field goal attempts. A long-forgotten guard, Max Zaslofsky, played for the Chicago Stags and earned All-BAA First Team honors that season. He would lead the league in scoring the following year.

The BAA/NBA struggled mightily in the early years. The level of interest nationwide was somewhere between badminton and croquet. Only three teams (the Knicks, Warriors, and Celtics) survive today from the charter list of eleven inaugural season entries. Only the New York Knicks and the Boston Celtics remain alive today in the city where they were born. Team owners had paid a now-laughable $10,000 franchise fee to enter the novice league. Today, that fee would be between $2 billion and $3 billion.

The games were met with a national yawn; teams averaged 3,000 to 4,000 fans a night in that maiden season. By the second year, the BAA dwindled to eight teams. I doubt you've heard of the short-lived Toronto Huskies, the Cleveland Rebels, the Detroit Falcons, or the Pittsburgh Ironmen. In some ways, though, the BAA was ahead of the times. The new league had a salary cap that first year: $55,000 per team. Scoring star Fulks was paid a princely salary of $8,000 in that first season, and that was $3,000 above the league average. The salary cap would last just that single year, and then it would be almost forty years before its re-birth in 1984.

Let me try to put all this in perspective. The top salaried players in the league today earn something in the vicinity of $40 million a year. That comes to almost $500,000 per game. That one-game earning bonanza for one player roughly matches the collective annual earnings of all the players in the league in those early formative years.

The BAA had competition early on from what was called the National Basketball League. Players would leverage their modest salary demands by pitting one league against the other. It was a bitter war between the leagues, but not nearly as unsettling as what would take place thirty years later between the National Basketball Association and the upstart American Basketball Association (more on that later). The BAA got the edge when it convinced four of the best NBL franchises to switch leagues. Among other things, that brought former DePaul University star George Mikan into the Basketball Association of America. Mikan would go on to become the pro game's first superstar big man. The rival leagues made peace in 1949, and merged to become the National Basketball Association.

The innovative BAA had also given birth to something called a territorial draft, which survived into the NBA until 1965—longer than the salary cap. The early pro hoop league had realized it had a long way to go in trying to capture the attention of sports fans throughout the country, so they created this territorial draft as a means of growing that fan base. A team would have a priority choice for a player from its designated market. That included wunderkinds who went to high school or attended college near an NBA team's hometown. Ball clubs had the first pick of players who were already well-known and beloved in their local marketplaces.

In 1950, Paul Arizin became one of the league's early major stars when he entered the NBA out of Villanova University along Philadelphia's exclusive Main Line. The hometown Warriors chose him as a territorial pick, and he was an immediate sensation—the league's best rookie in year one, scoring champion in year two, and NBA Champion in year four. Arizin twice led the league in scoring, and shot a then uncanny 44.8 percent from the floor in his first scoring title season (the league-wide average that year was 36.7 percent). Arizin logged over 20 points a game for ten straight years while spending his entire career with the Warriors.

The territorial draft would guide the placement of many future Hall of Fame basketball legends. Among the chosen few: Tom Gola from LaSalle College in Philly to the Warriors, Tom Heinsohn from Holy Cross to the Boston Celtics, Wilt Chamberlain from Overbrook High School in the City of Brotherly Love to the hometown Warriors, Oscar Robertson from the University of Cincinnati to the Cincinnati Royals, Dave DeBusschere from U of Detroit to the Pistons, Jerry Lucas from Ohio State to the Cincinnati Royals, Bill Bradley from Princeton to the New York Knicks, and Gail Goodrich from UCLA to the Los Angeles Lakers in 1965—the final pick of the nearly two-decade-old territorial draft rule.

Just imagine if, only four years later in 1969, the New York Knicks had the territorial rule and used it to draft former Power Memorial High School star Lew Alcindor (later known as Kareem Abdul-Jabbar). Hey, the Detroit Pistons could have taken Magic Johnson ten years later, and the Indiana Pacers could have tabbed Larry Bird.

The largely forgotten territorial draft did serve its purpose. It helped expand basketball fans' interest as players transitioned from college fame to the pros. It worked! You could now regularly read game stories and even find box scores in the newspapers. All the teams had their games broadcast on radio, and the league debuted on National Television in 1953. It was the beginning of the NBA's sometimes halting rise to relevance. By the mid-'50s, the eight-team league stretched from its East Coast origins westward, not only to Minneapolis, but also to Fort Wayne, Indiana, and St. Louis, Missouri.

The NBA was taking baby steps, but it was headed in the right direction.

Chapter 3

Go West, Young Man

MY PROFESSIONAL RADIO CAREER consumed my final two years at Bradley. I scheduled my classes around my radio responsibilities. I wound up with a full-time job as a midday disc jockey at WAAP in downtown Peoria, but my real joy came from a fifteen-minute nightly sports report.

The radio station was managed by a radio veteran named Dave Taylor. As I approached graduation at Bradley, he received a job offer in Riverside, California, and asked four of us to join him, including our station's Morning Man Gus Chan and news director Bob Steinbrinck, who was also my closest friend. The military draft was very much alive at the time, and they were drafting young men the day after they turned twenty-three. I was to turn twenty-three on April 21, 1961. I had to tell Dave that while I would love to move to California, I was going to have to go into the military. I was granted a deferment until my June graduation, and I chose to enlist in the Navy at that time rather than be drafted.

The week after getting my diploma, I was on a train headed to Chicago to undergo my induction physical. I spent the day walking around a musty old building with a few hundred other young men. We were all wearing nothing but our underwear while carrying a tube containing our specimen. It was not a fun day. Once I reached the final stop, a sergeant thumbed through my papers, looked up at me, and said, "Son, I have bad news for you." I could not imagine what could be worse than those past few hours. He continued: "I know you wanted to go into the Navy, but we are classifying you 4-F, meaning you are not acceptable for military service. Your records indicate you had a spontaneous pneumothorax [collapsed lung] a few years ago. I'm sorry!"

I could hardly believe my ears. I almost kissed that sergeant. Once I was back at the train depot, I raced to a phone booth. My first call was to Dave Taylor to ask if the job he had offered me was still available. It was, and it was mine. The pay was $125 per week. He wanted me in Riverside by mid-August.

That summer, I drove cross-country from Peoria, Illinois, to Riverside, California, after appearing in a summer stock theater-in-the-round presentation of the light-hearted comedy *Desk Set*. I was driving a brand-new Rambler American, a graduation present from my parents. It was snow-white with a racy red faux leather interior. The highlight for a twenty-three-year-old looking ahead to single life in Southern California was the fact that the front seats could fold down into a bed. I had the maturity of an eight-year-old with the raging libido of a teenager, and I was easy prey for most of the temptations that awaited me in sunny SoCal.

I headed for Riverside in early August. The drive west along Route 66 was memorable for a small-town boy from Peoria who was out on his own for the very first time. The endless miles sped by quickly, even through the barren flatlands of Oklahoma and Texas. I was getting more excited with each turn of the wheel. When I finally reached Riverside, Dave Taylor, Bob Steinbrinck, Gus Chan, and their wives welcomed me in the Presidential Lounge at Riverside's famed Mission Inn. We were not strangers in a strange land because we all had worked together in Peoria.

Riverside looked like paradise to me. In those days, the L.A. smog had yet to drift its way over Kellogg Hill. The skies were crystal-blue, and it seemed as if there were Orange Groves at the end of every street. And to think, I had expected to be at sea in the Navy right about now.

I eased into my new life comfortably. Gus Chan was the major personality of our radio station; Bob Steinbrinck reenacted his Peoria role as the station's news director; Jay Michael was on every afternoon; and Bob Allen, who had been a popular singer for the Hal Kemp dance band in the 1940s, was our colorful nighttime DJ. Dave Taylor was the manager, of course. We had a great group, and Dave was a natural-born promoter—and promote us he did.

The radio station was on the outskirts of the city. It was a free-standing building rising in the shadow of a single, giant 1,000-watt antenna. Built to be a radio station in 1941, the building included a large studio to house live audiences with a sizable stage and a grand piano. It was like stepping into another era. I was beside myself with joy and excitement.

We were very local, and with Steinbrinck's guidance, we were very good. I performed a daily sports report during a 6:00–6:30 PM news block. If some golfer in town had a hole in one, I was connected enough with all the golf clubs to have that golfer on the air that night to discuss the ace. I also signed the station on the air at 5:30 AM before working behind the scenes, operating the controls for Chan the Morning Man. Gus had originally hosted a national radio program in Chicago, and he was well-known in the business. Unfortunately, he got caught cursing on a mistakenly open mic from coast to coast, and he became taboo in the Windy City. That's when Dave Taylor reached out to him about a job at WAAP in Peoria, and then on to Riverside. Gus was probably forty-five to fifty years old at the time—wise, in my twenty-three-year-old eyes. He was one of the more enlightened people I have ever known. He never preached, but he was always there with sage words of counsel when needed. And I needed them, a lot.

I lived in a two-bedroom apartment in nearby San Bernardino, sharing the space with a tall, gangly sales manager from Nacogdoches, Texas, named Dick Lane. I worked a split shift at the station, from my morning sign-on at 5:30 AM to about 10:00 AM, when I would then record commercials and prepare for my nightly sports report no later than 3:00 PM. It was a crazy schedule, but I loved every second of it. I also loved my life outside of the radio station. I auditioned with the local community theater, the Riverside Players, which was offering a light comedy called *Marriage-Go-Round*. James Mason and Julie Newmar starred in the movie version that year, and I secured the James Mason role. A beauty from the Netherlands, Mieke Tunney, was perfect in the Newmar spot.

Mieke was married to a judge advocate officer in the Air Force, Captain Varick J. Tunney, who was the son of former heavyweight boxing champion Gene Tunney. Though I was totally smitten with Mieke, the three of us became good friends. Varick was stationed at March Air Force Base in Riverside, a major Strategic Air Command (SAC) base at the time. He was about to complete his stint in the Air Force and was searching for the next chapter of his charmed life.

Mieke and I sometimes went out for long lunches, driving to Lake Arrowhead or Lake Evans and just sitting in the car, talking for hours. She was the most beautiful woman I had ever known. I would have run off and married her in a heartbeat, but she was off-limits. I was lucky to have what we had.

One night, I was having dinner with Varick and Mieke at their Riverside home, a year or so after our run in *Marriage-Go-Round*. The phone rang; it was a call from Joe Kennedy, the father of President John F. Kennedy. Now, that knocked me out. Varick had been college roommates with the president's brother, Edward Kennedy, at the University of Virginia School of Law, and the Tunney and Kennedy families had remained close friends. Old Joe Kennedy was urging Varick to get into politics. He thought he would be a natural. There were dreams down the line that Teddy and Varick could team up on a presidential and vice-presidential ticket.

The three of us spent many an hour at the bar in the Mission Inn's Presidential Lounge, drinking the night away and dreaming about our respective futures. That's where I met a waitress named Judy. She worked every night until 1:00 am, and we would get together several nights a week after she got off work. Remember now, I was working that split shift that started at 5:30 AM and ended at 6:30 pm. Little wonder I was often late in getting the station on the air on time.

A couple of years later, after my second hiring at KPRO, Varick became John V. Tunney and a candidate for the U.S. House of Representatives. He would represent California's Thirty-Eighth District for three terms before running for the U.S. Senate. Though I was a Republican at the time, I enthusiastically attended his rallies. I remember the candidate Tunney asking a key aide, "Ralph's for me, isn't he?" After his successful run as a congressman, Tunney then succeeded George Murphy for one term as U.S. Senator from California in 1971.

Tunney's marriage with Mieke did not survive his Senate term. I somehow fought off the temptation to try to find her in the wistful hope of rekindling what might have been twelve years earlier. Sadly, both John and Mieke passed a few years ago.

In January of 1962, I was fired for being consistently late for work. I was very short on funds; I left my car with the Steinbrincks, and spent my last dollars on a train ticket from Riverside to Chillicothe, Illinois. It was another adventure for me and my bruised ego. My sister made the twenty-mile trip from Peoria to pick me up in Chillicothe. I was hardly coming home as a conquering hero. My career in Riverside had lasted a total of five months, but I harbored hopes for a second chance in Southern California.

I was welcomed home by my mom and dad, who gave me a temporary place to stay. I learned quickly that things had changed back in Peoria. LaVonne, my co-star in community theater a summer earlier, was getting a divorce. We started dating and quickly fell in love.

I was able to find employment at the radio station WMBD, working a six or seven-hour nighttime disc jockey job. Believe me, that's a long shift to sit there spinning records and reporting the news each hour on the hour. I vividly remember announcing the news of the death of movie idol Marilyn Monroe. The telephone immediately lit up with one person after another asking: "Is Marilyn Monroe really dead?"

The WMBD AM and FM studios were located in downtown Peoria, in what had been the Majestic Theater on Jefferson Avenue from 1906 to 1946. It had been a regular stop on the old vaudeville circuit. I liked to go exploring in the building after signing off at 1:00 am. My dad had spent his life in the movie business, rising from usher to theater owner, so I was fascinated with the old theater. With my heart beating out of my chest, I would pry open long-closed doors in the middle of the night and explore via flashlight, finding myself on a theater balcony one night and backstage the next. I found some of the original dressing rooms with autographs etched on the walls, including the names of such early show business luminaries as Eddie Cantor and Al Jolson. Then I found the greatest prize of all in the musty old theatrical catacombs: the theater's ledger books circa 1916.

Birth of a Nation was the first twelve-reel motion picture of all time. It had played at the Majestic, and there it was, with the dollars and cents memorialized on the brittle pages of the forty-six-year-old ledger. I brought it home and excitedly gave it to my dad, who had spent close to sixty years working in the theater business. He was thrilled beyond belief, and stashed it God knows where. Sadly, we have yet to rediscover this rare slice of motion picture history in our search through the family archives.

Meanwhile, my romance with LaVonne was in full bloom. We decided to get married, but I wanted to return to Riverside in the fall to take another swing at landing a job in Southern California. LaVonne was 100 percent in favor of beginning our new lives on the West Coast. In Riverside, Bob and Marge Steinbrinck took me in while I staged my job search. I had hardly started when KPRO's midday DJ, Bud Schenck, suddenly had a family emergency back East. Bob told Dave Taylor, who had fired me nine months earlier, that I was in town; I knew the format and the board equipment.

Before I knew it, I was hired as a temp to fill in for Bud. It went well and, God love Dave, he gave me a second chance at $130 a week. My job hunt was over! I called LaVonne and urged her to come out to Riverside to marry me. Bob and Marge were the only ones who knew about our wedding plans, which would take place on a crisp October night. That evening, the radio station had a promotion during an auto show downtown. We had a booth set up and were busy promoting our station. Around 8:45 pm, I went up to Dave Taylor and asked if I could bail out a few minutes early. He asked me why, and I said, "Well, I'm getting married at the Mission Inn at nine."

I had found a modest rental home in Riverside, about ten to fifteen minutes from the radio station. LaVonne arranged to have her Danish modern furniture shipped out from her home in Peoria, and we moved into the very first house I'd lived in since moving away from my mom and dad four or five years earlier. It was time to lead a responsible, adult life. I had a lot to learn.

The station thrived, and my role moved from DJ and nightly sports reporter to production director (making commercials) and then program director. I was loving it. The marriage was working, and we were happy. I think I was up to $150 a week, and the timing was good because weeks after getting married, LaVonne became pregnant. In those days, you did not know the sex of your baby in advance, but I was somehow certain we were going to have a son.

I was on the air spinning records when LaVonne called after a doctor visit to confirm she was pregnant. She asked that I not tell anyone just yet. I hung up the phone and announced, "We're having a baby!" Then I pulled out the cast album from the smash Broadway and motion picture hit *Carousel.* The song that immediately blared on the radio was Gordon MacRae singing "My Boy, Bill." I never could keep a secret as a young man. Nine months later, we welcomed Ralph William Lawler, named after my father.

The years in Riverside were filled with equal parts joy and angst amid the tumultuous 1960s. I was on the air at the instant both President John F. Kennedy and presidential candidate Robert F. Kennedy were assassinated. I was hosting my midday record show on KPRO on November 22, 1963. We were at a McMahon's Furniture Store in downtown Riverside, promoting their winter sales event. I would intro the records that were played back at the radio station. At some point I realized that I was hearing our midday newsman, Larry Smith, talking on the air. I could not make out what he was saying, but I did hear him cue me back at McMahon's. I blithely said: "Thanks very much, Larry, and now back to the music here on KPRO—here are the Four Fresh-man with 'Put On a Happy Face.'" I picked up the phone and asked Larry what was going on. He told me that the president had just been shot in Dallas, Texas. We scrapped the record program, and I spent the next couple of hours recording reactions from visitors at the furniture store. Some had heard the news and some had not. It was a stunning, life-changing event.

The California Primary Election of 1968 was held on June 6. I was anchoring our radio station's extensive election coverage from our sparkling new studios across the street from the Riverside Plaza shopping center. We were all over the local races in Riverside and San Bernardino counties. Late in the evening, we carried Senator Robert F. Kennedy's triumphant victory speech from the Ambassador Hotel in Los Angeles. He had won the California Presidential Primary. It was tantamount to winning the Democratic presidential nomination.

Moments later, I was handed a news bulletin, and the Associated Press reports were growing more unthinkable by the minute: "Robert Kennedy has been shot moments after claiming victory!" I read the sobering news to our sizable late-night audience. I almost choked on the words. The memories of his brother's death were still fresh in my mind. The nation held out hope after the man affectionately known as "Bobby" was rushed to Good Samaritan Hospital. The vigil would last for twenty-six hours before he died from the multiple gunshot wounds suffered on the night of his greatest political triumph. It left me sobered and shaken.

The '60s made up a frightening decade. Through it all, I was busy at the station by day and working play-by-play of local sports at night. Nighttime programming on small town radio was not much of a source of revenue. Local sports were perfect. High school, junior college, and UC Riverside sports were a fertile ground for fall football and winter basketball broadcasts. Rohr Aircraft became an advertising benefactor as sponsor for much of our local sports coverage. At $125 a game, Rohr provided the station with $75 in income at a time when it typically earned zero. They paid me a $25 talent fee, and the phone company $25 in phone line costs for the broadcasts.

Now this was fun! I had found an ideal training ground to develop my play-by-play skills. I was a glutton for punishment. There were annual high school basketball tournaments in the area over Christmas. Teams from throughout the state would make the trip to Riverside.

I saw an opportunity and grabbed it—I would contact a radio station in each team's hometown. It was a simple deal: the station would provide me with the broadcast lines, pay me $50, and I would give them a first-class broadcast of each game their team played. I would do five or six games a day and be thrilled every single second. Pretty sure I made more money in a day than I made in a typical week at the radio station.

One real highlight was broadcasting Riverside City College basketball games. The Tigers were coached by Jerry Tarkanian, who went on to a Hall of Fame career that included an NCAA Championship at UNLV. RCC won three straight California Junior College Championships in the mid-1960s. Eventually, I used recorded highlights of our broadcasts to produce a record that we sold at the school bookstore. It was cleverly called *Three in a Row*. I regret to add that I was a one-hit wonder. I have bumped into Tark's son, Danny, a few times over the years. The first words out of his mouth are always: "Three in a row!" Coach Tarkanian was a one of a kind. All coaches want to win, but Tark *had* to win. It was more than a passion; it was an obsession. I learned a lot about focus and determination just by watching and listening to the coach, who allowed me into the locker room at halftime. The team was coming off a state championship season in which his Tigers had gone 35–0. They finally lost a single game early the following season. The next contest was close at halftime. I was present when he angrily hurled his chalk at the blackboard and screeched, "Damn it, I'm tired of losing!"

That commitment to winning served Tark well over the years. He loved the teaching aspects of the college game. After his unforgettable career in Las Vegas was behind him, he traveled extensively with the Clippers during Larry Brown's second season. He wanted to get a close-up view of the NBA game, and he liked it more than he thought he would.

Tark had been offered the Los Angeles Laker job back in 1977, but he declined so he could remain in the college game. He felt there would not be much teaching in pro ball. Now he was giving the pro game a closer look, and he liked what he saw and let it be known. In 1992, he was hired to coach the San Antonio Spurs. It lasted only twenty games; he was tanked after a 9–11 start. He then returned to his alma mater, Fresno State, where he would go on to coach for seven years.

Jerry Tarkanian was inducted into the Basketball Hall of Fame in 2013, two years before his death at the age of eighty-four. He will long be remembered for his extraordinary success in Las Vegas with his Runnin' Rebels. He is a man I will never forget.

In 2012, I was invited back to Riverside City College to deliver their commencement address. It was an unprecedented honor. My nine years in Riverside were some of the very best of my young life. Things at KPRO were great in the early '60s, and my "take 2" was much better than the first. I even briefly was in the *Guinness Book of World Records* when fellow DJ Ken Collins and I rode motorcycles for thirty-six consecutive hours at the Riverside Plaza shopping center.

In 1964, we were all rocked and rolled when we heard the announcement that pop music icon Dick Clark was purchasing our radio station. There went our carefully crafted, middle-of-the-road adult music format. We expected the music to come right off Clark's hugely popular *American Bandstand* television series. Forget the news and sports, we thought; get ready to stock the record library with music by Elvis, the Supremes, and Herman's Hermits. Oh me, oh my!

Clark and his father, Richard A. Clark, came to visit the nervous KPRO staff. They assured us they were not going to challenge KMEN, the established teen station in the market. They were buying KPRO because they liked it the way it was. There was a collective sigh of deep relief in the room. Dick and his father became great supporters and mentors in the weeks, months, and years ahead. I learned so much working for them.

In the mid-1960s, there was talk that our KPRO staff was interested in organizing and joining AFTRA (the American Federation of Television and Radio Artists). The station prided itself on taking good care of its employees. We gave everybody on the air staff a raise to at least $200 a week, at a time when $10,000 a year was considered a mark of achievement. We never heard another peep about the union from anyone on the staff.

However, there were limitations on how much payroll a radio station in that marketplace could afford. Dick and his dad got creative to find ways to keep key employees in place, establishing American Race Casters to replace our in-house efforts at syndicating our auto racing broadcasts. Dick gave me and Dave Taylor a sizeable hunk of the sub-chapter S corporation. We had been broadcasting automobile races on the radio from the Riverside International Raceway, Laguna Seca, Las Vegas, and College Station, Texas. It was fun and exciting as we sold the broadcasts to stations across the country. Our NASCAR events were carried by upwards of 150 stations. Now this asset belonged to us rather than to the radio station.

Dick soon added to our incentive to remain at KPRO by giving me, the general manager, and the sales manager fancy vice president titles as well as a chance to be investors in a proposed chain of Arby's restaurants. We had the Riverside-San Bernardino territory.

At the time, my lifelong friend, Ando Teder, was just transitioning out of the military. He had served as a captain in the Marines, and before that had been a business major at Northwestern. He was headed from Hawaii to Chicago for a meeting with United Airlines, where he hoped to embark on a career in big business. I took advantage of our long friendship and arranged a meeting for Ando in Hollywood with the Clarks. He was impressive in the meeting and walked away with an offer to manage the day-to-day operations of the restaurant chain that was to open its first unit in San Bernardino. Ando would get a piece of the company as well; Dick retained a controlling interest, with the other four of us each receiving 12 percent. I would oversee the operation while continuing my role at the radio station.

We had a grand opening at our first store in San Bernardino. Dick Clark was there for me to serve him one of our first delicious roast beef sandwiches. Ando and I had attended Arby's Restaurant Management School together in Youngstown, Ohio. It was a whole new world for us, though I did have some past tangential involvement in my parent's successful ventures in Shakey's Pizza Parlors and Arby's restaurants in the Midwest. What could be better? I had a job I loved, and my family and I were able to purchase a home for the first time. On top of that, we had the Raceway Network, and we moved the radio station into brand-new quarters near the Riverside Shopping Plaza. Dave and I designed the office space and the broadcast studios.

As I approached thirty years of age, I was consumed with my multifaceted job. I was working on our popular two-man morning show with my pal, Steinbrinck. My days began with a 5:00 AM wake-up call and lasted well into the evening. It was more than I could gracefully handle, and it absolutely diminished my energy and focus on being a husband and a father. The first cracks in my marriage were forming.

By the late 1960s, I was getting a little big for my britches. I would question every move Dave Taylor made as general manager. My subordinates at the station would tell me, "You should be managing the radio station," and I eagerly soaked it all in. My long relationship with Dave was deteriorating. Late one night, I was working in my office when Dave stopped by unexpectedly and told me I was fired. He had cleared it with the owner, and I was to get my belongings out of the station that very night. Though I was staggered beyond belief because I felt that I was an indispensable part of our little empire, I fully understood. One of us—me or Dave—really had to go, and I was younger with a longer landing strip for recovery. Still, this was not good news to take home to my wife in the midst of our teetering marriage.

I was out of work for four months, and it was a much-needed and

TIME OUT Many a Strange Turn in the Road

Our venture into auto race broadcasting did not begin smoothly. The Riverside International Raceway boasted a world-renowned 2.7-mile twisting road course. Their two biggest annual events were the Los Angeles Times Grand Prix in October, and the Riverside 500 NASCAR event in January. I would go to the track on race day to broadcast updates on the races every half hour. The RIR public relations head was named Bob Russo, and we became good friends. One day he asked me why we didn't broadcast the races. Well, I had never thought about it, but . . . why not?

We went to work trying to figure out how to do it. It was a massive undertaking. I would anchor the broadcast from a pagoda at the start/finish line. We would have reporters at turn 6 and the back straightaway bridge, and in the pits. We had the sprawling course covered. Steve Gibson, the engineer for the radio station, proposed using two-way radios to go on the air at the remote locations. We tested the system a few days before the race, and it sounded great.

Our first event was to be the 500-mile stock car race in January of 1963. We planned an exhaustive six-hour broadcast. I worked through the night before the green flag fell on Sunday morning at 11:00 am. I called the start of the race with famed NASCAR driver Marvin Panch at my side. It was good to have at least one person around who knew what he was doing. I had prepared elaborate spotting sheets listing the car types, color, and number, as well as notes on each driver. Bring 'em on!

We went on the air with a fifteen-minute pre-race program. It sounded perfect. But then the race began, and it was a different story. As the forty-four starters weaved their way through a series of turns called the "esses," I turned the call over to Bob Steinbrinck at turn 6. Bob sounded like he knew what he was doing as the cars approached the sharp right-hand turn, encased by jam-packed grandstands. Once the cars got there, all we could hear was garbled and swallowed by the sound of the cars below. And then it was, "Back to you, Ralph." I turned it over to Howie Fisher on the Goodyear Bridge. Same result: "Thanks Ralph, here they come—*garble, garble*—back to you at the start/finish line." I quickly realized that it was going to be a long day.

But the worst was yet to come. The cars came by in the early laps, and it was easy to tell: "Gurney in first place in his Ford, followed by A. J. Foyt's Pontiac . . ." and so on. Well, before we knew it, the slower cars were being lapped. As they sped by our location, we had no idea who was first or who was last. It was like the Abbot and Costello comedy classic, "Who's on First?" Thankfully, the raceway would give us official standing updates every ten laps or so. The rest of the time, we faked it. For six hours!

We learned a lot of lessons that first day. We corrected our technical issues with wired connections and better microphones at each broadcast location, and found a terrific keeper of a lap chart in Bobbie Farley. What a concept. I could see, at a glance, the standing of every car in the race. We got much better in the years ahead, broadcasting six or seven events a year from racetracks throughout the Western United States. It was very cool that Dick Clark allowed us to be equity holders in the company that became known as American Racecasters. It was an exciting time for me as I approached my thirtieth birthday.

I was prepping for the 1968 Riverside 500 on the eve of the race when I received a phone call that our reporter on the back straight was not going to be available the next day because of an illness in his family back East. My mind raced as I tried to think of a reliable replacement. I had given tickets to the Saturday night race party to a friend named Fritz Duda, a young local attorney who was as glib as he was bright and confident. I called his home well after midnight, and his wife said he was not yet home from the party. I asked that she have him call me the minute he arrived home.

Fritz called an hour or so later, in a happy mood after several hours of hard partying. I explained my dilemma and he was intoxicated with the idea (or maybe it was the free drinks at the party). I told him I would pick him up at 7:00 AM to go to the raceway for a little broadcast prep.

The next morning, we went over the task. "Just remember Richard Petty in the Blue #14 Plymouth," I told him. "Simply describe what you see, and throw it back to me at the start/finish tower."

Fritz did an excellent job. Not only that, he wound up purchasing the Raceway 3 years later. He would operate RIR for almost two decades before closing it down to develop what is now the Moreno Valley Mall, a regional shopping center. That mall stands today because one of my fellow broadcasters had a death in the family before the 1968 Riverside 500. Go figure. ●

humbling wake-up call. Finally, the radio station WLW in Cincinnati
expressed some interest in me, which I think was piqued by my association with Dick Clark. They flew me back to Cincinnati, and I had a
good session with their general manager. We listened to my audition
tape and he gave me a solid professional critique. He fixed me up with
a ticket to the Cincinnati Royals NBA game that night. Things were
looking good, and I was thinking this might be the next chapter of
my career. I watched Bob Cousy and Oscar Robertson play for the
Royals. It was the first NBA game I had ever seen in person; little did
I know that I would see well over 3,000 more in the years ahead. Alas,
the WLW job was not to be. They felt that I was a little too green for
a major market radio station (and they were right).

Dick Clark invited me to work with him in Riverside, in his effort
to obtain the cable TV franchise for the city. I would run it once he
won his bid. It was a different path, but it sounded exciting. I thought
Dick's name and knowledge of television would give us an edge on the
competition, but unfortunately, that didn't happen.

Coincidental with all of this, I had prepared an audition tape
centered on a re-creation of a major league baseball game. It also
contained a part of a pre-race program for our coverage of the Los
Angeles Times Grand Prix at Riverside International Raceway and
my basketball play-by-play at Riverside City College. I sent my resume and the tape to three major league baseball teams: the Dodgers,
the Angels, and the Cubs. Though I'm still waiting for word from the
Angels and Cubs, the L.A. Dodgers gave me a phone call early in January of 1970. They were adding a third man to the Vin Scully and Jerry
Doggett radio booth on the 50,000W powerhouse KFI. They liked my
presentation and asked me to come in for an interview at the Dodgers
offices at Chavez Ravine.

My earliest broadcast dreams were to be a baseball announcer. I
listened for years to the amazing Harry Caray, who called St. Louis Cardinal games in the 1940s, '50s, and '60s. Then I would switch
to Burt Wilson or Jack Quinlan, who announced the games of the
Chicago Cubs during the era of my baseball passion. I would emulate
those announcer-heroes through endless hours playing a Cadaco board
game called All Star Baseball. I called every pitch and kept statistics
as religiously as the professional National and American Leagues. I

would spin the discs representing the game's greatest players until my fingers hurt. I truly dreamed of announcing games for the Chicago Cubs in Wrigley Field. Now, at the age of thirty-one, I was thrilled when the Los Angeles Dodgers came calling. I made the short one-hour drive from our Riverside home to Dodger Stadium with my heart in my throat.

The Dodgers broadcast coordinator greeted me upon my arrival. He took me in for a meeting with the team's general manager, Buzzie Bavasi. I was immediately put at ease when we realized we had both attended DePauw University. Buzzie and I had a great meeting, which led to an introduction to representatives of the Dodgers' leading sponsor, Union Oil. I had an association with the Union Oil people from my years involved in motor sports, and that made for another unexpectedly smooth meeting. Next up? Peter O'Malley. He was executive vice president of the team at the time, and second in command only to his father, the venerable Walter O'Malley. Peter and I were about the same age. We listened to a quick sample of my work, and everyone seemed like they were hearing what they wanted to hear. My excitement was growing with each meeting I had.

The final hurdle was a meeting with the big guy, the man who had brought Major League baseball to Los Angeles in 1957: Walter O'Malley. He was the same age as my father, and he bore an intimidating presence. I was so nervous that I don't remember much about the brief meeting, but apparently it went well enough that I was given all sorts of encouraging signs from the broadcast honcho who had contacted me in the first place. He said I could anticipate a formal offer next week; I would do two innings a game, home and away. *Vero Beach, here I come!*

I felt like the luckiest young broadcaster in the world as I navigated the freeway home over Kellogg Hill and into the Inland Empire. We met friends at a Shakey's Pizza in Riverside that night, and my excitement exploded with the news that I had a job with the Dodgers.

The following week, I received the anticipated phone call from the team, as promised. The caller sounded just about as disappointed as I was—there would be no offer. KFI was the Dodger radio station, and apparently when they heard that the team was about to go "outside" to hire a third voice for the broadcasts, they had a fit. Mike Walden was their established sports director, and if the team wanted an announcer to team up with Scully and Doggett, it had to be him. I was told that everybody I'd interviewed with had wanted to hire me, but they felt they could not betray their broadcast partner.

I don't think I have ever been so deflated in my entire life. In the end, Walden only lasted a single season on the Dodger broadcasts; I feel like I would have spent fifty years in Major League baseball. I very likely would have worked all those years side by side with Vin Scully, the greatest sportscaster to ever utter a word on the air. It is somehow ironic that I received the Vin Scully Lifetime Achievement Award from the Southern California Sports Broadcasters Association in 2020. In hindsight, I have no regrets. If I had gotten the job, I would never have broadcast a single NBA game. The demands of a 162-game baseball season would surely have sunk my already-listing marriage, and I suspect I would have been single all those years. I certainly would never have met Jo. The consequences of not landing that job were so much more far-reaching than I imagined at the time.

My job hunt continued into 1970. I felt that San Diego would be a good step up from Riverside, so I tried KOGO and KFMB, but there were no openings at either of the two major adult music format stations in the city. Then, I got lucky with a call from KDEO. They were looking for a program director who could help the small station compete with the bigger, established stations. They had made a mark by acquiring the broadcast rights to the San Diego Chargers of the NFL. That interested me, as did the presence in town of the San Diego Rockets of the NBA.

I got the job in February of 1970. I wound up working three seasons of San Diego Charger football broadcasts with the redoubtable Stu Nahan. It was my first "big league" assignment, and I loved it. The station had a great staff: Royce Johnson and Perry Allen were major market talents, and Mike McGregor, Gary Allyn, Ron Reina, John DeMott, and Sam Schwan were top-notch pros. We had our work cut out for us in carving out a niche in the very competitive San Diego radio market. KCBQ and KGB controlled the youth market, while the aforementioned KOGO and KFMB had a stranglehold on the adult listeners. Our inroads, if any, were very minor.

My jump from small-town Riverside to San Diego was well-timed.

This was a big-league city, and instead of high school and junior college sports, I was able to cover the big leagues. When Muhammad Ali came to town to fight Ken Norton, I was there.

We took the programming as far as we could in our 1,000-watt teapot of a station, starting off with an ill-fated "Have a Happy Day" jingle package. Luckily, in 1972 we developed a relationship with a program consultant named Buzz Bennet, who had a background in the famed Bill Drake Top 40 format. Buzz was moving into a more progressive area, and had some valuable guidance for us.

At the time, the FM stations played full-length album cuts of the hit artists of the day—which were anywhere from four to seven minutes long—while the AM stations usually played the shortened two-and-a-half-minute versions. The AM pop station formats simply would not accommodate the full-length recordings. The progressive music craze catered to young adult males aged eighteen to thirty-four, a key demographic favored by many advertisers. In those days, cars did not typically have FM radios. You either listened to music on a cassette tape player in your car, or you listened to music you did not like nearly as much. Here was the window of opportunity for our little radio station.

KDEO became one of the first progressive rock stations in the nation on the AM radio dial. We were playing four or five cuts off albums by Jefferson Airplane, Pink Floyd, Jethro Tull, Yes, and Genesis. The reaction to the revolutionary format was instantaneous. San Diego State students flocked to our station whenever they were in their cars, and we capitalized on that market by making a deal with a small club close to campus named Funky Quarters. We would book acts at the club and broadcast their early evening set live while promoting the late set. Cheech and Chong, Seals and Crofts, Harry Chapin, and Jim Croce were among the performers featured during our run at Funky Quarters through FQ owner Tony Habib.

It was a special time. I had grown my hair long, to ponytail length. I had a mustache, long sideburns, and a goatee. The dressing room at FQ was filled with drugs—a table was covered with lines of nose candy, assorted bongs, and joints. It marked my initiation into the drug scene. I never did more than smoke marijuana; I was afraid that if I tried anything beyond smoking some weed, I might like it too much.

It was a rare venture into moderation for me. That said, I was stoned a lot during that stage of my life.

Our radio station took the best of the Top 40 format and combined it with the most progressive music heard anywhere on the AM radio dial. When Chuck Berry released his controversial hit "My Ding-a-Ling," we played it every twenty minutes. Listeners could not wait to hear the double entendre recording. Many mainstream stations would not even play the record. KDEO 910 was on the local radio map.

Perry Allen, our creative morning disc jockey, always kept us and our listeners entertained with his antics. Once, he filled our parking lot and caused a traffic jam when he invited listeners to come by to see him feed a Venus flytrap. Young fans watched in rapt attention as Perry nourished the plant with a condemned fly. Another time, he noted that the time in Japan was sixteen hours later than the time in San Diego, and called a radio station in Japan at 8:00 AM to get the final score on that night's Monday night football game. And when a crazy rumor was circulating that a Loch Ness-like monster had been seen in the wilds of East County, Allen promoted a search for the beast. Cars lined up as far as you could see on Fletcher Parkway in El Cajon to follow Perry on his search for the Proctor Valley monster. We even wound up with a police escort.

It was the craziest of times. Stoned kids were skinny-dipping in a pond rather than hunting for the monster. It was just an excuse for a frolicking good time. Meanwhile, the station went deep underground at night with Rick Phelps playing the most progressive music of the day in a very cool, laid-back style. It was almost too good to be true. KDEO was earning a giant share of that coveted eighteen-to-thirty-four-year-old male audience. We could not offer the stereo quality that the FM stations could, but it was enough that the music was available on the car radios of young men throughout the county.

Alas, it was too good to last. Programming guru Ron Jacobs came to the area from Los Angeles, as the boss man at radio station KGB. I had programmed against him in the Riverside/San Bernardino market, when I was at KPRO and he was at KMEN. He had beat me then, and he beat me again at KGB, a 5,000-watt powerhouse compared to our under-powered radio station. They were an established rock operation, and Jacobs tweaked their format to a more progressive slant and stole our devoted, but fickle audience.

This led to our station owner investing in automation equipment, programming computers to play music and commercials. He fired most of the on-air staff. Mike McGregor and I were the last announcers standing—and we were standing in a cozy, barren building in the East County countryside, adjacent to the towering radio antennae.

My hardest job ever in broadcasting was ahead of me: Mike and I had to record the times of day for on-air use. When I say we had to record the times of day, I mean *every* time of the day—12:01 on the odd cassette, and 12:02 on the even. That's 720 combinations, 360 odd and 360 even, covering twelve hours. The recording process was repetitive, to say the least: "KDEO time is 12:02." "KDEO time is 12:04." "KDEO time is 12:06." And on and on, 360 times. If you blew one of them, you had to go back to the beginning. You needed to be perfect 360 times in a row. The further you got into the clock, the higher the pressure mounted. I get knots in my stomach just thinking about it now, almost fifty years after the fact.

I knew I had to get out of that automated hell. My career saw me as a jack-of-all-trades and a master of none. I could manage, sell, and program, and be a disc jockey, newsman, or sportscaster. It was clear that I needed to focus on one area to get my career back on track.

At the age of thirty-five, I felt that my best bet was in the field of sports. I had all those years of local high school and college sports in Riverside under my belt, plus a little San Diego State basketball and three seasons of San Diego Charger football during my time at KDEO. I rearranged my resume to accentuate my sports background, but I still received countless letters of rejection with promises to keep my resume on file in case an opening for someone with my background presented itself. Meanwhile, I was still sitting there daily with my buddy Mike, watching the computer produce the sounds that came out of the radio. I had spent four years at that station, and we had a solid AFTRA contract.

Then, the 50,000-watt clear-channel radio giant WCAU in Philadelphia came calling, wanting to bring me to Philly for an interview. Philadelphia seemed like the end of the world. All I knew were the W. C. Field jokes: "I spent a week there one night." My longtime friend and benefactor, Irv Kaze, encouraged me to take the interview.

He had spent years in New York and knew the East Coast media markets. Irv had hired me to work the San Diego Charger broadcasts, and told me that Philadelphia was a great sports town. He said that I would become a household name there in nothing flat.

The people at the radio station welcomed me with open arms. "Listen to that voice!" program director Allan Hotlen exclaimed. I was in the right place at the right time. They offered me the job of sports director for their iconic radio station. It was twenty-four-hour talk, with a heavy emphasis on sports. Of course, I accepted! I hardly needed an airplane to fly home. Because the job wouldn't open up for a few more weeks, I kept the news to myself.

So, for the meantime I was back in my little space in the country, watching the computer go round and round. The station owner, a man named Don Balsamo, was not what you would call a "people" person; he was much happier dealing with computers. One day, he called me into his office and told me he was going to have to let me go. He agreed that, based on our union contract, I had earned something like five or six weeks of severance pay. I then said, "No problem, Don. I've accepted a job in Philadelphia." His face turned white as a sheet. I thought he was going to pass out. Balsamo did not part with a dollar bill very easily. He asked if he could pay out my severance over time rather than in one lump sum, and I assured him that it was no problem for me. I was double-dipping all the way to Philadelphia! In the end, Balsamo actually helped us out with the down payment on our home in our new city.

Chapter 4

The City of Brotherly Love

PHILADELPHIA WAS EVERYTHING my trusted mentor Irv Kaze had said it would be. He'd said that Philly was a sports-mad city that was passionate about each of its teams. Sure enough, it seemed that *everyone* was a sports fan. As I was driving across the country from San Diego to Philadelphia, I found that I could tune in to WCAU radio as soon as I'd reached the Midwest. My new radio home was booming across the land thanks to its 50,000-watt clear-channel signal.

Fans calling in to the station were curious about the new guy coming in from California. I sensed that I would have some work to do, since I was not one of their own. This was not going to be like working sports in Southern California, but I was looking forward to the new set of challenges. It was also going to be the first time that my job would be 100 percent about sports. I could hardly wait to get started.

I arrived in Philadelphia late in February of 1974. The radio station put me up at a very nice hotel directly across the street from the CBS-owned television and radio studios, located on City Line Avenue in Philly's Bala Cynwyd community. Coming from the cramped, two-man transmitter building at KDEO in El Cajon, it was starting to hit me just what a great opportunity this was going to be. Talk about a move up in class. And my timing was extraordinary; Philadelphia was the fifth biggest market in the country at the time.

I did not know a soul in the city aside from Allan Hotlen, the program director who had hired me, and his boss, WCAU general manager Jack Downey. The first order of business was to find a new home. Our property in San Diego had sold quickly, and we were flush with cash to make an offer in our new city. My wife and son stayed back in SoCal while I adjusted to the Philly lifestyle and found us a home—a nice three-bedroom, two-story home in a suburban area called Gulph Mills, only twenty minutes away from work on the high-speed Schuylkill Expressway.

LaVonne and Ralph soon joined me, and all was well as we settled into our new life. My son, who was ten years old at the time, hated to leave San Diego's year-round sunny days and beautiful beaches. But he adjusted quickly. He went to games with me and became a big fan of all the local teams. He learned to ice skate in the winter and made friends with a variety of kids in our neighborhood. In the summer, he swam at a local pool and we made our way to the beaches along the South Jersey Shore from time to time.

The transition was less comfortable for LaVonne, who was certainly not a sports fan. She didn't know anyone in Philadelphia, and it was an isolated and lonely existence for her. Our only common cause was furnishing and redecorating our new home. We did most of it ourselves, from painting and wall papering to rewiring. I once spent an inordinate amount of time replacing a light switch in the dining room with a dimmer switch. Once I was finished, you would lower the dimmer switch in the dining room and the fan above the stove on the other side of the common wall would slow. Some things took two or three tries.

The job was going great, and I was loving it. The high-powered, clear-channel nature of WCAU allowed my parents to listen to me in their home in Peoria, Illinois—850 miles from Philadelphia—as if it were a local station. I was part of a three-man morning team: Joel A. Spivak was the morning host; Bob Schmidt provided the news; and I handled the sports and regular banter with Joel. We were on the air in the morning, from 5:30 to 9:30. Our three-man morning team was dubbed "SpivakLawlerSchmidt." One-third of my face became very well known thanks to our billboards throughout the city. The station was an institution in this sports-mad city.

My evenings were free to attend games. There was 76ers basketball and Big 5 college hoops at the colorful Palestra; Flyers hockey in the

winter; Phillies baseball in the summer; and Eagles NFL games and
Temple or Penn college football in the fall. We weren't in El Cajon
anymore, Toto.

The *Bulletin*, a leading local newspaper, sponsored a weekly hour-
long interview program on Monday evenings. I was the host, and we
had a who's who of Philadelphia sports with us as guests, including
Mario Andretti, local heavyweight champ Joe Frazier, Phillies slugger
Greg Luzinski, tennis great Billy Jean King, Phillies manager Danny
Ozark, Flyers captain Bobby Clark, Eagles coach Dick Vermeil . . .
well, you get the idea. This program made it easier for the local fans to
accept me as one of their own, despite my California pedigree.

The years in Philadelphia are like a blur in my overstuffed memory bank. So much was crammed into the fifty-six months I spent in
that city. There was the aborted flirtation with the ABA in 1975; the
historic Bi-Centennial Celebration of 1976 that featured the NCAA
Final Four Men's Basketball Tournament; the NBA, MLB, and NHL
All-Star Games; and a coast-to-coast wagon train route that ended
at nearby Valley Forge. They passed right by our neighborhood. The
culmination was the most spectacular Fourth of July fireworks show I
have ever seen, over the waters of the Delaware River.

Coincidental with my arrival in Philadelphia, World Team Tennis was born in 1974. It was the brainchild of tennis superstar Billie
Jean King. She was the heart and soul of the local team, dubbed the
Philadelphia Freedoms. Billie Jean's close friend, Elton John, wrote a
song to honor the team, a smash hit titled "Philadelphia Freedom."
The greatest thing about the WTT was that it put female players on
equal footing with the men. They were true teammates. The greatest
names in the sport were a part of the league: Jimmy Connors, Mar-
garet Court, Bjorn Borg, Chris Evert, and Rod Laver were among the
players who joined King in the new venture. Billie Jean enthusiastically promoted the team tennis concept. She was a hoot to be around, and
her energy was captivating.

While I was working at WCAU, Ed Snider, the owner of the Flyers and the Spectrum Arena, was developing a pay sports and movie
TV channel called PRISM. Somehow, I became the face of that timely
cable TV venture. We broadcast home games for the Flyers, 76ers,
and Phillies, as well as Big 5 college basketball and Spectrum boxing

featuring the likes of Marvin Hagler, Benny Briscoe, and Willy "The Worm" Monroe.

In the mid-'70s, when I was working the telecast of a 76er game at the Spectrum in Philadelphia, my son worked many games with me in the press box as my statistician. On one particular night, he wasn't working but was in the stands with a buddy of his. It was a basketball giveaway night. Ralph and his friend came to the press room door after the game to meet me. The usual attendant who knew Ralph was not on duty that night, and he didn't believe that young Ralph was my son. The attendant turned them away and basically threw them out of the arena.

It was a cold, wintery evening with snow on the ground. The teen-age boys walked around the building, hoping to find a friendly entrance manned by a familiar attendant. Suddenly, five guys descended on Ralph and his buddy, Cyrus, roughing them up and stealing their basketballs and a total of $25 cash. My son and his friend managed to make it around Spectrum to an entrance, where they found a familiar guard who let them in and relayed their story to me in the press box where I was finishing our post-game show. I was not very happy with the well-intentioned attendant who had thrown the boys out in the cold. Luckily, no serious damage was done.

In the summer of 1975—about a year and a half into my new life outside of Southern California for the first time in thirteen years—the upstart American Basketball Association was maneuvering toward a merger with the established National Basketball Association. That prospect attracted former Denver Nuggets owner Frank Goldberg, who saw an opportunity to enter the NBA through the back door. He firmly believed that any merger talks would include the San Diego market. Goldberg purchased and rebranded the ABA San Diego Conquistadors as the San Diego Sails. He hired Bill Musselman as head coach and my good friend Irv Kaze as general manager.

Irv arranged an attractive offer for me to return to San Diego. I would broadcast the Sails games, work a daily sports program on radio station KSDO, and call play-by-play again for the Chargers starting with the 1976 season. It was a Godfather offer I couldn't refuse, though the timing was awkward in Philadelphia; my departure came right in the middle of WCAU's vital fall rating sweeps. They asked that I work on the critical AM drive time program as often as possible through the early days of the ABA season. That meant every game would be a road game for me. I would fly from Philadelphia to San Diego for a "home" game, and then back to Philly to work a morning or two at WCAU. Then, it was off to Salt Lake City, San Antonio, or Norfolk for a Sails road game, and back and forth I would go. It was grueling, but it was only for eleven games and I was able to deal with it. What the heck—I was a pro basketball announcer.

One of the new team's first games was against the Spurs in San Antonio, at the old HemisFair Arena downtown. It was a special treat for me because I could get some good Tex Mex food along the colorful River Walk. I had not had even a mouthful of Mexican food since leaving San Diego twenty months earlier. It's no wonder that the Alamo City became one of my favorite stops along the NBA trail in the years ahead.

Another early game was in Louisville against the Kentucky Colonels, featuring the league's premier center: the towering Artis Gilmore. The Colonels were a really good team coached by Hubie Brown, who would become a dear friend years down the road. Aside from Gilmore, they also had Maurice Lucas, Louie Dampier, Jan Van Breda Kolff, Wil Jones, and Bird Averitt. They were loaded. They played at the Louisville Convention Center, which may have been the most NBA-ready arena in the league. I was especially excited about this game.

The customs of the day dictated that the visiting team would bring its own broadcast equipment to the arena, while the home team would provide the telephone lines at the press table. That meant I had to carry a heavy load of broadcast gear (an amplifier, microphones, and cables) from city to city, but it was a small price to pay to have this dream job. We arrived at the arenas roughly two and a half hours before tip-off time, allowing me sufficient time to get my gear hooked up and tested back at the radio station in San Diego.

However, on this particular night in Louisville, somebody dropped the ball. The home team had not ordered the critical phone lines for the visiting team. I scurried around, dealing with the engineer for the home team broadcast and a local guy from the phone company, but to no avail; there was no way on earth for me to broadcast the game from the assigned broadcast location along press row.

The rep from the phone company pointed me toward an out-of-the-way phone booth. It was located up an exit ramp, and he thought I might be able to see the court from there. Well, I could see about half the court. That became my broadcast location for the entire game. It was an imaginative broadcast, to say the least. I couldn't even see all of the scoreboard—I wonder who won? I also wonder what the tally was on that collect phone call?

The Sails played the Spirits of St. Louis on the road twice in their first eleven games. I had not been to St. Louis since high school, when we drove down to see a Cardinal game at Sportsman's Park. This was a Major League city, and the former home of the NBA's St. Louis Hawks. It felt good to be there for an early season game. It made me feel as if I had made it, as if it was my calling. I arrived at the arena with the team and was hard at work at the press table, setting up for the broadcast, when I looked down to the other end and saw a twenty-three-year-old guy named Bob Costas preparing to announce the Spirits game for radio station KMOX. I was thirty-seven at the time, and I wondered how this kid had landed the type of job I'd strived to acquire for more than fifteen years. Yes, I resented it.

The ABA was still such great fun. The players had huge Afros and wore gaudy jewelry around their necks. The red, white, and blue basketball served as a colorful trademark. The league played a wide-open style of entertaining basketball, giving 3 points for shots made beyond an arc on the court. They celebrated their annual All-Star Weekend with gala parties and an acrobatic slam dunk contest. They were ahead of their time. It was great.

The Sails had a return date in St. Louis on November 9. It was the end of my hectic back-and-forth schedule. I left my broadcast equipment with the team to take back to San Diego, where the next game was scheduled three nights later, and returned to Philadelphia for a final morning on the air and a farewell party planned by the radio station. Just then, I received a phone call from my sister in San Diego at our Philadelphia home. She said she had just heard on the radio that the Sails had folded eleven games into the season. The owners had learned they would not be one of the teams to be invited into the NBA and had said, "See ya!"

Talk about timing. WCAU had already hired my replacement, Steve Albert, out of New York. I called my boss and sheepishly announced that although the going away party sounded great, I had no place to go. The job had disappeared. "No problem," said the station manager, Bob Sherman. "Let's party and celebrate that you are staying." They withdrew the offer to Albert, and I was back at work the next morning. I was amazed at my luck. As I think back, I wonder . . . whatever happened to that Bob Costas kid?

As much as I was enjoying my busy broadcasting career, the problem was that I was still getting up at 4:30 AM for the WCAU morning program. That was more than enough work for one man, but then I took on another task when I was asked to be a sports anchor on weekend telecasts, first at WPVI and then at WCAU. I worked seven days a week for a straight seven or eight months. I wasn't just broadcasting those PRISM TV games—I needed to prepare for them as well. It was beyond exhausting, and emotionally draining. I was never home. My son did tag along to serve as a statistician for some of the games I broadcast, but my non-sports fan wife did not have a clue as to what or why I was doing whatever it was I was doing.

The cracks in the foundation of my marriage to LaVonne became a rapidly growing fissure. The wounds were further deepened because we had gone house hunting in San Diego and found a distinctive adobe brick home in the Mt. Helix area that we absolutely loved. So we had not only lost the ABA job, but also the "dream" house. In the end, Ralph was fine staying in Philly. I quickly overcame the disappointment of the San Diego Sails' failure and dove head-first into the diverse demands of my many roles on the local sports scene. LaVonne was understandably let down by the news that we would be staying in Philadelphia.

I was stretched too thin. One afternoon, I collapsed on an elevator in downtown Philadelphia on my way to a meeting. I was rushed to the hospital in an ambulance with concerns of a possible heart attack. It turned out to be an easily treated blood sugar issue, but also a warning sign that I was just doing too much.

That's when WCAU Channel 10 came to the rescue. They wanted

me to take over as sports director, and be the sports anchor on the 5:00 PM, 6:00 PM, and 11:00 PM newscasts. I would replace Ted Leitner, who went on to have decades of great success in San Diego. That meant no more hockey, basketball, baseball, or boxing play-by-play. No more getting up at 4:30 in the morning. It sounded like nirvana.

Sadly, nightly television and I were not a good pairing. I hated not being able to see the games. I would show up with a camera crew, film or tape a little snippet from the first part of the game, and then rush back to the studio to put together that night's sportscast. I found it confining and I wasn't very good at it, but I gave it my best shot and the CBS people were very supportive. They offered me every chance to succeed, pairing me up with legendary broadcast coach Lilyan Wilder.

Lilyan was remarkable. I would take the train to New York City once a week to work with her for an hour and a half. She would look at a video from my previous week of work and just mercilessly rip it apart. Luckily, I had thick skin and profited from every brutal critique. She helped me speak better, write better, and groom better, and guided me to more effective posture on the set. Remember the old saying, "You can't make a silk purse out of a cow's ear"? It applies. Still, she helped me get comfortable on television, and it served me well for all my years working the telecasts of Clippers games in San Diego and Los Angeles.

But even the great Lilyan Wilder could not make me good enough at sitting behind a desk on a news set to make a long-term living at it. By the middle of the summer of 1978, I knew that it was not my life's work. It might have been the only time in my broadcast career that I was not a happy worker. It was a job, and I had no idea what to do as an alternative. We had made a killing in the stock market—casino gambling was being legalized in New Jersey—which helped financially, but I was still not happy at work.

There was something going on behind the scenes in the National Basketball Association that was about to have a profound impact on my life. The owners of the Boston Celtics and the Buffalo Braves were conjuring up a bizarre franchise swap. The Kentucky Colonel, John Y. Brown, would trade his interest in the Braves to Irv Levin in exchange for his interest in the Celtics. Levin would then move his new team to San Diego to be closer to his Hollywood movie interests.

Once again, Irv Kaze was there for me. He was named the general manager of the new team in San Diego that would become the Clippers, and offered me a job as the full-time broadcaster for the team. That was the good news. The bad news was that the fledgling team could only pay me $25,000 a year to broadcast the games on radio. That was a 50 percent pay cut. Luckily, with the stock market bonanza from the Atlantic City casinos, we could afford the pay reduction. What the hell? I would be enjoying my work again, and my marriage might even be enlivened by a return to the San Diego sunshine. The latter, however, would prove to be wishful thinking.

We got off to a good start. Amazingly, the adobe home we had wanted to buy in our abortive ABA foray was available again. We visited the home for a Sunday open house, and the realtor was placing her signs in front of the home. I told her to put them away. "We are buying this house!" I proclaimed. And buy it we did, even though the property cost $40,000 more in 1978 than it would have in 1975.

Unfortunately, the home was not the answer, and our problems were more than just geographical. The travel requirements of my new job hastened the end of our nineteen-year marriage. I was in need of a soul mate. I would find her a year later, when I met my dear sweet Jo in San Diego. Much more about that later.

So, I joined the Clippers at the age of forty. I was thrilled to be the voice of an NBA team, and it would not have been possible without those years in Philadelphia. I will be grateful to that city forevermore.

OVERTIME Most Memorable 76ers

DARRYL DAWKINS

Darryl Dawkins was the fifth pick in the 1975 draft by the Philadelphia 76ers. He was an eighteen-year-old man-child fresh out
of high school in Orlando, Florida, where he had averaged over
30 points and 20 rebounds a game while leading his school to the
Florida State Championship. He was six foot ten and 240 pounds as
a high school senior, and he was still growing.

The Sixers were beside themselves with optimism; Dawkins
brought up images of Wilt Chamberlain. When he was introduced
to the Philly media, his personality also conjured up images of
heavyweight boxing champion Muhammad Ali.

The Philadelphia team was an emerging power under head
coach Gene Shue, and he was hesitant to use the raw-skilled teen in
his first two years in the league. Dawkins would play scant minutes,
but provided crowd-pleasing plays just about every time he stepped
onto the court. He was a slam-dunk machine, and the fans loved
him. They chanted his name, demanding his presence, but Shue
was focused on winning and deaf to the chants.

Dawkins time came after Shue was replaced by Billy Cunningham early in the 1977–1978 season. He was then twenty years old.
His minutes doubled, and so did his rebound and scoring figures.
He was a part of the rotation and the fans loved it. This was a team
that featured Julius Erving, George McGinnis, Doug Collins, Lloyd
Free, Steve Mix, Henry Bibby, and Harvey Catchings. But no player
was as adored by the fans as Darryl Dawkins. He fed off their love.

I hosted a live telecast of Dawkins' twenty-first birthday party
at a rollicking nightclub in downtown Philadelphia on January 11,
1978. Oh me, oh my. The celebrants fawned over him enthusiastically at the gala party. Everybody who was anybody in the city was
there to help celebrate the big man's ascension into adulthood. It
was a blast as Darryl's colorful personality filled the room with joy.

Fans throughout the league loved him. In today's media cli-
mate, he would have been a household name with a television persona somewhere akin to Charles Barkley or Shaquille O'Neal, and
with a social media presence to rival LeBron James.

Sports in the City of Brotherly Love is not a pastime, it's a reli-
gion. The fans care with a passion I have not seen in any other city in
the country. Darryl Dawkins was in the right place at the right time.
Former *Daily News* columnist Mark Whicker once wrote: "There

were only three people laughing in the entire building before tip-off—Darryl Dawkins, seated on the bench, and the two ball boys at his feet, listening to the Sixer center's nonstop patter." That perfectly captures the player, the man, the legend.

Darryl never won a championship. He never averaged 20 points a game. He never was an NBA All-Star. But he was "Chocolate Thunder." He was from the planet "Lovetron." He carried a boom box the size of a Volkswagen and actually suffered a shoulder injury as a result.

Dawkins is probably best remembered for his backboard-shattering slam dunks. This game-stopping destruction happened more than once. The game ops people had to wheel out and secure a back-up board and stanchion before the game could resume. Darryl is singularly responsible for the breakaway rims and shatterproof glass used on the boards to this day.

Dawkins went from the 76ers to New Jersey in 1982, just missing the Sixers' title season. He had a few decent years with the Nets. My next up-close encounter with him was in 1987, in Salt Lake City. The Utah Jazz had been involved in a massive seven-player, three-team trade that brought them the then-thirty-year-old, six-foot-eleven, 270-pound Darryl. The Clippers had an early season date with the Jazz in Utah. As we walked into the arena, I saw the hulking giant seated rather forlornly on the Jazz bench. I went over, sat down next to him, and asked what on earth he was doing in Salt Lake City, Utah. Darryl turned to me and said, "I have no effin' idea." He was made for the big Eastern cities, not for this Mormon outpost so far from home. He was soon sent to the Pistons in Detroit, but his NBA days were essentially over.

Darryl played only thirty-some games total in his final three seasons in the league. He would take his colorful fame to Italy, where he played until he was thirty-seven years old. By that time, he had spent over half his life as a professional basketball player. He left smiles on the faces of millions of basketball fans the world over, along with shattered backboards and bent rims. We lost Darryl Dawkins early in 2015; the world misses him.

JULIUS "DR. J" ERVING

Julius Erving was a mysterious legend in his five years in the old American Basketball Association. He was like the Loch Ness Monster. Everyone had heard of him, but nobody had seen him.

That all changed in 1976, when four ABA teams were absorbed

into the thirty-year-old National Basketball Association. After nine turbulent seasons, the ABA was dead and gone.

The Philadelphia 76ers had acquired two stars from the ABA the prior season: George McGinnis from the Indiana Pacers, and Caldwell Jones from the Spirits of St. Louis. They were going for the home run in 1976. The ABA's final season saw Erving average 29 points, 11 rebounds, and 5 assists a game. His dazzling dunks were too many to count.

The Nets were one of the four ABA teams given a ticket into the established NBA. The problem for the Nets was that the New York Knicks demanded several million dollars for the right to invade their coveted market in Gotham. Add that to the established fee to enter the league, and the Nets were in a major financial bind. They offered Dr. J to the Knicks in exchange for waiving the indemnity fee. The Knicks, to their ever-lasting regret, rejected the offer. The Nets then backed out of a promise to raise Erving's salary, and now everyone was unhappy. At least three teams lined up to bid for the twenty-six-year-old superstar's services: Milwaukee, the Los Angeles Lakers, and the Philadelphia 76ers. Just imagine Dr. J joining the unstoppable Kareem Abdul-Jabbar in L.A. It didn't happen.

Philadelphia blew everyone else out of the water by offering the Nets something in the range of $6 million for the fabled ABA star. It allowed them to cover most of their costs for entering the league in the nation's largest market.

At the time, I was in Philadelphia calling Sixer games on home TV. We were thrilled the prior year when the team brought in McGinnis, who was second only to Erving in ABA star power. The Philly team had won only nine games in the 1972–1973 season. They brought Gene Shue in as head coach, and the rebound began: twenty-five wins and thirty-four wins, respectively, in the first two seasons. And then they jumped to forty-six wins and a spot in the play-offs after the acquisition of big George. They knew they were getting close. The huge cost of attracting Erving would be well worth it if it led to the team's first NBA title since 1967.

The news conference in downtown Philadelphia to announce Erving's signing was almost surreal. McGinnis and Jones one year, and Dr. J. the next! The 76ers had fortified themselves with the ABA's top two stars in Erving and McGinnis, and with one of the junior league's best young centers in Jones. Caldwell had been the starting center for the San Diego Sails during my brief stint in the ABA, and I knew him to be a solid player and a good guy. I was thrilled to death. Add those three to Doug Collins, Lloyd Free, Henry Bibby, Steve Mix, and Darryl Dawkins, and you had a championship contender. Doc was a class act from day one, as he politely and intelligently answered questions from the horde of media members.

The spotlight could not find Dr. J during his years with the Squires in Norfolk, or even with the Nets. We would hear stories, almost fables, about this Dr. J guy, but never get to see him. So, to finally see him up close and personal, night after night, was one of the great thrills of my professional career.

October 23, 1976, saw Julius Erving make his NBA debut with the 76ers at the Spectrum in Philadelphia against the San Antonio Spurs, who were playing their first game in the NBA as well. Dr. J had a forgettable game, with only 17 points. It may have been the first and last time that his pre-game jitters carried over onto the basketball court. The career 78-percent foul shooter made only 5 of his 13 foul shots that night. I was excitedly working the telecast of the game on a new cable TV sports service called PRISM, with ten-time All-Star and Hall-of-Famer-to-be Hal Greer serving as my TV partner. He was a Philadelphia sports legend. We had a great time.

Legendary PA announcer Dave Zinkoff introduced Philadelphia's newest sports star to the sell-out crowd: "From the University of Massachusetts, Number 6, Julius ERRRRving!" The crowd went crazy. They could not wait to see what all the fuss was about when it came to this mythical star from the American Basketball Association. Doc made only 7 field goals that night, but at least 6 of them were the most spectacular dunks that NBA fans had ever seen. We had no commercial breaks on these PRISM telecasts, so we would just talk hoops and show the Doctor's dunks during the time-outs from every angle imaginable. Through three games, Dr. J. scored only 40 points and the 76ers were 1–2. It was too early to panic, but some did wonder if the NBA presented challenges Erving had never seen in the ABA.

Those concerns were put to rest in Game 4 in Houston, where Doc went for 27 points, 13 rebounds, 9 assists, and 2 blocks. The player and the team were on their way. It would be a fifty-win season that led to a trip to the NBA Finals against the Portland Trailblazers.

My most enduring memory of Julius that first year was the way he took a young rookie named Terry Furlow under his wing. I remember that he would always sit next to the twenty-two-year-old Furlow on the team bus, and they would be engaged in constant conversation. Furlow had led the Big Ten in scoring at Michigan

State the year before he was drafted #12 by the 76ers. Doc saw something special in the young player from Flint, Michigan, though Furlow played scant minutes in less than half of the team's games.

Come to think of it, maybe it was not so much that Erving saw something special; he may have seen something that worried him. Furlow was only with the team that one season. He had a few better years in Cleveland, Atlanta, and Utah, but it was all cut short when he lost his life in a traffic accident in Ohio in 1980. An autopsy showed evidence of cocaine and Valium in his bloodstream. Furlow's tragic end hurt Erving badly. He cared. That was typical of Julius.

The Doctor retired in 1987. He had a "retirement tour," and was honored at each of his final stops around the league. The Sixers had an early season date with the Clippers at the L.A. Sports Arena, and the team staged a special segment at halftime. I was on the court with Dr. J to express our thanks for the many hours of entertainment he had provided fans around the world. We presented him with the obligatory gift, and the crowd gave him a hearty ovation.

The Clippers played the Sixers in Philadelphia about seven weeks later, in early January. I went into the home team's locker room before the game to check with coach Matt Goukas. I had barely entered the room when a voice from the other side bellowed out my name. It was Doc. He called me over to say a special thanks for the ceremony in Los Angeles in November. He said it was one of the nicest he had experienced and he would never forget it. Erving came into the league with class, and he was going out the same way.

I would see Doc from time to time after his retirement. He came to Clipper games when he happened to be in Los Angeles, and we always found a minute to shake hands and exchange pleasant memories. His life suffered through significant losses, but he always managed to show a dignified face to all who met him. I last saw him, fittingly, at the Naismith Memorial Basketball Hall of Fame in Springfield, Massachusetts, in 2019.

WORLD B. FREE
I knew him as Lloyd Free when he came into the league in Philadelphia in 1975.

By year two, he would be a valuable player off the bench for the 76ers. A 16-points-a game scorer in less than thirty minutes a game. This is before the three-point shot.

Philly Coach Gene Shue wound up being the Clippers coach in their maiden season in San Diego (1978). He realized the first day of training camp that he needed added scoring punch, and he immediately thought of Free. The Clippers gave up a 1984 first-round draft pick for a player who had started only five games the prior season. Shue explained it to me succinctly: "If we are good five years from now, the pick won't be too valuable. If we are bad, I won't be here, so what the hell?"

History can be cruel, and it tells us now that the first-round pick the 76ers received for Free would be the fifth choice in that 1984 draft, and Philadelphia used it to acquire future Hall of Fame forward Charles Barkley. By that time, Free was a 20-points-a-game scorer for the Cleveland Cavaliers, and Shue had picked up his second NBA Coach of the Year honor with the Washington Bullets. Note also that the Clippers had moved to Los Angeles from San Diego.

It wasn't that Free was not impressive with the young Clippers. He went from 10–12 shot attempts a game to 20-plus a night in San Diego. His scoring exploded to 28.8 in year one, and a shade over 30 in year two. He was somehow not voted as an All-Star that first year, but he did achieve All-NBA Second Team honors.

The game before the All-Star break was in San Diego against Atlanta. The Clippers and their hardy core of fans were incensed that Free, now known as World B. Free, had been an All-Star snub. He led the team to a resounding win over the Hawks, and was clearly the best player on the court with 26 points. Shue took him out of the game once the win was secure. The crowd—and there were less than 7,000 of them on hand—screamed with joy as Free made his way around the entire perimeter of the court, high-fiving each fan in the front row seats. It was his All-Star game, and he made the most of it.

His back-to-back big seasons in San Diego started a string of eight straight years in which he would average 20 or more points a game on the season. Free and Shue were a perfect fit. Though the player was still earning a reserve player's salary when the Clippers acquired him, he realized quickly in San Diego that he was no longer a bench player, but a star. Free wanted to have his contract renegotiated. The dispute carried into his second season. He tried to make his point before a game in Phoenix by claiming he would not play because his back hurt, but Shue simply inserted second-year guard Freeman Williams into Free's spot in the starting lineup. The former NCAA scoring leader from Portland State responded with 51 points in, I think, his first NBA start. Predictably, Free's back felt a whole lot better during the next game in Chicago.

World was, and is, such a joy to be around. In those days, the traveling party consisted of a head coach, assistant coach, trainer, an announcer, and ten to twelve players. All flights were commercial, so teams would play a road game and stay there overnight before flying out the next day. It was a tight, compact group.

A broadcaster really got to know the players. I knew Free in his Philadelphia days, and he was easy to get to know. He knew no strangers. There would be drinks together at the hotel after the game, or breakfast in the hotel coffee shop, side by side at the counter in the morning. I missed him when Shue's successor, Paul Silas, decided that World wasn't his kind of ballplayer.

Free has been back in Philadelphia since his retirement in 1988. He is a well-recognized Goodwill Ambassador for the 76ers, and if ever a personality was perfectly fitted for that role, it belongs to my friend, World B. Free.

ALLEN IVERSON

Allen Iverson was a trend-setter unlike any others. He created new fans from the nation's streets and black-top playgrounds. He grew up in the projects in Hampton, Virginia. The streets were his home and he was often in trouble, to the point of spending four months in a correctional facility in Newport News while still in high school.

Basketball became Iverson's escape route to college when he was recruited by legendary Georgetown coach John Thompson. He entered the NBA draft after his sophomore season. In 1996, the six-foot Iverson would be the shortest number-one overall pick in the draft to ever play in the league. He would also become the shortest player to win the league scoring title—and he did that four times!

Allen was not the first player to sport tattoos. That recognition is generally given to Dennis Rodman, who was the first to openly display ample body art ten years before Iverson entered the NBA. However, A.I. popularized the concept. It is a rare player in the sport today who does not have a tattoo somewhere on his frame. Iverson brought the concept into the mainstream.

Young people from the inner city adopted Iverson as one of their own. I saw this firsthand in October of 2001, when the L.A. Clippers played an exhibition game against Cleveland in St. Louis, Missouri. The exciting young Clipper team featured a very youthful Darius Miles, who was just a year out of his high school across the river in East St. Louis, Illinois. He had been featured on the cover of

Sports Illustrated before his first season and was an all-rookie first-team choice in year one in the league. He was a featured player on a joyfully exuberant team that was easily the most popular Clipper edition since the franchise moved to Los Angeles in 1984.

The day before the game, I was with Darius for a visit at his old high school for an assembly honoring him less than a year and a half after his graduation. We stopped first to visit his mother at the house in which he grew up. He had spent a fair hunk of his early NBA earnings fixing up his childhood home. It was now the nicest home in the neighborhood by far, replete with a white picket fence. He was very proud and his mother, the formidable Ethel, was thrilled and grateful.

We left the happy home and headed to the high school, where it seemed like just yesterday Miles was earning Mr. Basketball of Illinois honors. As we strolled through the halls of the school, the older students all recognized him and stared adoringly. Teachers stopped to talk, while offering words of congratulations and encouragement.

By now, you must be wondering why I am telling you all about Darius Miles when we had been touting Allen Iverson. Well, here we go. D. Miles received a raucous welcome when introduced to the assembled body of students. They hung on his every word and reacted loudly as he talked about playing against the great players of the day: Shaq O'Neal ("ooooh"), Tracy McGrady ("ahhh"), Kobe Bryant ("wow"), and so on. But those reactions were nothing compared to when he mentioned Allen Iverson. The place went bonkers. The kids screamed and shouted and yelled at just the mention of A.I.'s name. You would have thought he'd just dribbled down the student aisle for a slam dunk, stage left. It took a while for the assembly hall to settle down enough for Miles to conclude his remarks.

That is just one example of the way things went throughout Iverson's fifteen-year NBA career. A.I.'s presence expanded the game's reach in ways nobody had imagined.

GENE SHUE

Gene Shue is one of the best friends I ever had in the game of basketball. I had the pleasure of working with him in three different NBA cities: Philadelphia, San Diego, and Los Angeles. He coached 1,645 NBA games and played in almost 700.

Shue spent sixty years in the NBA. Before that, he was a college star at the University of Maryland, where he set school scoring records and made first team All-ACC. In the pros, he was a five-time All-Star as a player, and a two-time NBA Coach of the Year. He then served a variety of roles for the Philadelphia 76ers, from scout to general manager. Somehow, all that has not gotten him into the Naismith Memorial Basketball Hall of Fame in Springfield, Massachusetts, though he's been nominated many times—first as a coach and then as a contributor. I'm amazed he has not been enshrined. He is the only two-time NBA Coach of the Year winner to not have been selected. It is shameful and cruel to a man who has given so much to the sport. Sadder still, we lost Gene in April of 2022 at the age of 90 after he succumbed to a long bout with cancer.

I first worked with Gene when he was coach of the 76ers in Philadelphia. He took over a team that was coming off an NBA record-worst 9–73 season. Four years later, the Sixers were in the NBA Finals, and I came in to announce the team's home games on television. Shue and I had a solid professional relationship that became personal in 1978, when we both coincidentally wound up working for the newly minted Clippers in San Diego. We bought homes on the same side of the city, which made it convenient for us to carpool to home games and to the airport for road games.

Gene was an exceptional athlete. His weight remained virtually unchanged from his playing days on into his eighties. He was a good golfer and a very good tennis player. I had played a fair amount of racquetball, and Gene, who had never learned the game, asked me to teach him how to play. He ended up beating me in our first game, and in every game thereafter. We played daily during his two seasons in San Diego. He wound up spotting me 4, then 6, then 8 points a game to make our race to 21 more interesting. In the meantime, our wives (now ex-wives) became close friends and remain so to this day. Our kids went to high school together. I still consider those years—1978 through 1980—as two of the most enjoyable years in my professional career.

This was a different world from what exists in the current day National Basketball Association. I remember one night after a game in New Orleans, Gene and I were sitting in a bar on Bourbon Street enjoying a little post-game libation. I had given my credit card to the waitress and asked her to keep the tab open. I asked her what time the bar closed. She had a shocked look at her face as she replied, "Close? Why would we close?" That was my introduction to the Big Easy. We were in for a long night. As the evening wore on, one Clipper player after another would stop by to join us for a drink and some basketball talk. We just had a great old time. Before we knew it, the clock showed 5:00 AM. The bill came. I gulped. Gene eventually found a way to bury the cost in his expense report.

There were so many things that happened then that would never happen today. League rules state that teams must suit up at least eight players or forfeit the game. The Clippers were dangerously short-handed for a game against the Suns in Phoenix in 1979. Assistant coach Bobby Weiss was just a season removed from playing, and was a regular participant in practices with the team. The plan was that Weiss would suit up if the Clippers were down to seven players. I was carrying a one-game contract for the coach in my suit pocket as we bused to the game. In the end, eight players were able to dress for the game and Weiss was not needed. I wish I had kept that contract as a memento.

Gene went on to coach the Bullets in Washington, where he won his second Coach of the Year award. We remained close, and looked forward to our twice-a-year visits when the two teams would meet. After Don Chaney was fired in 1987, I tossed Gene's name into the hat for the Clipper coaching job. It seemed a long shot that he would return to the team, but he interviewed brilliantly and got the job. I drove him down to San Diego so he could meet with his agent, Ron Grinker, and team president Alan Rothenberg to execute the paperwork. The deal was sealed for, as I recall, $170,000 a year, a figure that boggled my mind in 1987. Gene was thrilled.

I'm not sure I did Gene any favors by directing him to his Clippers return; the team was in total disarray. They won seventeen games in his first season. General manager Elgin Baylor desperately wanted to draft Scottie Pippen in the June draft that year. The owner had never heard of him and certainly had never heard of his college—Central Arkansas. He wanted, and got, Reggie Williams from Georgetown; he received a journeyman who played for six teams in ten years rather than a Hall-of-Fame, seven-time All-Star. That decision alone may have sealed coach Shue's fate.

There was a second chance with the 1988 draft. The Clippers' ineptitude the year before earned them the first overall pick in the draft that featured Danny Manning of NCAA champion Kansas as the clear top choice. No dispute from Sterling this time. Shue was in New York for the draft while Sterling and the rest of us were at a White Party at Sterling's swank Beverly Hills residence. Party time with the owner!

But the party had no sustaining power. Manning would hold out and miss all of training camp and the first week of the season. He joined a team that had dropped three of its first four games. His presence led to a rebound, with five wins in his first eight games. The big picture was looking better until Manning tore up a knee on a routine play in a game in Milwaukee at the old Mecca. A losing streak was underway. It would reach eleven games by mid-January, after a 15-point loss to the Lakers at the Forum.

After the game, I sat with Gene and his wife, Sandy, in their Marina Del Rey condo, drinking some wine. We knew he had likely coached his last game. Sure enough, the axe fell the next day with his good friend and able assistant, Don Casey, named to replace him. The eleven-game losing streak stretched to nineteen. Then there was a 3-point win, followed by 13 more losses. It was a low point for a team that had seen a lot of them.

Philadelphia came through by offering Gene their general manager post. He served there in a variety of positions for the better part of twenty-five years. When Jo and I were living in the Marina in our final six or seven years with the Clippers, we would get together with Gene and his dear Patti from time to time for dinner and laughs. It was one of those rare relationships where we related as if we were still playing racquetball every day. The quips and jabs flew back and forth, just like old times. My relationship with Gene Shue was truly a special one. ●

SECOND QUARTER

VOICE OF THE CLIPPERS

Chapter 5

Brotherhood of Broadcasters

THERE ARE THIRTY NBA TEAM television play-by-play broadcasters, and another thirty on the radio side. These are jobs young broadcasters across the country aspire to with zealous fervor. The instant a position opens, a hundred applicants are lined up immediately.

I always felt that being a team broadcaster was as close as you could come to playing the game. The advantage is that you can work into your sixties, seventies, and even eighties as a broadcaster, while players are typically out of the game sometime in their thirties. The players earn many times more money, but an NBA announcer's pay, especially in the major markets, provides a very nice lifestyle. The travel was first class, the accommodations on the road were sumptuous, the per diem was like free money, and you had five or six months off each year. No wonder people clamored for these jobs.

I recall being on the Clipper team bus talking to center Chris Kaman on the way to practice one day. He said, "I make a lot more money than you." I knew Chris was generously taking care of a very wide range of family and friends, with houses, cars, and advanced lifestyles provided to one and all. I replied, "Yes, but I bet I have more left over at the end of the year." He nodded in sad agreement.

The job with the Clippers in San Diego in 1978 was my first shot at being a full-time team announcer—not that I hadn't tried earlier. I'd made a bid for the San Diego Rocket NBA job when the team formed in 1967; it was a reach, and I came up short. I'd tried again in

Philadelphia with the 76ers in the 1970s, but had settled for working home games on television.

The welcoming committee for me in 1978 was led by Chick Hearn of the Lakers and Al McCoy of the Suns. I had known Chick from back in our Peoria days, and ran across him from time to time over the years. He was always an inspiration for me. He reached out when I got the position in San Diego with a pledge to help whenever needed. McCoy was even more welcoming, calling me up with the warmest of greetings. I didn't know him at all at the time, but he has become a great friend over the years and we would meet for dinner whenever our schedules would allow. The Hall of Fame broadcaster served the Suns for the fiftieth season in 2021–2022. He sounds as crisp and clean now as he did in the 1970s. Amazing.

Although there has never been a formal association of league broadcasters—there probably should be—we would meet annually in New York over the years for NBA broadcast meetings. The gatherings lasted two or three days, and were instructive and a great chance to spend some quality time with our peers.

I do not think there is a man or a woman in the announcer role today who feels that it is work. It is pure joy. Fans and some media members complain that the season is too long, but I never felt that way. There was one year when the Clippers went 12–70, and I hated to see the season end. Most of my contemporaries would have felt the same way. The relationships were exceptional, and they are one of the things I miss in retirement.

If you aspire to one of these jobs, I say go for it. I was truly blessed in my forty years in the business. I wish the same for you.

Young broadcasters often hunt for catchphrases to use, and would ask me what they could do to create them. The best answer I could give them was to not try too hard. The reality is that most of broadcasting's all-time greats had catchphrases. You can go all the way back to the first voice of the NBA, Marty Glickman. He coined phrases that are still commonplace in the game today.

Baseball announcers typically seek a signature home run call. I can still hear Harry Caray in St. Louis in the 1950s with Stan Musial at bat: "Fly ball to right field. It *might* be, it *could* be, it *is* a home run!" Chick Hearn gave basketball announcers a new vocabulary. Every time you hear an announcer today say, "slam dunk," "charity stripe," "air ball," or "no-look pass," it is right out of Chick Hearn's versatile vernacular. There is likely not an L.A. Dodger fan alive who doesn't hear Vin Scully's voice exclaim, "It's time for Dodger baseball!" before the first pitch of each game.

If an announcer tries to invent a catchphrase, it will sound contrived. The key is that it must sound spontaneous. It must originate spontaneously. I don't know when I first uttered the words "oh me, oh my!" on the air. They just popped out of my mouth from time to time.

Clipper marketing director Mitch Huberman told me one day in his office at the L.A. Sports Arena that he just loved it when I uttered my "oh me, oh my" catchphrase. That got me thinking: it could be delivered enthusiastically for a great play, or disappointedly for a poor play. It could be a shout of joy, or an expression of spiritless dismay. It turned into a valuable broadcasting tool.

In the early '90s, I was haggling with a car salesman over a purchase. He countered that he would make the deal I wanted if I would buy a vanity plate that read "OHMEOHMY." The closest we could come to at the DMV was "OHMEOMY," and the deal was done. All of my vehicles carried those plates as long as I was in Los Angeles.

"Bingo" happened organically. The NBA had instituted the 3-point field goal at the beginning of the 1979–1980 season, and the Clippers acquired a jump-shooting forward named Bobby "Bingo" Smith from Cleveland. Before long I'd call "Bingo" whenever he made a 3-pointer. It wasn't long before fans would greet me in the stands with "Bingo" shouts. It just expanded from there. Some fans wished I would only use it when a Clipper made a 3. I explained that it was not offered as a celebration, but as a description that a 3-point shot had been made. There was a big difference between an enthusiastic "Bingo" when Eric Piatkowski made 3 for the Clippers, and an agonizing "Bingo" describing a successful 3 by an opposing player.

Despite my mantra that catchphrases must be spontaneous, I must admit that I stole "Lawler's Law." A man named Al Domenico was the longtime trainer when I was calling 76ers games in Philadelphia in

---

TIME OUT **Bloopers Happen**

The Clippers were on the road in the early 1990s. I think the game was in Phoenix. I was working the telecast with the "Czar" Mike Fratello. I was to close an opening segment with a tagline for the sponsor, Reebok, that read: "Reebok—life is short. Play hard." I delivered it as effectively as I could, and we went to commercial break.

Fratello stood at my side in bemused silence. I asked him what was wrong. Mike replied, "Do you know what you said?" I had no idea what he was talking about. He told me that I had proclaimed, "Reebok—life is short. Stay hard."

I absolutely did not believe him. After the game, I flew home with the team and made the short drive to my Marina Del Rey apartment that I was sharing with Jo's son, David. He had watched and recorded the game. I asked if he'd heard our Reebok opening, and he said he certainly had. He confirmed Fratello's claim. I still did not believe it. We hit rewind on the video recorder, and I was ready to be vindicated. But there it was: Ralph standing tall on camera, saying, "Reebok—life is short. Stay hard."

It's the only time I was ever quoted in *Sports Illustrated*.

Similarly, Mike Smith and I were once working a Clippers–Knicks game at Madison Square Garden in the early 2000s. The first quarter ended with a player taking a desperation mid-court shot to beat the buzzer. Mike added to my description by marveling that the shot was from the "G" in the Madison Square Garden mid-court logo, to which I responded, "Oh, the G-Spot. I've been hunting for that for years!" ●

---

the mid 1970s. He challenged me once to watch how often the team that scores 100 points first goes on to win the game. I started with the Clippers in their first year in San Diego in 1978. I was the full-time broadcast voice of a team for the first time. I got to thinking about the premise proposed a couple of years earlier by Domenico, played with a little alliteration, and came up with "Lawler's Law." I explained it on-air: "First team 100 wins. It's the Law!" I had many opposing coaches taunt me by saying they'd "beat the Law" tonight. It was an identifying tool, and I still hear an occasional NBA announcer recall the "Law."

I will admit that it makes me happy.

Here are the four greatest voices in NBA broadcast history: Marty Glickman, Johnny Most, Chick Hearn, and Marv Albert.

The game desperately misses all four. The current-day NBA lacks the distinctive voices and vitality possessed by this mighty quartet. I don't care if we're talking about the network level or local team announcers; so many of today's play-by-play men sound cookie-cutter bland. They scream and shout, but lack not only the memorable voices and intonations of this legendary Mount Rushmore quartet, but also their prodigious personas. Who can replace the recently retired Marv Albert as the unquestioned voice and face of the league on the national NBA telecasts? Time will tell.

Hall of Famer Mike Breen has a unique and informative professorial style, while capably announcing more NBA Finals than anyone on earth. He works with his color commentators better than any play-by-play man who has ever lived. Sadly, there is no other worthy challenger to ascend to the national throne now that Marv has let go of his scepter.

Among the league's local team TV broadcasters, Joel Myers in New Orleans and Mark Followill in Dallas have the big voices, but Breen, better known for his excellent NBA network role on ESPN and ABC, is also the longtime voice of the New York Knicks. He started handling the team's play-by-play duties on radio, and has been their primary television face since replacing the redoubtable Marv Albert. Breen is solid on his own, but his pairing with former Knick great Walt "Clyde" Frazier (a living, breathing, talking thesaurus) is positively wondrous. The Breen and Frazier duo is spot-on perfect. Each ideally complements the other.

Local radio, meanwhile, has been dismissed by the league, moving from prized courtside press table broadcast locations to being hidden in the elevated cheap seats in virtually every NBA arena. In days long gone by, the local radio broadcaster would sit courtside, right next to the bench. Today's team radio announcers can only dream about that prized spot. The broadcaster could listen to the coach during time-outs, lean over to check with the trainer about the status of an injured player, or hail a referee for clarification of an official's call. Those were the days, my friend.

Despite this, one local NBA radio voice still shines: eighty-nine-year-old Al McCoy has been broadcasting Phoenix Suns games since

1972. His dulcet, pear-shaped tones continued to comfort Suns fans. The Hall of Fame announcer is one of the best to ever describe an NBA game.

The question "who's next?" begs for an answer. Twenty-five-year-old Los Angeles Clipper radio announcer Noah Eagle could be the one, if the team can keep him satisfied with working their games in relative anonymity on local radio. If the name sounds familiar, it may be because he's the son of well-known CBS and Brooklyn Nets announcer Ian Eagle.

That sums up where we are today in terms of the faces we see and the voices we hear providing the flipside of the game's soundtrack. The aforementioned historic foursome provided the "A" side and a melody the rest of the broadcasters can only hope to hum.

To be sure, Marty Glickman was the game's first voice. In that 1946 inaugural season, he broadcast New York Knicks games at the age of twenty-nine and then became the NBA's first national spokesman when he called the league's weekly Saturday afternoon TV games on the Dumont Network in 1953. The Bronx-born announcer had tasted fame much earlier, qualifying for the U.S. Men's Olympic Track and Field team as a sprinter in 1936. The games were played in Berlin. Glickman was scheduled to compete on the U.S. 4-by-100-meter relay team. The morning of the event, Glickman and his running mate, Sam Stoller, were stunningly scratched from the race. Both were Jewish, and it was widely believed that the Olympic committee had caved to pressure so as not to incite German chancellor Adolf Hitler, who loathed the prospect of seeing two Jews collecting gold medals in front of him in Berlin.

Glickman vowed to win his gold medal in the 1940 Olympics, which were scheduled to be held in Tokyo. When the beginning of the Second World War in 1939 erased both the 1940 and 1944 games, Glickman was left at Syracuse University, where he graduated in 1939. Marty's competitive juices still flowed. He dabbled in both professional football and basketball, but the pro leagues of the times simply did not provide a viable future for an ambitious young athlete.

Marty turned his attention to broadcasting, using his athletic fame to land a job airing sports reports for radio station WHN in New York City. By 1943, he had risen to the rank of sports director, which put

him in line to broadcast New York Knick games in the newly formed
Basketball Association of America in 1946. He would be the voice
of the Knicks for twenty-one years, and was a ubiquitous presence
as lead sportscaster in the nation's biggest market, where he would
call games of the NFL Giants, the AFL Jets, and the New York Nets
before the ABA/NBA merger. Glickman would also broadcast college
football and basketball games, and work pre- and post-game shows on
radio for baseball's Brooklyn Dodgers and New York Yankees. He even
worked the roller derby. The man was a broadcast junkie. He was literally everywhere, and by 1991, he was in the Basketball Hall of Fame as
the second winner of the coveted Curt Gowdy Award, given annually
to honor electronic and print journalists.

Marty Glickman was the game's first singular voice. Any list of the
NBA's greatest play-by-play men must include him.

Next up is Johnny Most, the "forever voice" of the fabled Boston
Celtics. Of course, it was not really forever, but it did touch five decades, from 1953 to 1990. Nobody can come close to having broadcast
the sixteen championships vividly described by Johnny.

The gravel-voiced Most was easily the most colorful and opinion-
ated announcer in NBA history. He was a Celtic "Homer" and proud
of it. All Celtic foes were the enemy to Johnny Most. If there was no
natural rivalry, he'd make up a desultory name for an opposing player
to create fan-fueled animosity.

The Celtics had no championship pedigree when Most joined
them in 1953. Boston was a hockey town at the time; the long-estab-
lished Bruins had won a couple of Stanley Cups with typical Garden
crowds in excess of 13,000. By contrast, the upstart Celtics were draw-
ing a reported 7,000 fans a night. Johnny Most fired up the fan base,
and Red Auerbach did the rest in building an unmatched basketball
powerhouse.

It is safe to say, there will never be another like Johnny. That may
separate this quartet of elite broadcasters from the rest more than anything else. The term "nonpareil" comes to mind.

Johnny smoked nonstop. I can still see him along the highly elevated radio row at the old Boston Garden—you had to literally climb
a steep metal ladder to get up there. It was a chore for me in the 1980s,
and Most was fifteen years my senior. But as I huffed and puffed my

way to my broadcast location, there he would be, seated some twenty yards to my right. I could see him through a cloud of smoke as he awaited the opening tip on the green-trimmed parquet floor far below. By his own admission, Johnny drank thirty cups of coffee and smoked eighty cigarettes a day. His smoking led to him actually setting himself on fire near the end of a Celtic-Milwaukee broadcast in 1988. He suddenly screamed into the live mic, "I'm on fire!" Sure enough, a red-hot ash had fallen from his cigarette onto his lap.

Happily, he survived that raging scare before passing in 1993 at the age of sixty-nine. I still stand in utter awe of Johnny Most and his unique body of work.

And then there is Chick Hearn. The longtime Los Angeles Laker broadcaster was positively one of a kind. His rat-a-tat-tat delivery introduced the Lakers and professional basketball to a West Coast city that had zero interest in the NBA when the club moved to Los Angeles from Minneapolis in 1960. It was Chick—more so than superstars Jerry West, Elgin Baylor, or Wilt Chamberlain—who carved a place in the hearts of the often laissez-faire Angelinos.

Hearn performed simulcasts of the Laker games. That is, his accounts were carried simultaneously on radio and television. He broadcast the games that way until the very end. Teams throughout the league had largely stopped using the cost-cutting simulcasts, but it was

---

TIME OUT Live Means *Live*

Live television sometimes presents the unexpected.

In the mid-'90s, I was working with former Clipper All-Star Marques Johnson, who was brand-new in broadcasting. The Clippers were facing the Lakers at the Forum, and we had repeated rehearsals for the on-camera open on the Laker hardwood.

Finally, at 7:30 sharp, we go on the air. I introduced Marques, and he said: "It is great to be here at the Sports Arena . . . oh shit, I meant the Forum. Let's do it again." I said something about the joys of live television, reminding him that we were on the air. He has since recovered from that first-time blooper and gone on to a successful broadcast career, now working the telecasts of the 2021 NBA champion Milwaukee Bucks. ●

simply unimaginable to separate the Laker TV and radio feeds. Who could possibly be accepted calling Laker games other than Chick Hearn? The easy answer was: nobody.

Chick worked with a variety of color commentators, including Al Michaels, Rod Hundley, Lynn Shackelford, Pat Riley, Keith Erickson, and finally Stu Lantz. It made little difference who the partner was, because it was clear that it was Chick's show. A largely apocryphal story was that his favorite response from a partner was always, "Right you are, Chick." His "Chickisms" became a part of the sports' lexicon: "slam dunk," "dribble drive," "air ball," "no harm, no foul," "finger roll," and "ticky-tack foul" were all his original utterances, and are now repeated by many who broadcast a basketball game. Most of those announcers are unaware that they are quoting one of the best to ever call a game. I remember Los Angeles sportscaster Tom Kelly marveling to me once that Chick could get more information into an end-line to end-line drive up the court than any announcer who had ever lived.

I had known Chick ever since I was a basketball-crazed kid growing up in Peoria, where he broadcast Bradley University games on the radio while also serving as a nightly sports anchor on the local NBC TV station. Chick actually broadcast a couple of high school games I played in at Peoria High School in the mid 1950s. I was more than a little thrilled to see him at the press table, where he would be calling his "words-eye view" of the game on radio. He would later be the guest speaker and presenter at our team's awards ceremony after the season.

However, my most enduring memory of Chick dates to 2002. This was forty-six years after he had the forgettable experience of broadcasting one of my high school basketball games. It was the very tail-end of his transcendent career as voice of the Lakers. I was at Staples Center early for a game between the Clippers and the Lakers. Presently, Chick and his dear wife, Marge, entered the arena and slowly, cautiously made their way down the steep arena steps to the court. Chick was slightly stoop-shouldered as he stopped by the press table to say his polite hello. He appeared to be every bit a little old man in his '80s as he took his seat at the far end of the press table, where he would call what was a Clipper home game.

Shortly before 7:30, he and partner Stu Lantz made their way onto the court for their television open. The lights went on, and this little old man rose up to his full six-foot-three height, the years fading away as he smiled and went on the air with a vibrance and presence shared by few others before or since.

No question, Chick Hearn was something special through his forty-two years of announcing Laker games in his truly inimitable style. I'm so sorry that his career is in the refrigerator—the door's closed, the lights are out, the eggs are cooling, the butter's getting hard, and the jello's jiggling.

That brings us to an announcer who has spanned the basketball ages and is familiar to all present-day NBA fans. Marv Albert was a genuine protégé of the original New York Knicks announcer Marty Glickman. He met the magnificent Voice of the City when he was a Knicks ball boy in the 1950s. Glickman helped him get into broadcasting and, in 1963, Marv was asked to sit in for Glickman calling a Knicks game because of a scheduling conflict. Four years later, Albert became the voice of the Knicks, a role he would fill for thirty-seven seasons. In 1990, NBC tabbed him as their lead play-by-play man on NBA games. He has since been known as "the Voice of the NBA."

The Albert family is laced through seven decades of sports broadcasting history. Brothers Steve and Al both had exemplary careers that included broadcasting NBA games. And Marv's versatile son, Kenny, has been active in broadcasting games in the NHL, NFL, MLB, and NBA. With apologies to the Bucks, the Barrys, and the Carays, the Alberts make up the greatest sportscasting family in American history.

Marv Albert brought a distinctive sound and a command of the game to the audience each telecast. His sense of the history of the sport is unparalleled. If I was told that I could watch just one more NBA game on television and it would be called by Marv Albert, I would instantly say: "YES!"

Chapter 6

The Big Redhead (Part One)

I FIRST HEARD OF BILL WALTON in the late 1960s, when I was working in Riverside. He was a high school phenom playing at Helix High School in San Diego. I drove down to see him play. He and his older brother, Bruce, demolished all comers. Helix would win back-to-back state championships. It was clear that the tall, skinny redhead was something special. Little did I know that he would become one of my life's greatest friends.

I followed his storied career at UCLA that included a record eighty-eight-game winning streak and two NCAA Championships. He and legendary Bruin coach John Wooden were an unlikely pair, but it worked in ways that may never be matched.

The Portland Trailblazers had the first pick in the 1974 NBA college draft. No team ever had an easier pick. There was no debate; Walton was the top pick in the draft. It was a time in the league when the number-one choice in the draft would be asked to appear in a pregame news conference during his first visit to each league city. That way, the player would not need to do twenty or thirty interviews on game day, but just one in front of the assembled media. This would be my next view of Bill Walton.

The news conference was scheduled for late afternoon at the Trailblazers' hotel in downtown Philadelphia, where I was working for WCAU radio. It was November 8, 1974. A very large crowd of newspaper, radio, television reporters, and assorted photographers

were jammed into a much-too-small room, waiting for the basketball prodigy. And wait we did. Walton finally appeared with his team's
PR head a good half hour after the scheduled start of the event. They
were greeted by a fidgeting and impatient gathering. Bill, dressed like
a lumberjack, sat down, stretched out the full length of his seven-foot
frame, and clearly looked like this was the last place on earth that he
wanted to be. His responses to the media questions were monotone
and monosyllabic. It was awful. Few Philly scribes were disappointed
to see Walton put in a forgettable 10-point performance that night in
a 20-point loss to the 76ers. My first impression of Bill Walton was
anything but positive.

The Blazers had losing records under Lenny Wilkins in Walton's
first two pro seasons. Losing was a foreign experience for a young man
who had been one of the game's all-time greatest high school and college players. He would lose more games in his first month in the NBA
than he had in all his years in high school and college.

Better times were ahead for the Big Redhead. Things turned around
in his third season coincidental with the arrival of coach Jack Ramsay.
The Blazers were in their seventh year in the NBA, and they won forty-nine games to log their first winning season. It was good enough for
third-best record in the West. Meanwhile, out East, the Philadelphia
76ers finished with the best record in the conference. As fate would
have it, the Sixers and the Blazers would meet in the NBA Finals.

Philly was the clear favorite and they looked the part, scoring a pair
of relatively easy home-court wins in games one and two in the City of
Brotherly Love. I had broadcast all the Sixer home games on television
that year and felt a vested interest in their success. I was on the team
plane flying to Portland, which was a little-known destination on the
opposite side of the country, if not the world. The Trailblazers gave the
76ers a rude and humbling welcome in the Rose City, winning Game
3 by 22 points and Game 4 by 32! The series was unimaginably even at
2–2 with Game 5 back in Philadelphia. At least the Sixers still had the
home-court advantage. That did not last long as the Blazers captured
the pivotal Game 5 by 6 points after leading by as many as 22.

The writing was now on the wall. The Sixers hoped to force a seventh game with a dramatic win in Portland in Game 6. It proved to
be the best game of the series. Julius Erving led Philadelphia with a

brilliant 40-point game, but Walton was supreme: 20 points, 23 rebounds, 7 Assists, and 8 blocked shots. Portland had the NBA Championship, and Walton was named Finals MVP.

I got up close and personal with Bill after the game in the champion's locker room. He was far more animated and articulate than he had been in that rookie meet and greet news conference twenty months earlier. He still suffered with a lifelong stutter and stammer affliction, but he was, at least, trying to communicate.

Walton would be the league MVP the following year, but injuries kept him and the Blazers from winning the anticipated back-to-back championships. They also kept him sidelined for the entire 1978–1979 season. That happened to be the birth year for the San Diego Clippers, and my first shot at being the full-time broadcast voice of an NBA team. Neither of us had any idea what lay ahead.

One day, while playing racquetball in San Diego with Clipper coach Gene Shue, he confided in me that he was very close to making a deal with Portland's free agent, All-NBA center Bill Walton. It was Shue's second shot at acquiring the big man. In 1973, immediately after Walton's second NCAA title win over Memphis, Shue and Philadelphia 76ers owner Irv Kosloff showed up at the junior center's hotel suite in St. Louis. The Sixers owned the first pick in the 1973 NBA draft, and the pair told Walton they wanted to choose him. They would make him healthy, wealthy, and wise. Well, wealthy, at least. But he would have to defy convention and come out of college a year early. Walton certainly had no aversion to going against convention, but he wanted to return for another year at UCLA with the goal of a third-straight national title. He turned them down.

Six years later, the situation was far different. Walton had a stormy final year in Portland after feeling he'd been forced to play and take injections in his foot against his better instincts. Walton was a free agent after the 1978–1979 season, and he wanted out. Here came Shue again, with the added bonus of offering Walton a chance to play in his hometown of San Diego. A seven-year, $7 million contract offer was the icing on the cake. The signature signing would finally put pro basketball on the map in the sleepy coastal community, where three professional basketball teams had failed.

A couple of days later, it was official. I could hardly believe my

ears. Airplanes towed banners heralding "Walton is a Clipper!" in view
of packed SoCal beaches. A major introductory news conference was
held at the Sports Arena. I introduced owner Levin, coach Shue, and
illustrious new Clipper Bill Walton to the assembled throng of reporters. Bill was dressed in a custom three-piece suit. It was difficult to believe this was the same player I'd seen introduced to the Philadelphia
media almost five years earlier.

After the event, a light lunch was held in the arena's private dining
room, and I found myself happily seated in a booth with Bill. Suddenly, he apologized for having to excuse himself. "What's up?" I asked.
The stunning response: "I have to go have surgery on my ankle." It was
an ominous sign of things to come. Fortunately, it was not a debilitating event, and Bill seemed fit as a fiddle when training camp opened
in mid-September.

The NBA rules of the day gave commissioner Larry O'Brien the
sole power to determine compensation for the loss of a free agent player. Four months had passed since the historic signing, but O'Brien
had not yet announced the compensation when training camp opened
in September. The entire roster assembled at the team's San Diego
training camp; it was an impressive group. The feeling had been that
the team would have Walton, physical power forward Kermit Washington, and guards World B. Free and Randy Smith as the foundation
of a championship contending team. That was a truly fearsome foursome. It would be easy to fill in the blanks after commissioner O'Brien
settled on the compensation. The team felt it would likely cost them
rugged rebounding center Swen Nater, high-scoring guard Freeman
Williams from Portland State, and maybe a first-round draft pick.
O'Brien had a different view. On about the third day of training camp,
assistant coach Bob Weiss started coming out and, one by one, calling players off the court for meetings. First there was Kevn Kunnert,
then Washington, and finally Smith. We all knew what was happening
right in front of our eyes.

Shue and the Clippers were stunned by the decision: the San Diego team would send Washington, Kunnert, two first-round picks, and
cash to the Blazers and also be required to move All-Star guard Smith
to Cleveland to acquire one of those required draft picks. Losing
Washington and Smith was unimaginable to the Clippers. They were

the perfect complements to Walton. Washington was to be what Maurice Lucas had been to Big Bill on the 1977 Championship Blazers, and Smith was a reasonable clone for Lionel Hollins on that title team. Still, Walton, Free, Williams, and Nater could serve as a foundation for a potentially competitive Clipper team. Walton himself was enough to legitimize the team in San Diego.

In 1979, the Clippers landed the cover of *Sports Illustrated*—unimaginable a year earlier. The past was the past, and the future was now; the local media had discovered the fledgling NBA team, a hoop hero had returned home, and the Clippers had the attention of the city. Those of us with the Clippers were so energized. Coach Shue and assistant Weiss were hard at work devising plays and a style to best utilize Walton's broad range of skills. Bill seemed healthy as the team continued its training camp.

There was such hope for the future when Walton played well in the early exhibition games. Then, in Game 4 against the Lakers, he broke the navicular bone in his left foot. The team's dreams and hopes came crashing down in an avalanche of disappointment. The league had arranged the 1979–1980 schedule so it would feature the Lakers against the Clippers on opening night on national TV. It was another sign that pro basketball was finally poised for success in the coastal Navy town. The game was to match two former UCLA centers against each other at the San Diego Sports Arena. And it did—but it was Swen Nater, rather than Walton, who represented the Clippers against Kareem Abdul-Jabbar of the Lakers.

Walton would play only fourteen games that first season, and that was fourteen more than he would play in either of the next two seasons. Despite his absence on opening night, the Clippers and Lakers put on a spectacular show for the national television audience. The game also featured the NBA debut of NCAA champion Magic Johnson. Kareem's last-second sky hook earned the Lakers a thrilling 103–102 victory. Johnson leapt into Kareem's arms at game's end, as if he had just won another title. Kareem admonished him: "Hey, we still have eighty-one more games to play."

Significantly, despite the surge in season ticket sales in the wake of Walton's signing, the much-ballyhooed season opener attracted barely 8,500 fans. Instead of the beginning, this may have been the beginning of the end of pro basketball in San Diego. Today, Walton still blames himself for failing his hometown. He believes that, had he been healthy, the team would have survived and thrived in San Diego. We will never know.

Despite Bill's recurring injuries, the team endeavored to capitalize on his presence on the roster and the hope of his eventual return. Hal Kolker, the team's marketing and sales whiz, arranged for Bill and me to appear on a weekly program on radio station KSDO. It was a one-hour gabfest featuring Bill, special friends, and players from around the NBA, as well as social commentary from Bill himself. I was there to moderate the program. We were well-compensated, so much so that owner Levin declared to Kolker, "You sure are being good to those guys." Well, "those guys" worked hard each week to present an informative and entertaining hour on the radio. Bill would line up a couple of guests for telephone interviews, and we would outline a format for the program. Then we would spend up to two and a half hours recording the elements of the program. After Bill left, I would spend an additional four or five hours in the studio editing our recordings into a meaningful package. The program was wildly popular with the meager San Diego Clipper fan base, but not so popular with the conservative local populace who resented Bill's progressive social and political views.

Bill was still cursed with his stutter and stammer affliction, and that needed to be edited out of the program. If he said, "It is g-g-g-great to have M-m-m-m-Maurice L-l-l-Lucas with us t-t-t-tonight," I would use a razor blade on the quarter-inch recording tape and literally cut out each stutter. The end result was Bill fluently saying: "It is great to have Maurice Lucas with us tonight." It was radio magic.

One day, the doorbell rang at our adobe brick Mt. Helix-area home, and it was a messenger delivering a large, heavy box. I had no idea what it was. We opened the cumbersome package to discover a brand-new Betamax video recorder/player. It was from Bill, with thanks for my hard work on our radio program. It was my first glimpse of the big man's extraordinary generosity. Videocassette recorders were a popular fad of the day, but they were far too expensive for me to consider purchasing. Some weeks later, I was hosting a small family gathering at a fashionable beachside restaurant in Del Mar when we noticed Bill with a group at a table across the room. We settled merely for waves and smiles. When I asked for the check at the end of the evening, I was informed that Mr. Walton had taken care of it. This was my second glimpse at his generosity, which seemed to know no bounds.

Bill's time with his hometown team was tortured. Though his mid-season debut was greeted by the biggest ovation ever heard from a San Diego basketball crowd, he would appear in just fourteen games that first season. Coach Shue was limited to using Walton in five-minute bursts. Talk about load management. Bill would just be getting warmed up and into the flow of the game when trainer Roberts would let the coach know that it was time to bring the big center back to the bench. He was in, and then he was out. It was crazy, and though Walton played well in those brief spurts, it was not a winning way.

It also didn't last past those fateful fourteen games; Walton would not play at all in the two seasons that followed. It really seemed that Bill's career was over at the age of twenty-seven. He remained on the Clipper roster even when he enrolled in law school at Stanford in 1981. But an odd thing was about to happen: having benefited from countless hours of walking barefoot on San Diego's endless miles of soft sand beaches, Bill's feet became pain-free. He began to wonder if he might be able to play again, while dealing with questions about torts and contracts at Stanford.

Walton was a part of the Clipper training camp in Yuma, Arizona, in the fall of 1982. At the time, Paul Silas was in his third season as Clipper coach, and not a single Walton teammate from the 1979–1980 season was still on the roster. When camp opened at Arizona Western College on a sauna-like day in late September, Bill quickly challenged Silas's authority. The coach dragged the player to the lobby just outside the gym, and I stood there in stunned silence as the coach yelled at Bill, informing him that he would do things the Silas way or he could just go home. Bill essentially nodded and said, "Yessir!" and the conflict was resolved.

Bill was always one to test authority. He had done it with Coach Shue during his first Clipper training camp. On Bill's first bus ride with the Clippers, he plopped down in the coach's seat a row ahead of me. "Uh-oh," I thought. The head coach always sat in the front-row seat on the team bus—it was just one of the unwritten codes in the

NBA of the day. Sure enough, when Coach Shue stepped on the bus and saw Bill in his seat, he smiled and motioned the player to the rear of the bus. Bill moved without a problem—he just had to see. He had to test.

The bottom line in 1982 was that Bill was excited to be back playing basketball. His feet felt good. However, he was not ready to give up his backup plan, which was getting his law degree at Stanford. An unusual compromise was reached: Walton would be a law student during the week, and a basketball player on the weekend. That season, he would squeeze thirty-three games into his law school calendar.

Bill played twenty-eight minutes in the season opener, contributing 20 points, 9 rebounds, and 2 blocked shots. He was playing almost exclusively in home games, and the team struggled mightily despite the presence of quality players such as Tom Chambers, Terry Cummings, and Craig Hodges. A rare highlight occurred on the day after Christmas, when Big Bill led the Clippers to a 112–105 win in San Diego over his old Portland Trailblazer team. He contributed 25 points and 7 suffocating blocked shots in the winning effort that left the Clippers with a record of five wins and twenty-three losses. The team finished a disappointing 25–57.

Owner Donald Sterling dismissed Silas at season's end, and replaced him with the respected Portland assistant Jim Lynam. Walton had gotten through his comeback season without major injury, and was ready to be a full-time NBA player again. The Clippers traded Chambers to Seattle in exchange for big center James Donaldson. It was a worthwhile insurance policy considering Walton's history.

By this time, Bill and I had developed an enduring friendship. I loved seeing his preparation for each game. He would share his thoughts with me before a game, and it helped me become a better broadcaster. His prep before facing his longtime UCLA friend and foe Kareem Abdul-Jabbar was expansive. He would work to limit Kareem's lethal right-hand skyhook, and encourage him to shoot it left-handed instead. The two had some classic match-ups over the years, and it was a privilege to watch from my front-row courtside seat.

The following season, Sterling kidnapped the Clippers, moving them to Los Angeles. As Walton reluctantly left his hometown, I stayed behind to pursue my new career in real estate. The Big Redhead played in sixty-seven games in that first year in L.A.; he would only play more games than that in a season once in his decade-plus pro career. We stayed in touch, as I worked maybe a dozen games that year. I returned to the team full-time the following year, but Bill had moved on to Boston, where he would play in a record eighty games while winning the NBA Sixth Man of the Year award, as well as his second NBA championship. That was the final highlight of his oft-interrupted career.

I was happily back in the NBA in Los Angeles, having transitioned from doing strictly radio to adding television play-by-play to my duties. I had worked with Junior Bridgeman one year and former player and coach Kevin Loughery the next. We were looking for a full-time partner for the thirty-five games we would have on KTLA each season.

Meanwhile, Walton was contemplating an uncertain future in San Diego at the sprawling home he had purchased when he first joined the Clippers roughly nine years earlier. Bill and I were living in separate worlds for a while, but that all changed one summer day in 1990. My sweet Jo and I were enjoying a delightful day at Pacific Beach in San Diego. It was a warm day at the beach, and we walked to a nearby 7/11 to get something to drink. Who did we see there but our old friend, Bill Walton!

It was great to see him. He was a bit of a lost soul. Bill had been an exceptional athlete for as long as he could remember, but his days of athletic excellence were behind him and he really had no idea what road to take on his continued journey through life. We were talking animatedly in this busy convenience store when I burst out with, "How about broadcasting?" The thought had never entered his mind, but it intrigued him.

Bill would go on to work Continental Basketball League games on the radio for free, just to get a feel for the craft. We would talk from time to time about his transition into the broadcast medium; it would have been impossible to comprehend back in 1974, when I first heard the NBA's number-one draft pick speak at that news conference in Philadelphia. Now, he had worked with sportscasting giant Marty Glickman to overcome his speech defects, and he was finding a way to continue being a part of the game he loved.

Soon, the Clippers hired Walton to serve as my broadcast partner, a role he filled for thirteen happy, wacky, fun-filled seasons. It took a while to find our way with each other. I was a serious-minded broadcaster and tried to do things by the book. Luckily, Laker broadcaster Chick Hearn and his wife, Marge, helped me climb out of that restrictive hole about the same time as Bill's return to the Clippers as a broadcaster. One evening, the three of us were sharing dinner in the press room at the Forum before a Clipper-Laker game. Chick excused himself to get up to his broadcast perch high above the western sidelines. Marge and I talked about our younger days in Peoria, and then she offered some words that helped change my view of my role as the voice of the Clippers. She observed that I had a good sense of humor, and encouraged me to use it on the air. I thought of Chick's groan-worthy shaggy dog tales during games and thanked her for the sage advice. That background helped me adjust to working on the air with Walton. Bill showed me that the game we both loved was not all that serious. It was a game and it was okay to have fun.

Remember now, this was long before the brilliant TNT quartet proved the concept night after night on their insightful and delightful *Inside the NBA* telecasts. Sure enough, Walton and I had fun. For example: After a rebound by Michael Olowokandi in the second half of a 1999 game, Bill said, "And *that's* why the Clippers made him the number-one pick in the draft!" I replied, "Bill, that's his first rebound of the game and we're in the fourth quarter." Bill said, "Oh."

And so it went, for thirteen vividly memorable seasons. It was not always easy for the Clipper front office, but they learned to grin and bear it. Bill had worked some telecasts for the Dallas Mavericks along the way, and got fired virtually every game until he and the Mavs separated for good. The Clippers were seldom a good team over the Walton years, but their TV ratings from the period dwarf any of those from even the Lob City or Kawhi years. It totally changed my concept of being a team broadcaster. Bill changed my view on a lot of things.

Chapter 7

So Close to Bird, Duncan, and Kobe

THE CLIPPERS WERE OH SO CLOSE to greatness, even in
their early years in San Diego. When Irv Levin and John Y. Brown
were hatching their bizarre NBA franchise swap in 1978, one of the
key decisions involved players and draft picks. The Celtics had two
first-round picks in the draft that year. They chose Larry Bird with
one of them and NCAA scoring champion Freeman Williams with
the other. Bird was to return to Indiana State for another season, and
it would be a full year before he would join the pro game. The gamble
on choosing him was made by Celtic hoop maven Red Auerbach. He
envisioned Bird's future greatness. Neither Levin nor Brown knew
enough to care much which of the draft picks would be transferred
to Levin and the transplanted Buffalo Braves in San Diego. Rather
than wait a year for Bird, Levin chose Williams. It could have been
Larry Bird.

Twenty years later, the Los Angeles Clippers had the first overall
pick in the June draft. The year was 1998. A year earlier, they had
chosen Maurice Taylor out of Michigan with the fourteenth pick
in the first round, while the San Antonio Spurs took full advantage
of David Robinson's lost season because of injury, to earn the prized
number-one choice: Tim Duncan. The Clippers could not even be
bad, I mean really bad, at the right time. In 1998, they had the first
pick. Instead of Tim Duncan, the draft board was topped by Michael
Olowokandi. What a difference a year makes.

TIME OUT Best of the Best Teams

There have been some historically great NBA teams over the years. I have seen them all, from the dominant Minneapolis Laker teams in the 1950s to the Boston Celtics—who won eight titles in a row—and on through the best of the modern-era teams.

There are a lot to choose from. The Lakers, Warriors, Celtics, Spurs, and Bulls all had some terrific teams over the seventy-five years of NBA history. It is a major challenge to rank one better than the other, and the final decision is certain to anger some fans of a team not listed at the top of the heap. The leading candidates are the 1995–1996 Chicago Bulls (72–10), the 1971–1972 Los Angeles Lakers (69–13), the 1985–1986 Boston Celtics (67–15), and the more recent vintage 2016–2017 Golden State Warriors (67–15). That is some quartet.

I want to start with the 1971–1972 Laker team. This is the club that ran off an NBA best-ever winning streak of thirty-three games, a record that may never be broken. I had a little taste of what a streak such as that feels like when the L.A. Clippers won seventeen straight under Vinny Del Negro in 2012. There was a sense of invincibility each time that team walked into the gym. This Laker team almost doubled that string of wins! A closer look at that thirty-three game stretch of excellence reveals one win in overtime and only one other decided by as few as 4 points. It was total dominance by a dominant team, led by Jerry West and Wilt Chamberlain.

But were they the best team in league history? I don't think so. Most longtime Celtic fans point to the 1985–1986 Boston team being their best ever. That is no slight to the amazing Red Auerbach teams that won an unprecedented eight titles in a row from the 1950s into the '60s. This Celtic team had it all. Their front line of Larry Bird, Kevin McHale, and Robert Parish may have been the best trio in the history of the league. Danny Ainge and Dennis Johnson were superlative in the backcourt, and Hall of Famer Bill Walton was sixth man of the year off the bench. It is not easy to spot a weakness with this group. Still, I don't think they were the best team in league history.

The Golden State Warriors were good when Kevin Durant joined them as a free agent from Oklahoma City in 2016. They had won a league record seventy-three games the season before, and then they added one of the greatest offensive players the game had ever seen in Durant. The Warriors had opened the prior year with twenty-four straight wins. They were a tough act to follow, despite their flame-out in the 2016 playoffs. Their potent offense became unstoppable with the addition of the impossible-to-guard KD. They had three consistent 20-point-a-game scorers in Curry, Durant, and Thompson. Each was lethal from 3-point range. They had defensive excellence from Draymond Green, Andre Iguodala, Matt Barnes, and Shaun Livingston. The bench was deep, and Steve Kerr was the perfect coach for this group. They are hard to top.

Only the 1995–1996 Chicago Bulls can do it. Phil Jackson's Bulls won six NBA titles in the 1990s. Everybody else was basically playing for second place during the run of the Bulls. The 1995–1996 team stands out from the rest. They won seventy-two games, and that seemed an unassailable mark prior to the 2015–2016 Golden State juggernaut. Michael Jordan and Scottie Pippen were two of the most complete all-around players to ever play on the same team. Great offense and defense were provided by both. Some will compare the Los Angeles Clipper two-way duo of Kawhi Leonard and Paul George, or the Lakers' pairing of LeBron James and Anthony Davis. They are worthy of the mention, but Jordan and Pippen have the clear edge in longevity and championships won.

The Bulls were not just a two-man team. Dennis Rodman was one of the game's all-time great rebounders and defensive stoppers. Toni Kukoc stormed off the bench and made 40 percent of his 3-pointers. Luc Longley, Ron Harper, Steve Kerr, John Salley, and Bill Wennington provided quality depth.

Harper is a particularly interesting figure on this team. He had been a scorer in his first eight years in the league with the Cleveland Cavaliers and the L.A. Clippers. He checked out new Clipper head coach Bill Fitch in the summer of 1994. He was a free agent after five seasons in Los Angeles. The coaching change intrigued him. I was encouraged when he showed up at the Clipper news conference announcing Fitch as head coach. However, days later, Ron Harper, a lifelong shooting guard, signed with the Chicago Bulls, who had a pretty good shooting guard of their own wearing number 23. It did not take Coach Jackson long to convert Harper to point guard. It is a position he would perform with excellence during the Bulls' final three championship seasons, including that best of the best 1995–1996 Bulls team. Harper had become a playmaker and defensive specialist; the shooter/scorer classically reinvented himself and was vital in making this the best team in NBA history. ●

One of the biggest Clippers moments that never came to fruition was back at the beginning of Kobe Bryant's career in 1996. When he came into the Sports Arena, I remember Elgin Baylor saying the teen prodigy put on the greatest pre-draft workout he had ever seen in his life. The entire coaching staff was blown away by Kobe, including coach Bill Fitch. Assistant coach Barry Hecker looked on in amazement as the seventeen-year-old Bryant skied for a one-hand slam dunk. Elgin wanted him so badly.

For years when we played the Lakers, I wanted to use this workout video footage on our pregame program, but the idea was always nixed by the team. They said it would make us look bad. But hey, history is history. The never-before-seen video would have been great television.

While Elgin and the rest of the staff wanted Kobe, Fitch believed he was too young, even though he thought Kobe was brilliant. So, who did the Clippers draft? Lorenzen Wright. He was also a teenager, just a year older than Bryant. Lorenzen never really had much of a career and wound up being tragically murdered in 2010.

The Lakers had the wisdom and wherewithal to trade with Charlotte. They gave up starting center Vlade Divac to obtain the rights to Kobe. A bunch of us watched that deal and said, "But now they will have no center for the kid to play off of!" I remember talking to people at summer league, wondering what on earth the Lakers were doing. But, of course, they were great chess players. They were just paving the way for the creation of a mini dynasty. Laker general manager Jerry West was trying desperately to make an offer acceptable to free-agent Orlando center Shaquille O'Neal; he kept coming up just short. Owner Jerry Buss insisted that he find a way. They moved key rotation players George Lynch and Anthony Peeler for future second-round draft picks. It was a virtual giveaway, but it created the dollars needed to make a godfather offer to Shaq.

The Clippers did not have the ownership that allowed for that kind of aggressiveness and foresight. I still often wonder what it would've been like having Brent Barry in the backcourt with Kobe. It would not have mattered who the point guard or the off guard was. Together, they just would have been remarkable. That could have been one of the most exciting teams of the era. We were all crushed that Fitch had nixed that deal and that Sterling had gone along with him. You must understand the era back then: Clippers coaches were under pressure to make short-term decisions to save their asses. Quick fixes. With Sterling, you didn't dare take long-range risks. That shortsightedness permeated the entire organization, and that's part of why they lost out on Kobe Bryant. The first time.

Incredibly, another shot presented itself. By 2004, Kobe had become unhappy playing with Shaq, and he was an unrestricted free agent. We heard that he didn't want to leave Orange County, where he lived, so the Clippers made their move. Elgin Baylor, Andy Roeser, owner Sterling, coach Dunleavy, and legal counsel Bob Platt set up a very private meeting with Kobe at the Four Seasons Hotel in Newport Beach. The Clippers made their case, and as someone who was in the room told me directly, Kobe loved the pitch. In fact, he got so excited at the idea of having a chance to beat the Lakers as a member of their crosstown competition, he said on the way out of the meeting, "Don't worry, I'm a Clipper." Evidently, Sterling really pressed him, saying, "I hope you're going to come over, Kobe," and when the player spoke those words, everybody felt secure that it was a go. I got the news of the meeting that night and thought to myself, *Holy shit! This is going to be big.*

At the time, Laker owner Jerry Buss was in Europe on vacation. Evidently, the next day, after a trans-Atlantic phone call with Kobe, Shaq was traded. Then, a day later, the Lakers had a news conference to announce that they had re-signed Kobe Bryant. Fans can draw their own conclusions about what transpired on that phone call or what Kobe's demands may have been, but all I know is, it pains me to this day. I threw things at the television set when I saw the news on ESPN.

It was just the latest in a series of what-might-have-beens for the Clippers.

Chapter 8

Elgin and Jerry

ELGIN BAYLOR AND JERRY WEST will forever go hand in hand in the minds of basketball fans. They formed one of the greatest duos ever seen on the basketball court during their twelve years together with the Los Angeles Lakers. They both went on to coach in the league, and each moved to front office roles that earned them NBA Executive of the Year awards. Both were ten-time All-NBA First Team choices as players.

I first met this amazing pair in 1961, at the Lakers' pre-season media day ahead of the team's second season in Los Angeles. I had seen Elgin play when he was at Seattle University. He came to Peoria to meet Bradley, and simply destroyed the Brave's All-American star, Barney Cable. I felt a special connection to West. We were the same age and about the same size. As I recall, he was a better player than I, but I could relate to him. I was instantly a Laker fan. There was no way to imagine that our paths and careers would cross in the decades to come.

My next encounter with Elgin Baylor was when he was the head coach of the New Orleans Jazz in 1978 or '79. The San Diego Clippers had a couple of days off in the Big Easy before meeting the Jazz. Head coach Gene Shue and I went to the Superdome to "scout" the Jazz. The team was led by the incomparable Pistol Pete Maravich. Afterwards, we made our way to the New Orleans locker room to talk to Baylor. Shue had played against him for many years in the late '50s and early '60s.

Elgin was great. Despite the Jazz problems on the court, it was a good time in his life. He had met and married his wife, the wonderful Elaine, who would be his life's loving companion. You could just tell how content he was. That was early 1979; just over seven years later, we were together again, when Elg was named general manager of the Los Angeles Clippers in October of 1986. I had seen him a couple of times the prior year, when he was the courtside guest of owner Donald T. Sterling at Clippers games in the L.A. Sports Arena. Nobody thought much about that. Sterling loved being with well-known people. It was a bolt out of the blue when Elgin was named the team's general manager. There had been some rumors that he could be a Clipper coaching candidate, but nothing had ever tied him to the team's general manager position.

I was pleased because, at least, I had a little history with Baylor and had great respect for him as a keen basketball mind. He traveled a lot with the team, and we spent many a night together at hotel bars around the world, rehashing the latest game and talking about a wide range of topics. Elgin loved trivia and would come up with some of the damnedest things. "Did you know that the average person will spend six months of their life stopped at a red light?" he would say. He could go on and on with facts known almost only to himself. It was fun.

Baylor was a vital part of the fabric of the franchise. It bothers me a little that he is remembered in Los Angeles almost exclusively for his days as a Laker when, in fact, he spent many more years with the Clippers. In my mind, he will always be a Clipper. I loved him dearly.

Elgin had one of the most challenging jobs in sports. The owner tied his hands from day one and then expected him to put a winning team on the court. Sterling always said he would pay a star's salary to star players. The owner was so excited when his team traded for the thirty-four-year-old, nine-time All-Star Dominique Wilkins in 1994. He rushed over to me before Nique's first game and gushed that he was so thrilled to finally have a superstar player. I was crestfallen that we had traded away Danny Manning, a player in his prime, to acquire a fading star in the autumn of his career. And, of course, Wilkins was gone by season's end; he would go on to play for five different teams in his final four years in the league, an unfortunate conclusion to a spectacular career.

Sterling let one talented player after another slip though his fingers, year after year: Tom Chambers, Terry Cummings, Bill Walton, Danny Manning, Charles Smith, Doc Rivers, Mark Jackson, Brent Barry, Mo Taylor, Elton Brand, Lamar Odom, Loy Vaught, Sam Cassell, and on and on. It was never Elgin's fault, but he always got the blame. I was very happy when he received the NBA Executive of the Year award in 2006. He had helped put together a very good team that won forty-seven games in the regular season and advanced to the second round of the playoffs. I was deeply saddened two years later when he "resigned" under a cloud of mystery, ending his twenty-two years in the Clipper front office.

It was a career where Elgin was always under-paid and under-staffed. Had he been given the authority to go along with the responsibility, I think he would have been a highly respected basketball executive. The man knew talent. I would be sitting with him at a summer league game and be amazed how quickly he could pick up on a player's unique skills or subtle weaknesses. This was an amazing man and a marvelous athlete. I think that, today, he is one of the game's all-time most underrated superstar players. If you actually saw him play, you would agree. Baylor was in his fifties when he joined the Clippers. The GM would consistently challenge incoming players to shooting games in the gym, and I never saw anybody beat him.

Elgin's fractious break-up with the Clippers was a sorry chapter in franchise history. Happily, some of that was repaired in my later years with the team. It was a joyous day when the Clippers first invited him to a game. In 2019, I had a chance to make a couple of appearances with him. It was great to see him, though it was clear his health was failing him as he was in his mid-'80s. He was only really comfortable when his wife, Elaine, was within arm's reach.

Elgin and Jerry West remained friends from the beginning in 1960 to the end in 2021. West stopped by the Clipper training camp in Santa Barbara in the fall of 2000, not long after his departure from the Lakers. It was special seeing this great pair of Hall of Famers side by side in the training camp gym. I wanted to lock the doors so that he could not get away. But it was not the time. Jerry finally joined the Clippers in June of 2017; it was a long time coming.

West spent forty years with the Lakers as player, scout, coach, and general manager. It was always rewarding to find a chance to talk to him. He might be the most frank and direct-to-the-point person I have ever dealt with in sports. I can remember talking to him after a Clipper-Laker game in his Laker GM days, and he would offer a brutally honest assessment of one of his players.

Jerry's greatest strength may have been his refusal to live with a mistake. I sat with him at a California summer league game in 2002, when he was brand-new as the top man with the Memphis Grizzlies. His first act was to draft Drew Gooden with the fourth pick in the June draft. Just a couple of weeks later, we were watching his prized rookie play. Jerry was excited about just how good this six-foot-ten forward from Kansas was going to be. He felt Gooden could be a big star. But early in that season, it became clear to Jerry that Drew Gooden was not the star material he'd hoped he would be. He moved the rookie to Orlando in mid-season for two players and two draft picks before the rest of the league knew what he knew. Gooden went on to play for ten teams in a journeyman's fourteen-year career.

The point is, not only did West make great and historic moves for the likes of Kobe Bryant and Shaq O'Neal, he was also willing to get out from under a rare mistake in judgment. He also knew what *not* to do. His greatest contribution as a valued consultant in Golden State may well have been his insistence that the Warriors should not trade Klay Thompson to Minnesota for Kevin Love. Nobody is right 100 percent of the time, but West has one of the best batting averages in sports history.

One afternoon in 2001, I received a phone call at home from Clipper team president Andy Roeser. He said the team had a chance to hire Jerry West. My first reaction was: "What about Elgin?" Andy replied that Baylor was all for it and thought the two old friends could make a great team.

Jerry chose the opportunity in Memphis instead. It does make you wonder how differently that Alvin Gentry Clipper era with Brand, Maggette, Odom, Miles, Richardson, and Piatkowski might have worked out if West had been working as a second voice in Sterling's ear. But Jerry was gone to Memphis, where he would have full control of the team's basketball operation. He stayed five seasons. I never saw his home there, but he told me I would not believe it; you got a lot more house for your money in Memphis than you did in L.A.

Nevertheless, Jerry missed Los Angeles, and by 2007 he was back and out of basketball. A year later, Elgin and the Clippers parted company acrimoniously, there was an opening, and Jerry West was a free agent. There were talks. There was mutual interest. But character has a way of shining through; Jerry simply felt it would be disloyal to Elgin if he were named as his replacement.

West did not work in the league again until 2011, when he joined the Golden State Warriors in a position that allowed him to still spend significant time at home in Los Angeles. He was instrumental in the Warriors' NBA titles in 2015 and 2017. Surprisingly, after their second championship, Jerry left the Warriors, and the time was finally right for him to come home full-time as a trusted consultant for the Los Angeles Clippers.

In September of 2017, West was at the Clipper training camp in Hawaii. It was almost surreal to look down on the court and see him in Clippers gear. During scrimmages, he would come over to sit and talk with me, and it was enlightening to hear his take on various players. Brian Sieman and I absorbed it all gratefully.

Jerry was there when the Clippers needed him. I would often see him at team shoot-arounds or practices at the team's training center in Playa Vista. One memorable day, he came over and sat next to me. During our conversation, he said that in all his years with the Lakers, he thought Chick Hearn was the best NBA play-by-play man in the business. Then he said, "Ralph you are every bit as good as Chick, maybe better." To this day, it is my most prized review of my career. It was always so great to see Jerry in my final years with the team. It took a long time for us to get together, but it was well worth the wait.

We lost Elgin in 2021. I was at our home in Florida when the news was delivered by numerous friends calling from Los Angeles. It rocked me to my very core; I had memories of Baylor dating back to the mid-'50s. We had been friends for over thirty-five years. I hate when fans dismiss his abilities as a basketball sage in the front office. He did as well as possible, considering the circumstances. I thought the Clippers dropped the ball in the aftermath of his passing. Instead of taking the lead in mourning his death and praising his years of service to the game, they let the Lakers command the stage. Elgin was lauded far and wide for his fourteen years (twelve, really) playing for the Lakers, with hardly a mention of his twenty-two years in the L.A. Clipper front office. The formal announcement of the loss of this basketball great was made by the Los Angeles Lakers, though he had not been a part of the Laker organization for fifty years. I felt that Elgin Baylor had been slighted as a player, slighted as a front office executive, and now slighted a final time in his passing. It bothers me to this day.

OVERTIME Most Memorable Clippers

BRENT BARRY

Brent Barry spent three years with the Clippers. He was a breath of fresh air for a franchise that desperately needed it.

As a rookie, Brent won the Slam Dunk crown during All-Star weekend. It elevated his stature around the league, and gave the Clippers some hope. I recall discussing the team with head coach Bill Fitch that year. We agreed that the team—well, the franchise—needed a star player, and Fitch was hoping Barry could fill that bill.

The coach treated the twenty-four-year-old rookie with constant criticism. I have never seen a coach be so hard on a player. Every mistake was drawn to the attention of Brent and all of his teammates. His accomplishments were downplayed, as if they weren't good enough. Some players can handle that, but I don't think it was the best approach with Barry. Brent had a promising rookie season, averaging 10 points a game and showing great potential as a 3-point shooter. He was named to the NBA's All-Rookie second team.

Brent was one of five sons of Hall of Fame player Rick Barry, who may be the most underrated star player in the history of the NBA. Rick could play with anybody who ever played the game. He cast a long shadow, under which his sons struggled to be seen.

It was not easy being Rick Barry's son. In fact, nothing was easy around the elder Barry. I worked a few games with him on television and had no problems; I thought he was a terrific commentator. However, wherever Rick went, he seemed to piss off somebody. His television career was cut short by those who had problems with his personality.

Brent was just the opposite. Nicknamed "Bones" due to his skinny frame, he was friendly, kind, outgoing, and just a pleasure to be around. After the Clippers finished his second season with a game in Seattle against the Sonics, Brent came up to me on our charter flight home and handed me a handwritten note thanking me for my support on the air over the past two years. It was extraordinary for a player to do that. He added that he was going to work on a special off-season strengthening program, and promised that I would not recognize him when training camp opened in October. I think I did recognize him that fall, but neither his game nor his frame matched hopes or expectations. He was traded mid-season to the Miami Heat for center Isaac Austin, for whom the Clippers started a vigorous "I Like Ike" campaign.

They did not like him so well at season's end, letting him leave as a free agent. The Clippers had also received a first-round draft pick from Miami in the Barry trade. They used that to choose power forward Brian Skinner out of Baylor. The bottom line is the Clippers never received adequate compensation for Brent Barry, who went on to a solid career that included stops in Seattle, San Antonio, and Houston. He helped win two NBA championships with the Spurs.

In retirement, Barry had a successful run as a TV commentator at TNT before joining the Spurs' front office. He has a bright future as an NBA executive. I always loved bumping into him along the NBA trail. Brent is one of the league's very best people.

LARRY BROWN

As a basketball coach, the nomadic Larry Brown has few peers. He won an NCAA men's championship at Kansas, and an NBA title in Detroit. He's a three-time Coach of the Year winner in the old American Basketball Association. Today, he's back in college in his eighties, working as assistant coach of the Memphis Tigers. Larry loves to coach.

I only have a season and a half of Larry Brown memories, but they are rich and treasured. He took over for Mike Schuler as coach of the Clippers in mid-season of 1992. The team was floundering; the players had totally tuned out Coach Schuler. Even his assistant coaches were not speaking to him. Basketball-wise, it was absolutely the low point in my years with the team.

On February 5, 1992, we announced the hiring of Larry Brown at halftime during our KCOP telecast of the Clipper-Laker game. General manager Elgin Baylor made the announcement on television, introducing Larry as the new Clipper head coach. I proclaimed it as the most important day in Clipper history. The local media was incensed that the local telecast had exclusive access to the monumental announcement.

The new coach took advantage of a break in the schedule to hold a mid-season mini-camp before coaching his first Clipper game. He went back to the familiar UCLA Pauley Pavilion to stage this re-birth. It worked. I was in the gym and saw that it was a better team after practice number one, before it had even left the court. Brown was the ultimate teacher; no subtle details escaped his watchful eyes. Off the court, Larry was very personable. He was great to be around, but his mind was never too far removed from the game he loved. If a fan or a cab driver suggested a play they had used in high school, he would write it down. Some even made their way onto his team's playbook.

Larry Brown had style, with a capital "S." We would return from a road trip at LAX at two in the morning, and his girlfriend (now wife) Shelly would pull up on the tarmac in his Mercedes convertible with the top down. I remember thinking, "Now, that's living."

Coach Brown was also known for his fickle nature. It might be vanilla today, but don't be surprised if it's strawberry tomorrow. He always wanted to change players and, of course, change jobs. I recall one time, after a game, we were standing side by side at adjacent urinals in the MGM terminal at LAX. He was enthusiastically telling me that he thought he could trade this player or that for whoever. But I didn't put much stake in what he said, because I knew the flavor would change tomorrow.

Brown's complicated relationship with Clipper star Danny Manning was volatile, to put it mildly. The two had teamed up to win a college title at Kansas and were now reunited in the NBA. The tension between the two was palpable. It all came to a head when the team arrived in Milwaukee late one April night in 1992. The team trainer was checking the traveling party into their rooms as the group ambled around the lobby of the historic Pfister Hotel. Suddenly, Brown and Manning began arguing loudly in the middle of the lobby. It became a shoving match, bordering on an out-and-out brawl. Thankfully, it was broken up, and my broadcast partner Bill Walton and I had time for a more peaceful nightcap. We had no problem finding something to talk about.

The Brown/Manning saga lasted another year. It marked the Clippers' first two seasons in the playoffs since their move west in 1978. Larry was gone as the coach after the 1992–1993 season, and Manning was moved to the absolute top of his game in the middle of the following season. The whole story is so Larry Brown.

That said, I loved my time with him and think he is one of the game's all-time greatest coaches.

BARON DAVIS

Baron Davis was a schoolboy basketball hero in Los Angeles, starring at Crossroad High School in Santa Monica in the mid-1990s. He then had a stellar two years at UCLA, where he was All-Pac-10 and third-team All-American as a sophomore. Davis turned pro at the age of twenty, when he was the third overall pick in the NBA draft by the Charlotte Bobcats.

Jo and I had some up-close fun with the young BD the following summer, when we were all on a relaxing NBA cruise of the Caribbean. We had a few responsibilities as a part of the league-sponsored cruise, but still had ample time to experience the joys of ocean cruising. One day, Jo and I were walking along the shoreline in St. Martin with Baron. The weather and the beach were both spectacular. The three of us suddenly realized that the bathers were not wearing swimwear. We had happened upon a nude beach. We had a good chuckle and a few glances here and there before reversing our direction. It made for some good conversation during our daily radio broadcasts aboard the Norwegian Cruise Lines' magnificent SS Norway. We would have pleasant reunions each time the Clippers played Baron's Charlotte, New Orleans, or Golden State Warrior teams.

The Clippers enjoyed a rare serving of the sweet taste of success in 2006, when Elton Brand led the Mike Dunleavy-coached team to a 47–35 season and a run into the second round of the NBA playoffs. It marked the most wins in a season, and the deepest run into the playoffs in the team's twenty-eight years on the West Coast. Optimism filled the hearts of the growing number of residents in Clipper Nation. The following season was a major step back as they missed the playoffs by two games. The 2007–2008 season became a certifiable disaster when Brand tore his Achilles before the season began. He would play just eight games at season's end, and that in itself renewed some hope for the following season. EB would be a free agent, but he had spent seven seasons in Los Angeles. Brand and his wife loved L.A., and there was little concern that he would leave.

Hopes soared when it was learned that the team was close to signing Golden State star Baron Davis. Brand helped recruit the free agent point guard. It was a perfect homecoming at a position of need. I was spending the summer in Bend, Oregon, and considering the trip to Los Angeles for the news conference announcing Brand's new contract with the team. The thought of the team announcing Brand *and* Davis had me checking the flight schedules. Sure enough, Baron decided to come home. Presumably, it was to join Brand, Kaman, Thornton, Mobley, and rookie Eric Gordon on what would be a sure-fire playoff contender.

Oh-oh! Brand took a last second offer from Philadelphia. He would be a 76er. The starting backcourt of Davis and Mobley missed eight-eight games between them, and this edition of the Clippers never got off the launch pad.

Baron would try to come back. I remember asking him what he was missing on the court, and he said, "Explosiveness." I am not sure he ever got it back. He was such a talented player when healthy. He would finish his NBA career with the Knicks in New York in 2012, at the age of thirty-three. I would bump into him often around town in the years that followed. He always indicated the belief that he could still play and longed for a comeback opportunity. Sadly, it never happened. I miss Baron Davis. His good career could easily have been a great one.

BILL FITCH

Coach Bill Fitch was an interesting guy. He was brought in to get the Clippers on track in 1994, after a season and a half of Larry Brown and a single season of Bob Weiss. Fitch was fiery, and very intense. His personality and approach were so different from his two predecessors.

Fitch had won a championship with the Boston Celtics in 1981, and was named one of the NBA's top ten coaches in the league's first fifty years. That was a high honor, and it increased the size of the hammer he used on Clipper players and coaches.

Fitch insisted that each of his coaching assistants live within two miles of him so he could have them over to his house at a moment's notice. When we flew for road games, even if we got in well after midnight, he would summon the staff, everybody, to his hotel room to watch videos of the upcoming team we would be playing.

Fitch was the original Captain Video. He kept all kinds of charts and stats along with the opposing team videos, putting analytics to work years before they became popular. Just a brilliant guy. I used to watch him dissect a box score after a game. Fitch would share this with me on the team bus as he added up all of a player's good stats (points, rebounds, assists, blocked shots) and subtracted their bad stat (turnovers) before comparing the sum total to minutes played. If the total exceeded the number of minutes, Fitch considered it a superstar-level game. It was really an early-day version of the now popular Player Efficiency Rating (PER).

Coach Fitch and I had a defining moment one night on a charter flight, when he called me up to the coach's area of the plane and got in my face. At the time, Paul Sunderland was my broadcast partner; he had come over to join us after some years with the Lakers. We had played an exhibition game against the Lakers in St. Louis. Fitch had just viewed and listened to the video of the game, and started off by attacking Paul's work. He said he sounded like a Laker announcer. I explained that he had a background with them and was able to offer an interesting perspective on the team we were playing. I thought he had done a very good job.

Fitch then said that i wasn't all that good, either. He questioned my loyalty to the team. That's all I had to hear. I fired right back at him with our faces inches apart, standing in the aisle of the coaching section of the aircraft. "Wait a fucking minute, how dare you?" I said. "I *am* loyal to the Clippers. Don't you ever doubt that!" The staff and coaches in the section told me later that they wanted to give me a standing ovation. That was our moment. From that point on, Fitch and I were totally cool.

The man had been coaching since 1956. He claimed that he remembered scouting me during my senior year of high school in Peoria. He was a young assistant coach at Creighton at the time. I am not sure I believed that, but I appreciated the story.

In September of 2019, Bill Fitch and I were both honored by the Naismith Memorial Basketball Hall of Fame. The old coach was eighty-seven years old and living in Houston. Poor health would not allow him to be there for the induction ceremonies. I was truly sorry that I didn't get to see him on the day we shared our career's greatest honor. Happily, his daughter and son-in-law stopped by our table after the ceremonies to tell me Bill had asked them to be sure to seek me out to say hello and congratulations. Sadly, the old coach passed in Houston in February of 2022.

BLAKE GRIFFIN

Blake Griffin was twenty when the Clippers drafted him, and his pre-draft workout became like a coronation. Sponsors and season ticket holders were there to watch the session, and everybody went crazy. He went through the paces with the Clipper coaching staff. Then he asked head coach Mike Dunleavy if he could do one more thing. He wanted to show his ball-handling ability by dribbling two basketballs at once, first between his legs and then behind his back. He made his point.

General manager Neil Olshey wanted to introduce me to the unquestioned number-one player in the June draft. I found him to be a nice young man. He was polite, engaged, and genuinely down to earth. Later, at a summer league practice in Las Vegas, I remember he ran all the way across the gym to shake my hand and say hi. I was so impressed. Later, prior to a pre-season game, Jo was sitting a couple of rows up in the bleachers reading a book when I told Blake that I wanted to introduce him to my wife. He hopped over the press table to give her a hug. I just thought to myself, this guy is truly amazing. At a pre-season scrimmage down at the Camp Pendleton military base, I was sitting with Coach Dunleavy and said to him, "I think he's the best kid on the team." Mike looked at me and said, "Oh, he's the best guy and there's not even a close second."

Griffin broke his left kneecap during a subsequent pre-season game and missed his rookie season. He spent some time with us on the air during his rehabilitation; I was pulling hard for a full and complete recovery. His coming-out party the following year was the game against the New York Knicks on November 21, 2010. The Clippers didn't win, but Blake made a name for himself that night, dropping 44 points, 14 rebounds, and a veritable highlight reel of ferocious dunks. Everybody took notice after the game. Blake Griffin was going to be a powerful presence in the NBA, there was no doubt about it.

But over the years, something changed in Blake. He was on many national television commercials. He was a stand-up comic. Maybe things went to his head, I don't know. It happens. He clearly felt betrayed when the Clippers traded him to Detroit in 2018. Not too many people with a five-year, $171 million contract feel betrayed, but he did.

The Clippers played the Pistons in downtown Detroit on February 8, 2018. It would be our first look at Blake Griffin in an opposing team's uniform. I was looking forward to seeing him. Brian Sieman and I saw him before the game in the passageway leading to the court. It was a narrow hallway, and as he jogged by we said hello and held out a hand for a high five. He didn't even look at us. I know he saw and heard us. It was like we didn't exist.

Once the Pistons came back to Los Angeles, Steve Ballmer went over shake Blake's hand, but the player blew him off. It was very disappointing. Again, you never know what's going on inside someone's head, but given how wonderful, warm, and unspoiled Griffin was in the beginning, this was one of the biggest personality changes I've ever witnessed in my life.

NORM NIXON

Norm Nixon holds the little-known distinction of being the only player to earn NBA All-Star status with both the Los Angeles Clippers and the Los Angeles Lakers. The six-two guard was the Lakers' point guard when they drafted Magic Johnson in 1979. It made for a talented, if imperfect pairing. Both were All-Star players, and both needed the ball in their hands to be most effective.

Nixon was a Laker All-Star in the 1981–1982 season. The Clippers had a rotating cast of players at the play-making position over this period. The San Diego Clippers chose Byron Scott out of Arizona State with the fourth overall pick in the 1983 NBA draft. I remember asking him, on draft day in a hotel ballroom in San Diego's Mission Valley, whether he saw himself in the NBA as a shooting guard or a point guard. Without hesitation he said, "Both. I am just a guard."

It was good, if not accurate news for a team in desperate need of a point guard. But Scott never played either position for the Clippers. He was traded to the Lakers for Norm Nixon just before the team's final season in San Diego. Scott was never an All-Star with the Lakers, but he was a more perfect back-court partner for Magic Johnson. The two paired for three NBA titles in Los Angeles. The swap wound up being a good move for both teams.

Nixon had perhaps his best NBA season that first year in San Diego. He averaged 17 points and a league-leading 11 assists per game while playing in all eighty-two games. Norm gave the team some much-needed star power when they moved to Los Angeles the next season. He was an All-Star that first year in L.A.

By the promising 1985–1986 season, Norm and I had become pals. We would eat together, drink together, attend college games together, sit within a row of each other on team buses, and just generally enjoy each other's company. I got to know his multi-talented wife, Debbie Allen. The accomplished dancer and choreographer was on the way to becoming a show business giant with multiple Emmy and Golden Globe Awards. I knew her best as an amazing

cook. She would dish out delicious meals for team members in the
Nixon kitchen. They were a special and enduring pair in a glitzy city
not known for long-term marriages.

In February of 1986, the team was in New York City, and Norm
wanted to go out with me on our first night in the city. He had a
special place he wanted to take me. It wound up being a dance club
that was popular among the players in the NBA. As it turned out, I
was the only White person in the room. Norm delighted at my obvi-
ous awkwardness. It was a very worthwhile experience; I had never
been the only White guy in a room, and it gave me a sense of what
many African Americans experience being alone in a room—and
world—of White people. It gave new meaning to the term "minori-
ty." I later thanked Norm for the experience.

Injuries hastened Nixon's retirement in 1989, at the age of
thirty-three. He spent a couple of years working on Clipper radio
broadcasts in 2004 and 2005, paired with Mel Proctor. I always felt
that he would find a spot in the Clipper front office or a role as an
assistant coach. I'm sorry that never came to be.

Norm remains a special part of my long list of NBA memories.

LAMAR ODOM

I loved Lamar Odom. Everybody did. I remember telling Sterling
how excited I was when we got him on draft day in 1999. Sterling
was a bit skeptical; though he found Odom exciting, he was concerned about the player's background. His concerns proved to be
well-founded.

There was a lot of tragedy surrounding Lamar, from the early
death of his mother, to the murder of a close cousin, and several
other incidents as well. There were things he couldn't control. I remember when he first got busted for drugs. I was there at the news
conference, and I simply said to him, "I love you, man, and we will
always be with you." He just stared blankly into space.

Years later, when he made it back to the team for a second run,
it didn't take long for the new crop of players and staff to fall in love
with him. But again, he just couldn't keep it together. I will always
have a soft spot for that young man. Lamar has a big heart and is a
very sensitive guy. He's just made some bad decisions.

I like to remember Lamar's sense of humor. He was soft-spo-
ken with the media, but behind the scenes he was the class clown.
I remember hearing him in the back of the bus during pre-season,
loudly imitating Donald Sterling: "Oh, my beautiful players, you are

so beautiful. Don't you just love it here in Los Angeles?" Everybody would be in stitches listening to him. He sometimes performed his impersonation of the owner using the bus driver's microphone. We all laughed until we hurt.

In Odom's first few years with the Clippers, we used to tease him about being strictly a left-handed player. He could do nothing on the court with his right hand. I was in my early sixties at the time and am also left-handed. At the conclusion of a Clipper practice one day, the guys were kidding him about it and I chimed in: "Hey, Odom, I'm a lefty and I bet I can beat you in a game of H-O-R-S-E, with both of us shooting right-handed." He agreed, and his delighted team-mates circled around us to watch. They were 100 percent rooting for me. They cheered my every make and his every miss. It was a close match, and it got down to S to S. He finally shot me out of the game, but the point had been made: he had barely beat the sixty-year-old broadcaster. It was great fun, and the entire team was in on it. That was a happy time with a very young team.

MICHAEL OLOWOKANDI

Sometimes you are good. Sometimes you are lucky. Sometimes you are the Clippers in the 1990s and you are neither. If they'd had the first pick in the draft in 1997, the clear number-one choice would have been Tim Duncan, who went to the San Antonio Spurs that year. But this was not 1997. It was 1998, and Michael Olowokandi was the first overall pick in the NBA draft by the LA Clippers.

The seven-foot, 270-pound center had a sound career nearby at University of the Pacific, where he had been Big West Player of the Year as a senior. He was highly rated on all the draft boards heading into the 1998 NBA draft. The Clippers had him in for a very impressive pre-draft workout, and he was outstanding. He had the right-hand jump hook and the left-hand jump hook. He could face up and make the mid-range jump shot. Not only could he jump, he also had a quick second jump.

Olowokandi had big, soft hands and ran the court like a deer. The only other serious consideration for the top pick was University of Arizona guard Mike Bibby, who was the son of former Clipper player Henry Bibby. The team had Mike in for a workout and had him play one-on-one with Clipper assistant coach Rex Kalamian. When the workout ended, Rex came up to me and asked for my opinion. I said, "Well, he's better than you." It was just very difficult to judge without seeing Mike compete against players of similar or greater skill levels. But one thing seemed clear: Olowokandi was a better pick than Bibby.

The Clippers got the colorfully nicknamed "Kandiman." It was perfect Hollywood casting. The team then brought in the NBA's all-time scoring leader, Kareem Abdul-Jabbar, to tutor and refine the talent of the gifted big man. Wow! What a great idea. Kareem had longed for a chance to coach in the league, and this was the perfect opportunity. Everybody loved the idea—except Michael Olowokandi. Believe it or not, he had little to no interest in anything one of the greatest players in basketball history had to say.

The son of a British diplomat from Nigeria, Michael was very bright and well-bred. He had been raised in high society in London. I really think he felt he was the smartest person in the room, no matter who else was there. Surprisingly, he did not love the game of basketball. It was not the most important thing in his life, and it showed. He also had a bit of a nasty streak, which can be good on the basketball court, but it tended to show elsewhere. After a road game one night, I was following my TV partner Mike Smith up the stairs at the rear of a charter plane. Mike was directly behind Olowokandi and accidentally bumped him on the way up. Olowokandi swung around and appeared ready to slug the lanky broadcaster. They exchanged words. Smith was stunned and shaken over how an innocent bump could provoke such a reaction. The Clipper center would have similar encounters with teammates and staff.

It just made no sense. But then, little about Michael Olowokandi makes sense in hindsight. That includes his spot atop the draft list, a list that included one future Hall of Fame player in Vince Carter and two current members of the esteemed Hall in Dirk Nowitzki and Paul Pierce.

Oh me, Olowokandi.

GLEN "DOC" RIVERS

Vinny Del Negro coached the Clippers for three seasons. By any measure, years two and three were among the best seasons in the team's previous thirty-three years in Southern California. The 2012–2013 team won a franchise-record fifty-six games. The reward? Vinny was fired at season's end. There was a feeling in the front office that Vinny had done a great job, but to get over the hump with a roster featuring Blake Griffin, Chris Paul, Jamal Crawford, DeAndre Jordan, Chauncey Billups, Caron Butler, Matt Barnes, Eric Bledsoe, Lamar Odom, and Rony Turiaf, the team needed a championship-level coach.

Doc Rivers had won the NBA championship five years earlier as head coach of the Boston Celtics. He was restless for a change, and not enthralled with the idea of a Celtic re-build. The Clippers and Celtics agreed to an unusual trade: Boston would send Rivers, plus the three years and $21 million left on his contract, to the Clippers in exchange for a 2015 first-round draft pick.

For the record, it wound up being the twenty-eighth pick in the draft that year. Boston chose a six-foot-five guard named R. J. Hunter, but he never made a name for himself in the league and wound up playing in Australia. It painted a happy face on the deal for the Clippers; they essentially got Doc Rivers for nothing.

Doc was impressive. He was the first former Clipper player to coach the team. His first four years saw fifty-seven, fifty-six, fifty-three, and fifty-one wins, respectively. Doc coached the team to seven consecutive winning seasons. The problem was, he never got them past the second round of the NBA playoffs. But he did win an impressive 64 percent of the games he coached.

The most memorable thing Doc did was serve as a calming hand in the face of disaster amid the playoffs in 2014. The revelations of the racist rants of owner Donald Sterling before Game 4 of the playoffs against Golden State brought the team and much of the league to its knees. It was devastating. The team had fashioned a 2–1 series lead, with Game 4 set for a Sunday afternoon in Oakland. Sterling kept making matters worse in follow-up interviews that were intended to pacify—but ended up intensifying—the nationwide furor over the multi-millionaire's standing in the popular American sport. Sterling would quickly be given a life sentence by NBA commissioner Adam Silver. He was banned from the league and would never again even be allowed to attend a game. Sterling was ordered to sell the franchise.

The players played Game 4, but without focus. They went home with the series tied at 2–2. We are all badly shaken. The longer we had been with the team, it seemed the more it hurt. That's when Doc came to the rescue. He was a consoling messenger for anyone and everyone in the organization. I cannot tell you how impressive he was, standing there in the middle of the virtual Fires of Rome without a burn mark on his body. I was disconsolate, and Doc was there to say we would get through this. There were some good people lining up to bid for the franchise, he would tell us. He was there for the top-level executives in the front office and the everyday worker bees who tried valiantly to keep the organization humming.

Meanwhile, Doc had a team to coach. It was now a three-game series against one of the league's rising young powers. Somehow, he massaged his players in such a way that they were flexible enough to recover with home-court wins in games five and seven to advance into the second round against a very good Oklahoma City team. The news media spent as much attention on the owner's troubles as they did on the playoff series. Coach Rivers had his hands full getting the players to recover from a highly emotional seven-game series with the Warriors to concentrate on Kevin Durant, Russell Westbrook, and the Thunder.

The series opened in OKC on May 5, 2014. Stunningly, the Clippers were able to score a convincing 122–105 Game 1 win, stealing the Thunder's home-court advantage in the first game of the series. Every button Doc pushed was the right one; it looked like his players had recovered from the atomic bombshell that had rocked them just over a week earlier. Maybe, maybe not. The Thunder rumbled to wins in games two and three. Two nights later, the Clips scored a narrow 2-point win in Game 4 at Staples Center to force a pivotal Game 5. I marveled at how Doc and his staff exhibited laser focus on the task at hand while the media was filled with stories about the unrest in the city's junior NBA franchise.

The players showed nerves of steel through all of it. Their confidence seemed unshakable. The Clippers stormed out to an early lead in the raucous and jam-packed Chesapeake Energy Arena in Game 5. They still held a seven-point lead with forty-nine seconds to play. One improbable play after another and two very questionable calls by the referees, and the Thunder scored a stunning 105–104 victory. It was one emotional event too far—they were done. Oklahoma City won Game 6 in L.A. to advance to the Western Conference Finals.

Doc Rivers overcame substantial odds to get his team to a Game 5 in the second round and, even though the season was over, his job was far from done. The team had no owner. The team president was moved aside, and the future was filled with dark, gray thunderclouds.

I spent some time with Doc during this unwanted siege. He was on top of the negotiations that were ongoing for the sale of the team. There were at least three groups seriously interested in the franchise. The Clippers were a good team, and they were in Los Angeles; that was enough to create a serous bidding war. We heard rumors of

$1.4 and $1.5 billion. This was for a team that Sterling had bought in San Diego years earlier for $1 million cash and the assumption of $12 million in debts. Former Microsoft CEO Steve Ballmer ended the bidding with a mind-boggling $2 billion. Doc Rivers was cautiously hopeful that this was the right man. Doc was soon given a raise, and a new title as president of basketball operations. His leadership during the crisis had not gone unnoticed by the new owner.

Doc was a media members dream. He was friendly, available, quotable, and cooperative. We can question his judgment as the president of basketball operations, and maybe his decision to bring in his son, Austin, to play for the team, but he was a bright, hard-working coach who consistently assembled exceptional staffs to serve under him. As team basketball boss, Doc went to the owner each off-season and expressed a need to expand his basketball operations staff. He needed more personnel in analytics one year, and in the medical and training areas the next. He was responsible for building a championship-level operation during his years with the team, which was vital if they were to compete with the likes of Golden State, Oklahoma City, San Antonio, and Houston. Those teams were the leaders in organizing the modern blueprint needed to compete at the highest level. Others, like the Lakers, have caught up, but Doc Rivers was the person whose leadership and organizational skills will allow the Clippers to succeed long after left for Philadelphia in 2020.

Few are aware that Doc was also fantastic at home interior design. He did it at his lovely family home in Winter Park, Florida, made changes to his first home in Brentwood after acquiring the Clipper job, and then spent months reworking the interior of his beach home in Malibu. Doc loved L.A., but his wife, Kris, loved Florida. They spent months away from each other in the respective cities, grew further apart, and finally divorced to end their thirty-four-year marriage.

Doc is a charismatic personality, and he often attracted Hollywood stars. He would tell stories about his dinners with the late comedian Don Rickles, football games with Larry David, and golf dates with close friend and network sportscasting icon Al Michaels. He's just fun to be around, and has many interesting dimensions. He is very aware of the ills of society and is active in trying to correct them. My relationship with him was multifaceted. I broadcast his games when he played for the Clippers in 1991 and 1992. He worked a couple of games with me on television after his retirement as a player, and then we had six winning seasons together in a broadcaster/coach relationship. Each facet was a delight.

Doc is the tenth coach in NBA history to have coached 1,000 wins. That is a key number in gaining entry to the Naismith Memorial Basketball Hall of Fame. Another championship would clinch it. He belongs. He is certainly in my personal Hall of Fame.

DEREK SMITH

The Derek Smith story is a terribly sad one. Few present-day fans have ever even heard of him. I first saw him play in 1983 when, at six foot six and 205 pounds, he was miscast as a power forward by the Golden State Warriors. The second-round draft choice did little that was memorable for the Oakland-based team. He averaged about 2 points a game in twenty-seven brief appearances in his rookie season. He did not last the year, as the Warriors released him in mid-season.

Clipper head coach Jimmy Lynam was given a tip, and decided to bring Smith in on a non-guaranteed contract to open training camp in the University of San Diego gym in 1983. The coach quickly realized that he was undersized as a power forward. Lynam moved him to the shooting guard spot, where his size would be an advantage rather than a disadvantage. I can clearly envision one of the plays during a scrimmage. Smith had the ball at mid-court. He accelerated past two or three defenders, rose in the paint, and threw down a thundering slam dunk. Everybody in the gym was aghast! The coach wore a knowing grin; he knew he had found something special.

The former University of Louisville star came off the bench most of the year. Lynam wanted to bring him along slowly, starting him in nineteen of the final twenty games. There was no doubt that this young man had game. He averaged 17 points a night in that finishing stretch.

It was to be the Clippers final year in San Diego, and they opened the 1984–1985 season in Los Angeles. Derek Smith played in and started in eighty games and averaged over 22 points a game while making 54 percent of his shot attempts. A star had been born in a city where the Clippers knew they desperately needed one. The signature game for Smith took place on November 30, 1984, at the L.A. Sports Arena against the Chicago Bulls and their rookie superstar, Michael Jordan. It was no contest; Derek was so much stronger than MJ. He handily outscored Jordan—who went on to become the game's greatest player—33 points to 20. Afterwards, Jordan called Smith the most underrated player in the NBA.

Derek was now an elite shooting guard in the league. He averaged 22 points a game in his first year as a full-time starter. Those of us who followed him believed he was on his way to sharing the NBA stage with Jordan. If Michael represented Coke, Derek would do the same for Pepsi. If MJ was the Nike guy, Smith would be the Adidas guy. The two were so close to being equals. The league had already benefited with the Magic Johnson-Larry Bird pairing. Now, here was another.

Derek was a special young man. He had grown up in rural Georgia, in a small house with a dirt floor and no indoor plumbing. He rose from those humble beginnings to graduate from college and win an NCAA basketball title at Louisville. It was a storybook success story, and I was loving the chance to live it with the twenty-three-year-old who had married his college sweetheart, Monica. She was every bit as real as her loving husband.

Derek Smith's second season with the Clippers in Los Angeles started off even better than the first. The team roared off to a 5–0 start. Derek was battling for the NBA scoring lead at 28 points a game. He was named the NBA Player of the Week for the season's first week. Here come the Clippers!

One injury after another hit this promising team, now coached by Don Chaney. No injury hurt worse than Smith's torn-up knee nine games into the season. Surgery would be required, but the early estimate was that he would be able to return in no more than six weeks. The season still had hope, but the estimate was clearly optimistic.

By mid-December, the team was getting impatient. The Clippers had a Christmas Day game scheduled in Portland, and the team badly wanted Smith to be back on the court for that game. I remember sitting across the table from Derek at a team dinner on Christmas Eve. I was expressing how great it was going to be to see him back on the court. He did not share my joy, saying he just was not sure he was ready, but he would give it a try. The next day, he only came off the bench to play eleven tentative minutes, but at least he was playing.

Smith would play briefly in only one more game before he was ruled out for the season; the knee and then a bout with mononucleosis had taken its toll. It got ugly, as the team felt Derek might be faking or exaggerating his injury or illness. Those of us who knew the quality and competitive nature of this extraordinary young man also knew faking was impossibly out of character for Derek.

At season's end, Smith was a restricted free agent. A year earlier, it had looked like a big payday would be in the offing, but now, things were not so clear. He received a modest offer-sheet from the Sacramento Kings, which the Clippers quickly matched and traded their sullied star in exchange for Junior Bridgeman, Mike Woodson, and Larry Drew, a first-round pick and second-round pick. It was a major haul for a player who had appeared in only eleven games the previous season.

It broke my heart to see him leave, but Derek was happy to have a new start. I drove him to the airport for his departure to Sacramento. He was appreciative of my support and genuinely happy for the chance to revive his career with the Kings.

The Sacramento team and their fans thought they had acquired a superstar. Expectations were through the roof, but Smith was no longer capable of meeting such lofty hopes. The fans blamed him for being only a 16-point and 12-point-a-game scorer in his two years in the state capital. He was not the same player, and he never would be again. He was still young enough, but his explosiveness and athleticism were gone. He was out of the league by the time he turned thirty.

Jimmy Lynam came in to resuscitate Smith's career a second time in 1994, when he hired him to be a part of his coaching staff with the Washington Bullets. I sat with him for fifteen or twenty minutes when his team came to Los Angeles to play the Clippers that December. He was full of warmth and joy. He was raising a young family, and life was good. We talked about what might have been in his unfulfilled rivalry with Michael Jordan, who by then was racking up NBA titles with the Chicago Bulls. Derek was a little wistful about it, but there was not a hint of resentment or any "why me" sentiments.

Derek died aboard a team-sponsored Caribbean Cruise in August of 1996. He was seated across the dinner table from a Bullet player named Tim Legler. They were engaged in a casual conversation when Derek suddenly collapsed. They say he was dead by the time his face hit the table between them. It was devastating news to all those on board, and his death was felt around the league.

I met Derek's son, Nolan, when he played with the Portland Trailblazers from 2011 to 2013. It was such a pleasure to tell him how much I admired his father and to give him a first-hand account of just how good he was on the basketball court. Nolan had his dad's good nature, if not his physical and basketball attributes—he was inches shorter and twenty pounds lighter than his uber-athletic father. Nolan always stopped by the press table to say hello whenever the Blazers and Clippers met. He is now an assistant coach at Duke, where he played from 2007 to 2011. I would not be surprised if he becomes a head coach somewhere along the line. He certainly has good bloodlines. I will carefully watch his progress, in as much as I feel cheated that I never got to see the full career story written by his father.

BRIAN WILLIAMS (BISON DELE)

Brian Williams was one of the most interesting young men to ever play for the Clippers. He was the son of Eugene Williams, who was a member of the popular musical recording quartet The Platters for eighteen years. The Clippers visited the Cavaliers in Cleveland during his season with the team, and Brian insisted I go visit the Rock and Roll Hall of Fame there to see his Dad's spot in the music shrine. My partner, Rory Marcus, and I ventured over to do just that. It was a kick, and Brian was really pleased that we made the visit.

Rory and I were working radio that game, and we did manage to sneak in a few bars of one of the Platters hits. I think it was "Only You" on that night's broadcast. We did get a call from Brian's mother, Patricia Phillips, correcting some minor "fact" we had misstated in the story about her husband, but she was always supportive of her son and I never failed to have interesting interactions with Patricia.

The six-ten Williams averaged almost 16 points a game for the Clippers during his lone season with the team in 1995 and 1996. He was the team's number-two scorer, barely behind Loy Vaught. I just found him fascinating.

I used to routinely deliver birthday cards to players' lockers on their special day. I did so with Brian in Dallas on his birthday, late in the 1995–1996 season. He was generally very intense and serious-minded. When he found the card, he came over and gave me a big man-hug and thanked me with a happy grin on his face. It was a rare, intimate moment between broadcaster and player.

Sadly, the team would not meet Brian's salary demands after that year, and he sat out before signing late the following season with the Chicago Bulls. He would go on to help them win an NBA championship with Michael, Scottie, and Coach Jackson. Then it was on to Detroit, where he changed his name to Bison Dele and had two impressive seasons before retiring at the age of thirty in 1999. He walked away from the remaining $35 million on his contract.

Brian was not your usual NBA player. He reportedly dated Madonna, and used the musical genes he'd gotten from his father to play trumpet, saxophone, and violin. He was also a world traveler, and that's where the story met a mysterious and tragic ending. In the summer of 2002, Brian was sailing his catamaran off the coast of Tahiti. He was with his girlfriend, his brother, and the boat's skipper. Two weeks later, the brother, Miles Dabord, sailed the boat into Tahiti alone—he was the only one on board. It remains a remarkable, unsolved mystery. The most popular theory is that Brian, his girlfriend, and the skipper were murdered by Dabord and then thrown overboard. We will never know.

Dabord died in a California hospital of a drug overdose on September 27, 2002. I could not imagine the depth of despair Brian's mother must have experienced. Other Clipper players have also had tragic events change or end their lives: Malik Sealy (auto accident), Rodney Rogers (paralyzing dirt bike crash), Lorenzen Wright (murdered), but none carries the mystery or intrigue of the life and times of Brian Williams. ●

Chapter 9

The Clippers' Growth Chart: 1990s and 2000s

THE '90S REPRESENTED A TUMULTUOUS CHAPTER in Clipper history. It started with some hope, as former NBA Coach of the Year Mike Schuler took over as head coach. He had made the Portland Trailblazers a high-scoring offensive juggernaut (117.9 points per game in 1986–1987) and promised more of the same with the Clippers. He also made it clear that his reputation of being gruff and unresponsive to the media was overstated, and we would all soon see the difference. He really seemed like a very personable and capable new coaching hope for the team.

Schuler was rightfully full of hope, because the roster boasted some talented young players: Danny Manning (twenty-four years old), Charles Smith (twenty-five), Ron Harper (twenty-six), Ken Norman (twenty-six), Gary Grant (twenty-five), Benoit Benjamin (twenty-five), Loy Vaught (twenty-two), and Olden Polynice (twenty-five). They were old enough to know the NBA ropes, but young enough to have room to grow. None of them had reached their prime athletic years yet. Schuler was excited, I was excited, and the jaded SoCal media was paying a little attention to a team that had averaged only twenty-four wins a season in its first six years in Los Angeles.

I went on a summer outing with the coach and trainer Keith Jones to survey the Clipper pre-season training site at Cal Poly Pomona. Keith and I had our fingers crossed, but Schuler was understandably stunned and dismayed by the quality of the facility. It was acceptable as a small college gym, but not close to NBA training camp standards; the teams typically benefited from two full courts and multiple baskets. The motel where the team was to stay was even more concerning. It was small and frequented by budget-minded families and truckers. I can still see Mike shaking his head in absolute disillusionment. He was wondering what on earth he had gotten himself into.

It also brought about a return of his dour personality. The season gave the coach little reason to turn those frowns into smiles; the team was eleven games under .500 by the first week of January. They were no way near the offensive powerhouse the coach had expected (103.5 points per game).

I got along fine with Mike, and his wife, Gloria, was a delight. The further you could get him away from the game, the more normal he became. He did not know how to balance his work with life and fun. I ran into him on the road in the hotel lobby one night and told him about this great meal I had just had at a very good restaurant. He said, "I won't waste my money on places like that. I eat at fast food joints. That food all comes out the same in the end." A lovely vision if ever I heard one, but it does help paint a picture of Coach Schuler's personality.

His first season ended with a record of thirty-one wins and fifty-one losses. Sadly, that was the highlight of his season and a half at the helm. The 1991–1992 season was far worse. Oh, the team was better—an eight-game winning streak lifted them four games over .500 by mid-December. But by the end of January, they were four games under .500. Schuler's relationship with his players and his assistant coaches deteriorated day by day. It got to the point that neither the players nor the members of his staff were speaking to him. Not a one.

We arrived late one night in Houston after a loss to the Spurs in San Antonio. The coaching staff would normally join the head coach in his hotel suite to review video of the prior game and start planning for the next. But things were so bad, the coach only invited me to his suite upon our arrival. It was just the two of us, and it was about as awkward as it sounds. There we were, the head coach and the broadcaster. We sat. We stared at each other. Neither of us knew what to say. I think we both knew that things had to change. Meanwhile, before their win over the Clippers the night before, the Spurs had fired their coach, Larry Brown. It wasn't on our radar at the time, but it registered loud and clear a few days later.

Schuler was fired on February 2 after a home win over New Jersey, and assistant coach Mack Calvin was named interim coach. General manager Elgin Baylor made it crystal clear that Calvin was not a candidate for the job on a full-time basis. No matter; the former USC star campaigned unashamedly for the job, and even had one of his players, Olden Polynice, go on the radio to tout him for the job.

The night before meeting the Lakers at the Forum, Calvin led the Clippers to a win over Dallas. He still somehow harbored hopes of landing the head coaching job. We televised the game against the Lakers and introduced Larry Brown as head coach of the Clippers. It was huge news. Larry was widely regarded as one of the game's greatest coaches, and now he was a Clipper! It is hardly shocking that Brown's tenure with the team lasted only a season and a half, despite back-to-back appearances in the playoffs.

My pal, Bob Weiss, replaced Brown but was only given a one-year trial before the team bought him out of his contract following a twenty-seven-win season. The four-year Bill Fitch reign followed. It was four straight losing seasons, tempered only by a brief playoff appearance in 1997. The Clippers made the playoffs, despite winning only thirty-six games in the regular season. They were predictably swept in the first round by the heavily favored Utah Jazz. Before Game 1 in Salt Lake City, I was interviewed on Jazz TV and asked about concerns over a sweep. "Oh," I said, "I don't think the Clippers are going to sweep the Jazz." It provided a rare bit of levity in a decade that was void of much to smile about. Fitch was gone after going 17–65 in 1997–1998.

Labor problems took over the NBA headlines in the off-season, and the league locked the players out at season's end. The Clippers owner dragged his feet on hiring a replacement, because he would have to pay him once he hired him. The team went 263 days without hiring a coach for the shortened fifty-game season that began the first week of February.

Former Boston and Milwaukee coach Chris Ford was given the job in late January. He did not have a chance; the hodge-podge roster was simply not good enough. The team went 9–41. When Ford was let go late the following season, Jim Todd would become the team's ninth coach of the decade. The 1980s were rough for the Clippers, but they were parade-worthy compared to the '90s. A January 2000 *Sports Illustrated* cover told the story of the '90s for all to see, labeling the Clippers "The Worst Franchise in Sports History."

The move to Staples Center and the hiring of Alvin Gentry as head coach signaled a new era, and it was none too soon. The Clippers were fun for the first time since the quick-as-a-blink sixteen months of Larry Brown nearly a decade earlier.

The Clippers added exciting young talent through the draft and deft trades. In came nineteen-year-old Darius Miles, joined by a trio of twenty-year-olds: Corey Maggette, Quentin Richardson, and Keyon Dooling. They complimented a twenty-year-old hold-over named Lamar Odom. These young players had all known each other since their AAU days, when they were in their early teens.

The Clippers' future had never looked brighter. Miles landed on the cover of *Sports Illustrated* with Kevin Garnett. He was the first Clipper player on the prestigious magazine's cover since Bill Walton in 1979. On the court, the team was too young to win consistently, but they more than doubled the previous season's win total. Miles made the all-rookie first team, and Odom led the club in scoring and rebounding. The stage was set for a run at the NBA playoffs. The next season, Elgin Baylor took a big step forward in a draft day trade in 2001 for another young warrior, twenty-two-year-old Elton Brand. He was the perfect fit.

These guys were so much fun to be around. Darius and Q were inseparable. Despite the forty-year age gap between us, I had a great relationship with the two, who had also grown up in Illinois. They respectfully called me "The Man." The two pals now live near each other in Florida, where they host a popular podcast called *Knuckleheads*. I was thrilled when they flew across country to be there for my final regular season home game broadcast on April 10, 2019.

The head-bumping pair was the focal point of that 2001–2002 Clipper team, and the nation was taking notice. ESPN developed a weekly reality television program called *Sidelines: L.A. Hoops*, and their camera crew and producer had full access to the colorful young team. They were with us at games, practices, team flights, and bus rides. It was the first time that many fans became aware of the existence of L.A's "other" team. Fans could not wait for the weekly program to air.

The free-spirited Gentry was the perfect coach for the happy-go-lucky Clippers. He was in his early forties and had a good understanding of his young team's psyche. The cameras rolled almost nonstop. Miles's #21 jersey became one of the league's top sellers. That was virtually unimaginable in years past. Darius and Q became the young darlings of the league, as fans became fascinated by their celebratory double-fisted head bumps after a made 3 or a thundering slam dunk. Kids were copying the act in high school gyms all around the country. Some fans were touting the Clippers kids as "America's team." Brand had a brilliant All-Star season. If Odom had not battled injuries and a five-game drug suspension (he missed fifty-three games), this team would have made the playoffs. As it was, they were three games over .500 in late March and right in the middle of the playoff race. They would sadly drop ten of their final thirteen games to finish ninth with the top eight making up the playoff field.

No matter—the joy was there. The Clippers sold out twenty-five games that year, a total that matched their prior five seasons combined. The team was on the local map at last. The final home game was one of the happiest nights in team history. The Clippers beat Memphis to finish 25–16 on their home court. At game's end, Odom jumped up on the press table in celebration; Miles went back to the locker room time and again to grab sneakers, wristbands, and t-shirts to toss to the fans in the stands. Nobody wanted to leave the building, and I didn't want to leave the air. No one wanted to let go of this exuberant young team. Little did we know, we would never see them together again. Four months later, the Clippers traded Miles to Cleveland for NBA assist leader Andre Miller. The magic vanished.

Veteran coach Mike Dunleavy further elevated the stature of the franchise with his hiring in 2003. I had known Mike since he had come into the league as a sixth-round draft pick with the 76ers in Philadelphia in 1976. He had a solid NBA head coaching resume built around impressive runs with the Lakers and Portland, sandwiched around some troubled years in Milwaukee. His Clipper teams improved modestly in year one, dramatically in year two, and spec-tacularly in year three. He brought in veteran Sam Cassell in a trade with Minnesota for Marko Jaric in 2005, and that jump-started what was the team's best season to date on the West Coast. They won for-ty-seven games. The veteran point guard joined Elton Brand and Co-rey Maggette, who were hold-overs from Alvin Gentry's young squad four years earlier.

The Clips finished ahead of the Lakers for only the second time in their years in Los Angeles. It seemed the two teams were poised to meet in the playoffs for the first time. The Clippers were up 3–1 against Denver, and the Lakers were up 3–1 on Phoenix. Each just a win away from an L.A. city-series face-off in round two. It would have been great for pro basketball in the city, and it would give a big boost to the Clippers' emerging credibility. Sadly, the Lakers lost three in a row, and the Suns advanced to face the Clippers, who were easy 4–2 winners over the Nuggets. It is the closest the two L.A. teams had come to a dramatic playoff battle.

The Clippers' Game 5 double-overtime loss in Phoenix goes down, in my mind, as the most painful playoff defeat in franchise history. The Clippers led by 3 with 3.9 seconds to go in the first overtime period. The stars had flocked to the Valley of the Sun in hopes that the Clip-pers could take a 3–2 lead with Game 6 back in Los Angeles. Billy Crystal was there, as were Penny Marshall and James Brooks. Even the Lakers' most famed fan, Jack Nicholson, had a front-row seat. Clippers fans will forever blame Coach Dunleavy for letting young Daniel Ewing chase Raja Bell into the corner, where the Suns guard made the game-tying 3-pointer. I blame the coach as well, but not for having Ewing on Bell; he had a mis-positioned Cat Mobley, covering in-bounds passer Boris Diaw rather than seven-footer Chris Kaman, who could have obscured the six-foot-eight Diaw's vision and defend-ed against the easy pass into the corner. It was a heart-breaker of a shoulda-couldas.

The series marked the zenith in a decade that actually bore some hope. Dunleavy's hiring was the first step toward respectability. The luck of the draw, and the drafting of Blake Griffin in 2009, was the big step that eventually led to the Lob City era and years of winning Clipper basketball.

Chapter 10

Memories of Lob City

I WAS LUCKY ENOUGH to spend most of my adult life as a broadcaster in professional sports, and I can tell you that, from inside the pro sports bubble, there is nothing better than winning. Likewise, few things feel worse than losing. Forget about the old adage that "it's not whether you win or lose, but how you played the game." At the professional level, victory is an absolute obsession. I've had both coaches and players lament over the years that the thrill of winning does not come close to compensating for the agony of losing. Winners just immediately start worrying about losing their next game. Philadelphia 76ers coach Doc Rivers told me he's spent far more time lamenting the title his Boston Celtics lost to the Lakers in 2010 than he has his Celtic title against the Lakers two years earlier. Losing engulfs your soul, and its pain diminishes any fleeting joy derived from a victory.

Winning is just as addictive to the fans. I became a sports fan in 1945, at the age of seven. I'd listen to Chicago Cub baseball broadcasts on the radio, and announcer Burt Wilson brought the games to life for me. The Cubs reached the World Series that year, though they lost in seven games to the Detroit Tigers. I was heartbroken by the Cubs' loss, without realizing how good we Cub fans had it—they would not make another World Series appearance until 2016! Still, I was in love with the Cubbies through all those seventy gruesome losing seasons in between. It was a long and painful lesson, learned from childhood to senior citizenship, about the elusive nature of success in the world of sports. It was also maybe a prep course for my first thirty years as the voice of the perpetually losing Clippers in San Diego and Los Angeles.

I would say the L.A. Clippers were mired in mediocrity for most of their first twenty-five years in Los Angeles, but that would be generous; they seldom rose to mediocre status. The team went through sixteen head coaches between 1984 and 2013, when Doc Rivers was brought in from Boston to replace Vinny Del Negro. Doc adopted a very good team that had won fifty-six games the prior season. The hope was that the man who had won a championship in Boston five years earlier could help the Clippers win their first NBA title.

The team was led by a Big Two of Blake Griffin and Chris Paul. Rivers quickly helped center DeAndre Jordan up his expectations and his game to make it a Big Three. Doc challenged D. J. to model his game after Bill Russell, who had led the Celtics to eleven titles in his thirteen seasons with a total focus on rebounding and rim protection. That was the challenge for the twenty-five-year-old center.

Doc started by changing Jordan's number to Russell's number 6. The transformation was immediate—DeAndre led the NBA in rebounding that year and next. He would make All-NBA first team in 2016, and represent the U.S. as a member of the Olympic Gold Medal team that summer. D.J. was an All-Star in 2017. Yes, the Clippers had a Big 3.

DeAndre came up with the "Lob City" moniker in 2011, when it was announced that the Clippers had traded for New Orleans star point guard Chris Paul. It gave the team an identity. Paul gave Jordan and Griffin countless opportunities to posterize opponents, one after another. The acrobatic feats were so spectacular that they carried the names of the victims: Knight, Gasol, Plumlee, Mozgov. The Lob City Clippers were a broadcaster's delight. I remember the executive producer at Fox Sports West once telling us to not show so many slam dunks on television. Huh?

Griffin, Jordan, and Paul were such fun to watch. They gave the team unprecedented exposure on national TV, and became the replay darlings of ESPN's *SportsCenter*. They were also fun to be around. Early in their years together in 2012, the Clippers played a pair of pre-season games in China against the Miami Heat. The two teams split the pair of games in Shanghai and Beijing. The results were secondary to the NBA-crazed fans in China, who were split in their fascination with LeBron James of the Heat and the Clippers' amazing Lob City high-wire act. It was a long flight home to Los Angeles after the second game on October 11, 2012. I was taking a nap on the plane when Griffin, Jordan, and Paul added me to their poster list by taking a photo of me sleeping while they held a sign above my head that read, "#Oh Me. #Oh My!!!"

However, it was not all fun and games. There were the inevitable personality conflicts. There was the highly publicized Blake Griffin punch-out of assistant equipment manager Matias Testi in Toronto in

---

TIME OUT Worst of the Worst Teams

Over the years, I've seen a lot of great basketball, and I've seen a lot of very bad basketball. It is not easy to quantify teams that excelled or floundered the most from one decade to the next, but this is my courtside view.

Hands down, the worst NBA team I ever saw came from the labor strife-shortened 2011–2012 season. I will grant you that the L.A. Clippers had some bad teams during my forty years broadcasting their games, but none were as bad as the Charlotte Bobcats in this sixty-six-game season. The team started slowly, and then went into a slump. The highlight was a 2–4 start through the season's first six games.

Paul Silas was stuck coaching the Bobcats after owner Michael Jordan had traded away the team's best players over the past couple of years. The roster was virtually bare of quality NBA talent. They were on pace to compete with the 1972–1973 Philadelphia 76ers (9–73) for the worst record in league history throughout much of the season. They clinched matters by losing their final twenty-three games. The final tally was seven wins and fifty-nine losses. That .106 winning percentage goes down as the worst in NBA history. They lacked offensive punch. They were a sieve on defense, and they did not rebound the ball. It was as bad as it gets.

It was not easy being worse than those 1972–1973 Philadelphia 76ers. This vagabond group of players started off losing their first fifteen games of the season. Amazingly, that was not the low point. They later would endure a twenty-game losing streak.

A man named Roy Ruben had somehow been named head

2016. It left the diminutive Testi bruised and battered, and left Griffin with a broken hand. Blake had been everywhere, as a spokesman on one national television commercial after another. Those days ended that January night in Toronto. It's one day in his Lob City life that Blake Griffin would like to change.

DeAndre Jordan came into the league as a happy-go-lucky, nineteen-year-old second-round draft pick. He was full of life and always seemed ready with a lovable smile. His role with the team and expectations were lifted substantially when Doc Rivers took over as head coach in 2013. It gave us a more serious DeAndre Jordan. The

coach at the start of the season. He had once written a book about how to play defense, but I don't think his players read the book. Ruben was fired after a dismal 4–47 start. One of his players, an aging Kevin Loughery, was named to replace him as player-coach. They went 5–26 the rest of the way.

The 76ers only once won consecutive games. That pair of victories in March left them at 9–60 on the year. They would not win another game. The Sixers finished with a mark of nine wins and seventy-three losses. It was the worst record over an eighty-two-game season in the history of the league.

Attendance had fallen below 6,000 fans a night. I got to Philly the following year, when attendance had plummeted further to about 4,600 per game. That historically futile season had soured the long-faithful 76er fan base, but they came back to the Spectrum as a team improved under head coach Gene Shue. Attendance more than tripled by the time of their march to the NBA Finals in 1977. The collateral damage from that dismal 1972–1973 season was four full years in recovery.

The other team that comes to mind is the 1981–1982 San Diego Clipper team. They were simply bad in the season's first half, under novice head coach Paul Silas. At the midway point, the record stood at 12–29. This is the time they became the worst Clipper team of all time. The Clips went 5–36 the rest of the way. Injuries took a mighty toll, and Silas was forced to go with a backcourt of Jim Brogan and John Douglas for the balance of the season. They averaged less than 14 points a game between them. The Clippers went 2–12 in February, 1–15 in March, and finished April in a 1–8 flourish. I have not seen a Clipper team as bad as that one. ●

demands and expectations left him more vulnerable—or maybe sensitive—to critiques on his game. After hearing, or imagining, some "slight" on one of our telecasts, he became upset and did not speak to me for weeks on end. I went over to him at St. Elmo's restaurant in downtown Indianapolis one night to tell him I loved him and was open to talking about it whenever he was ready. There was no defining moment, but D.J. was there to offer me hearty congratulations as my final Clipper broadcast approached. That meant a lot to me.

Chris Paul was the most consistent personality of this talented trio. He is as competitive as anyone who ever played the game, and demanded much of himself and his teammates, which would sometimes rub people the wrong way. Though the oldest of the Clipper Big Three, he's the one who has been able to continue to perform at an All-Star level. The facts show that teams get better as soon as he joins them. I think he is the greatest player in franchise history. I Love CP3.

The trio won fifty or more games in five consecutive seasons, but never got over the second-round playoff hump. Paul, Griffin, and Jordan get all the attention from the Lob City era, but it took more than *SportsCenter* highlight plays to win as consistently as this group did. Doc River's first team may have been his best. I think they were the best Clippers team of all time, certainly the deepest. Jamal Crawford was the team's second leading scorer and NBA Sixth Man of the Year. He was also one of the most down-to-earth players to ever wear a Clipper uniform. I emceed the ceremonies on NBA-TV when he received the well-deserved Sixth Man honor. His entire family was present, and it was a big day in the thirty-four-year-old player's life. Afterward, he thanked me so profusely that you would have thought I was responsible for him getting the award. He won it again two years later, and we repeated the process all over again on national television. This would mark the third time that the scoring sensation from Seattle would receive the Sixth Man recognition. He brought along his prior two trophies to load a table with his third. Jamal had a way about him of making people around him feel special. I always thought that sharing those two award ceremonies with him gave us a special bond.

Crawford was such a creative scorer. His longevity earns him the title of being the greatest bench player the game has ever seen. He

Baby Ralph home from the hospital, April 1938.

Young Ralph at three years old as WWII begins.

Five-year-old Ralph with Dad on moving day, 1943.

Fishing was a passion even before basketball.

Early Peoria.

Great group of lifelong friends from the Peoria years.

Thomas Jefferson Grade School team 1951–52.

Peoria Central High School sectional champs, 1956.

Seventeen-year-old high school player.

Always a "ham."
Riverside players,
1961.

(Staff Photo)

OFFER — Ralph Lawler, as Paul, discusses an offer by Mieke Tunney (Katrin) in Leslie Stevens' "The Marriage-Go-Round," which is playing at Riverside Community Players Theater. Katrin, who is brainy as well as beautiful, wants to have a child by Paul, who is also bright, but married. It's all in the interest of genetics — and laughs.

"Mr. Roberts" at Bradley, 1959.

First full-time radio job at WAAP while a college student.

My move to California led to association with Dick Clark.

One of many promotions at KPRO in the '60s.

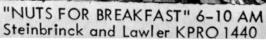

Two-man morning show with Bob Steinbrinck.

Opening of Arby's Restaurant in 1968.

Publicity photo for WCAU Channel 10 in Philadelphia, 1977–78.

Still loved playing the
game during Philly years.

Phillies spring training in Clearwater, Florida, 1978.

Ad for morning show at WCAU Radio, 1974–75.

WHO ARE THIS MAN?

SpivakLawlerSchmidt.
The best newsman in town.

WCAU Radio gives you a morning man who's a triple threat. We give you the brilliance of Joel A. Spivak, the enthusiasm of Sports Director Ralph Lawler and the nose-for-news of our Managing Editor, Bob Schmidt.

Professionals. Who combine to give you the best morning radio your dial has to offer.

And they're not all you get. We throw in the best of CBS News. People you already know as the best in the news business. Like Dallas Townsend, (8 AM) Dan Rather, (6:23 AM) Charles Osgood, (8:40 AM)

We give you more time checks. To help you start the day out right.

More local weather reports. Six, between 5:30 and 8:31 AM, with CBS Meteorologist Tom Barnes. His accuracy average is

Eight complete Go Patrol Traffic Reports between 6:52 and 8:51 AM.

Dennis Cunningham and the world of entertainment. (6:56-8:56)

And plenty of surprises. Like newsmaker calls to the White House. (Or a live volcano if there is one.)

What we give you is the world. Every morning.

That's our business.
What you do with it is up to you.

JOEL A. SPIVAK'S MORNING NEWSBEAT 5-30-9-30

WCAU RADIO 121

RALPH LAWLER —
"VOICE" of the SAILS

For Ralph Lawler, his absence from San Diego may have seemed like a long time, but he crammed his schedule full enough to make the time fly. Recalled to his favorite city to become the radio "voice" of the San Diego Sails, he returned after serving as sports director of WCAU in Philadelphia for two years.

What did he do at WCAU? He aired daily sports shows, sports commentaries, play-by-play for the Philadelphia Flyers of the National Hockey League, Temple University football, and Big Five basketball. He also hosted a weekly college football highlights show on television.

A 15 year radio veteran, Ralph has also broadcast major automobile races from tracks through out the United States and hosted a daily, syndicated world-wide, program titled "World of Wheels."

Before beginning his sojurn in Philadelphia, Ralph was extremely active in sports broadcasting in San Diego. He was sports director of KDEO-Radio, doing daily sportscasts, as well as San Diego State basketball and San Diego Chargers football.

An Associated Press and Golden Mike award winner, his return to San Diego was greeted warmly by both KSDO General Manager Jack Sabella and Sails General Manager Irv Kaze.

"We're extremely pleased that Ralph is willing to leave Philadelphia and help us launch the Sails," said Sabella.

Kaze commented, "Ralph's professionalism and major league approach will add tremendously to our fans enjoyment of games."

Ralph gathered his degree in communications from Bradley University in Peoria, Ill. He is married, with one child. He lists his hobbies as theater, politics, and sports — but not always in that order.

GET BUSHWAKKED
...AFTER THE GAME.
new adventure in dining.
BUSHWAKKER
SEAFOOD · STEAKS · SPIRITS
Lunch, Monday–Friday · Dinner and entertainment, nightly.
TELEPHONE: 299-3544
1299 Camino del Rio South, across from Mission Valley Center

Short-lived flirtation with ABA in 1975.

xiii

Rainy day at Laguna Seca sports car race, late 1960s.

My varied career included calling San Diego Charger games in '71–'73.

Finally, in 1978, I was a full-time NBA announcer in San Diego.

On to Los Angeles in 1984–85.

Worked with so many greats. Here I am with Mike Fratello.

Dominique Wilkins.

Hubie Brown.

Billy Crystal.

Thanking Bradley University with fellow grad Charlie Steiner and benefactor Larry King.

NBA team elders: George Blaha, me, Joe Tate, and Al McCoy, 2010.

I met so many great people. Here I am with Dodger manager Tommy Lasorda.

Honoring the great Kareem during his retirement tour, 1988–89.

Ali in San Diego for a bout with Ken Norton.

Final season with the brilliant Jerry West.

An unforgettable night to honor John Wooden and Vin Scully.

Oh, what might have been.

Clippers LOG

JUNE 1979   VOL. 1, NO. 1

WALTON SIGNED TO SEVEN-YEAR CLIPPERS CONTRACT

Clippers head coach Gene Shue, Bill Walton, and president Irv Levin measure the newly-acquired center for his uniform jersey.

Bill Walton is coming home.

The announcement on Mothers' Day, Sunday, May 13, that Walton had signed a seven-year contract with the Clippers resulted in a wave of season ticket sales.

The first four weeks after the announcement of Walton's signing, San Diego area fans responded with the purchase of 1,500 season tickets. These were all new season ticket purchases and in addition to the 3,000 sold during the Clippers first season.

Walton's contract with the Clippers makes him the highest paid player in the history of the NBA.

Clippers president Irv Levin, who made the announcement at a press conference that included live coverage by CBS-TV, noted, "All of us in the Clippers organization are excited about the advent of Bill Walton to an already solid team which won 43 games this past season.

"There is no question that Bill is one of the outstanding players in basketball."

Clippers coach Gene Shue noted, "This is terrific news for our club and for our fans. Bill is a great individual player, but at the same time is an extremely unselfish player who believes in the team concept."

Walton, obviously pleased to be returning home to continue his NBA career, stated, "I'm really looking forward to playing in San Diego. I have a great deal of respect for Irv Levin and Gene Shue, and the entire organization and I am very happy that we were able to work things out so that I could play in San Diego as a winner.

At Helix high school in La Mesa, Walton led his team to 43 consecutive victories. Then at UCLA, he paced the Bruins to a pair of NCAA championships. And he owns an NBA championship ring for his efforts with the Portland Trail Blazers during the 1976-77 season.

(continued on next page)

NBA REGULAR SEASON STATISTICS

SEA.	TEAM	G	MIN.	FGA	FGM	PCT.	FTA	FTM	PCT.	OFF.	REBOUNDS DEF.	TOT	AST.	PF	DQ	STL	BLK	PTS	AVG.
74-75	Portland	35	1153	345	177	.513	137	94	.686	92	349	441	145	113	3	23	34	443	12.8
75-76	Portland	51	1687	732	345	.471	228	133	.583	132	549	681	220	174	6	48	111	1035	20.3
76-77	Portland	65	2264	930	491	.528	327	228	.697	211	723	934	245	174	5	60	211	1210	18.6
77-78	Portland	58	1929	882	460	.552	246	177	.720	118	648	766	291	145	5	60	146	1097	18.9
	Totals	209	7033	2889	1473	.510	938	632	.674	553	2269	2822	901	616	19	224	533	3785	17.5

NBA PLAYOFF STATISTICS

SEA.	TEAM	G	MIN.	FGA	FGM	PCT.	FTA	FTM	PCT.	OFF.	REBOUNDS DEF.	TOT	AST.	PF	DQ	STL	BLK	PTS	AVG.
76-77	Portland	19	755	302	153	.507	57	39	.684	56	210	266	65	61	3	21	65	345	18.2
77-78	Portland	2	49	18	11	.611	7	5	.714	5	39	44	5	10	0	1	4	27	13.5
	Totals	21	804	320	164	.513	64	44	.688	61	249	310	70	71	3	22	69	372	17.7

NBA ALL-STAR GAME STATISTICS

SEA.	TEAM	G	MIN.	FGA	FGM	PCT.	FTA	FTM	PCT.	OFF.	REBOUNDS DEF.	TOT	AST.	PF	DQ	STL	BLK	PTS
1977	Portland	Selected-Injured: Did Not Play																
1978	Portland		31	14	6	.429	3	3	1.000	2	8	10	2	3	0	3	2	15

Bill Walton back home in San Diego.

It seemed odd to see Chris Paul in a foreign uniform.

The Lob City era was so special.

Jerry West visited Clippers training camp in 2001 and we all wondered.

Blake Griffin's Rookie of the Year season was worth waiting for.

The Lob City trio had a playful side. Here we are on a flight back from China.

The Doc Rivers-led elimination of Golden State in the playoffs in 2014.

Doc saved the franchise that year and made my final season special.

The years with Doc are truly treasured.

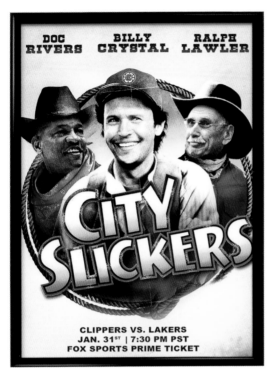

Comedic genius Billy Crystal was front and center for my year 40.

Command appearance at one of Donald Sterling's many parties.

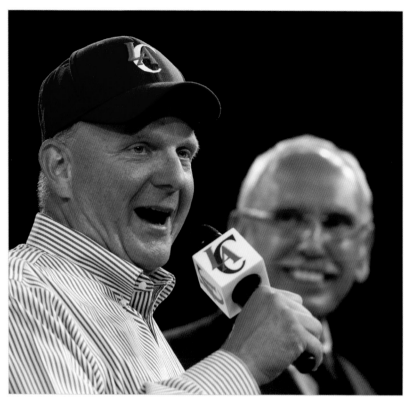

Steve Ballmer's ownership gave the franchise newfound direction.

Clippers trip to Russia in 2006. (I am third from the right.)

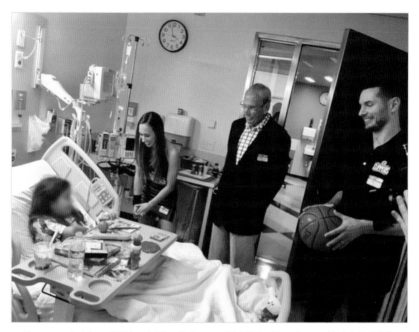

The annual visit to Children's Hospital was a highlight. Here I am with J.J. Reddick.

The joy of spending time with the broadcast crew on the road.

So honored that Q. Richardson and D. Miles traveled 2,500 miles to pay respects.

There is nothing that I miss more than L.A. Clippers fans.

The years flew by. This is game 2,000.

Game 3,000 with my son Ralph.

The April 10, 2019 finale with my sweet Jo.

It was not easy to say "Goodbye."

The honors started with the California Sports Hall of Fame.

They culminated
with the Naismith
Memorial Basketball
Hall of Fame
in Springfield,
Massachusetts, 2019.

In between the thrill of a star on the Hollywood Walk of Fame.

Former and current players were there.

Five years with Bill Walton as a Clippers player
and thirteen with him as a broadcast partner.

His wit, whimsey, and wisdom were on full display each night.

I never felt so short or so fortunate.

It was so appreciated that he came back for my final regular season broadcast.

A night to honor UCLA greats Annie Meyers-Drysdale and Big Bill.

Eighteen days, seventeen nights on the Colorado River through the Grand Canyon.

Bill and Lori Walton visit after my surgery for prostate cancer in 2007.

Elgin and Elaine Baylor at our wedding in Dana Point in 2001.

With Elgin Baylor in Japan, 1994.

Happy times with former Clippers coach Gene Shue.

Loved having Hall of Famer Harvey Pollak as a friend.

Walton hosted a family lunch on the day of my Hall of Fame induction in 2019.

A Christmas Day off was a special time for the family.

We had our annual Lawler/Bell reunion in Oregon each year.

Much of my career was shared with family and friends.

Three generations of the Lawler fishing clan.

Three generations of Ralph Lawler, 1998.

Marie and Ralph Lawler in the 1960s.

The joy of May 26, 2001.

Oh Happy Day!

This is the night in 2000 on an NBA cruise when we decided to get married.

Honeymoon in Tahiti, 2001.

Our great adventure in the Grand Canyon, 2004.

Life's joys all shared with Jo.

A respite at the Stagecoach Festival, 2011.

may also have had the best handle of anyone to ever play the game. He controlled the basketball as if it were a yo-yo tied to his hand. I do not think I've ever seen a player who enjoyed playing the game as much as Jamal (maybe Pete Maravich). So many players look forward to the end of the season so they can get away from the daily grind. Not this guy. Crawford played virtually every day during the off-season. He also played all eighty-two games in his final season in a Clipper uniform.

J. J. Redick was a major addition to that first Lob City team. Rivers' first act as head coach was to arrange a three-team trade that brought Redick to the Clippers from Milwaukee. Team owner Sterling first approved and then disapproved the transaction. The Rivers era almost ended before it began. I remember how excited Doc was about acquiring the perpetual motion shooting ace. He made it clear that he would quit on the spot if Sterling did not approve the carefully thought-out swap. They made peace, and the trade was consummated.

Redick was the perfect fit; he established himself as the greatest three-point shooter in franchise history during his four years in Los Angeles. That fifty-seven-win, 2013–2014 Clipper team also had an outstanding back-up point guard in Darren Collison, a feisty wing in Matt Barnes, the veteran savvy of Jared Dudley, the length of Ryan Hollins, the vital contribution of the multitalented Hedo Turkoglu, and the spot appearances of Glen Davis, Danny Granger, Willie Green, and Antawn Jamison. That totals fourteen quality NBA players on that roster. Why didn't they win it all?

The Sterling post-season debacle wore them out. They somehow recovered to win their opening-round series from Golden State, but the emotionally drained team ran out of fuel and focus in a pivotal late-game-five meltdown to the Thunder in Oklahoma City. They almost certainly would have won that series if they just could have held on to a seven-point lead in the final minute of Game 5 and gone on to play San Antonio in the Conference Finals. This is the same Spurs team the Clippers defeated in seven games in the opening round of the 2015 playoffs—the same Spurs that easily ousted OKC and Miami en route to their fourth NBA title. My point is, this was the best chance the L.A. Clippers have ever had to win the league championship. They had all the pieces. Quality ownership was the one missing link. Players would come and go in the ensuing years. Austin Rivers, Paul Pierce, Luc Mbah a Moute, and Mo Speights all contributed in the last three Lob City years. Each was a playoff season, but each was sabotaged by one thing or another, most often an injury to Paul or Griffin.

The exciting era ended when Paul was traded to Houston in 2017. The team sold out every home game through Paul's six seasons in Los Angeles. But now, Lob City was over. It was such a fun time. When I reflect on my forty years with the Clippers, those six Lob City seasons are the first that come to mind. I almost missed it all.

I had privately made the decision to retire at the end of the 2012–2013 season. Only Jo was in on the secret. I had just had enough. It was a great run, and I was happy with where I was in life at the age of seventy-five. It really was time to move on. We had moved from La Quinta in January of 2013 into an apartment in Marina Del Rey. We signed only a six-month lease.

Then, all of a sudden, Doc River's name started appearing in the mix when the Clippers were searching for a coach to replace Vinny Del Negro. Now, that was interesting. I got a call from Fox Sports West, and they asked me to act as a host for the TV news conference to announce Doc's arrival once everything was official. At that point, again, nobody knew I was retiring. Jo and I had been busy boxing up our belongings for our anticipated move to Bend, Oregon. I went to the training center as requested. Once there, I asked for a few minutes with Doc before we appeared on television in the formal news conference. I was excited that he was going to coach the Clippers. I loved him both as a player and a coach, and we had always had a solid, friendly relationship. He is total class act with incredible leadership skills. I've often told people that if he wasn't a basketball coach then he easily could have been the chairman or CEO of any number of major corporations. He just had the capacity to see the big picture, with leadership chops that are equaled by few.

Anyway, we hugged when we saw each other, and I started thinking to myself, how on earth can I walk away from this? So, I had a question for Doc. I confided to him what my plans were, but then I said to him: "If I were staying on, would it still be possible for my wife to travel with us the way she has been for years?" Doc got a surprised look on his face, took a step back, and said with a big smile, "Are you kidding? Of course! We're not going to change that!" And so, I went home and asked Jo to stop packing. We weren't quite done yet with Los Angeles or the Clippers.

Doc wasted no time in taking things over and getting things done. One of the very first things he did, which I absolutely loved, had to do with Staples Center. One of my biggest pet peeves was the fact that it always felt like we were playing in somebody else's building, thanks to all of the Laker banners that hung from the ceiling. I don't begrudge the fact that it's a legendary franchise with many superstars who deserve to be up there. I just never felt like we were made to feel welcome in that building. For years, I had campaigned to have those banners covered when the Clippers played home games there, so that at least it would look like our arena. But club president Andy Roeser always pushed back, saying, "There's no way that's going to happen. The Lakers will never allow that."

Well, like I said, Doc had an immediate and immense impact. Right after he was hired, he walked in and had those banners masked whenever we played a game there. They would be covered by bigger-than-life replicas of Clipper players that loomed over the nightly sell-out crowds for Clipper games at Staples. The building became a home court for the first time since it opened in 1999. There was no discussion; Doc just ordered it done, and it was done. How could you not love that?

Something else that had always bothered me over the years was what happened when you compared a Clipper media guide with a Laker media guide. The Clippers guide was so much thinner than their building mate's. That's because they had a much bigger staff (and more history), so their guide required many more pages. Well, Doc wasn't going to have that, either. He met with plenty of resistance from owner Sterling right from the get-go. He would battle through one barricade after another.

It was so much easier once Steve Balmer controlled the team and the purse strings. The coach and president of basketball operations began hiring staff that the team desperately needed. He wanted a competitive analytics department. He wanted all the support staff that it would take to put the team on par with other teams around the league. Steve Ballmer always listened to Doc, and once he was convinced that the request was reasonable and a step toward building a long-term winner, he would give his approval.

It was truly a new day for the Los Angeles Clippers. I am so glad that I stuck around to experience it.

Chapter 11

The Sterling Stigma

THE CLIPPERS' FIRST OWNER IN SAN DIEGO was movie producer Irv Levin. He was personable enough, and he certainly wanted to see his team succeed. He formed a company in 1980 to sell advertising for Clippers Radio and TV with team executive Irv Kaze, Clipper marketing head Hal Kolker, and me, the team's broadcaster. We each put in $10,000 and Levin funded the rest. Kaze handled the business side, Kolker the sales, and I was in charge of production.

Things did not start off well. Kolker obligated us with splashy high-rise office space near Hotel Circle, in the heart of the city. He hired a sales aid and an executive assistant, and then took a girlfriend on an around-the-world tour. Our company credit card was used during this prime advertising selling season. Kaze and I worked our tails off trying to keep things afloat. I had gone to St. Louis with Kolker to make a pitch to Anheuser-Bush, but that was the extent of my involvement in sales for the fledgling company. Sales contracts were arriving in Kolker's absence; Irv signed some and I signed some to keep the business going. We hired Stu Lantz to be my color commentator on our telecasts. It was interesting, as I was basically producing our telecasts. I was arranging facilities for each of our road games. I was hiring directors and all the personnel needed to get our games on the air.

Once the season got underway, advertising revenues lagged. The San Diego Clippers were not an easy sell. During the holidays, the team was fifteen games under .500. Levin pulled the plug in January.

No more television for the Clippers for the rest of the 1980–1981 season. Levin shut down the company and proceeded to sue Kaze, Kolker, and me. I was paralyzed with fear; the $10,000 entry fee into this business venture had been an intimidating obligation to begin with. I was comforted when Levin's top lieutenant, Lou Lennart, told me, "Don't worry, you are not at risk here—we know you were trying hard to keep us going. Kolker is the guy we are going after."

Problem was, my name was on numerous sales contracts because Kolker had been on his lengthy world jaunt with a former Clipper cheerleader. So, they sued us for the failure of the company. I was called in for a deposition in Levin's fancy Beverly Hills offices. Levin and Lennart were there, and we were all sworn in to tell the truth, the whole truth, and nothing but the truth. I thought this would be easily resolved. Lennart would certainly verify our meeting in San Diego.

"As I'm sure Lou recalls," I said under oath, "when I expressed my concern, he told me not to worry—they knew I was acting in good faith, and it wasn't me that they were after." Lennart looked me square in the eye and said he did not recall any part of that meeting or that conversation. He was lying. He knew that I knew he was lying, but he simply did not care.

I had one more hope outside of that deposition. The team's sales manager was named Paul Mendez. He was a friend, and he was in attendance during the meeting in question. Surely he would support my version. For whatever reason, he told me he could not testify on my behalf. I was stunned again.

In the end, Levin agreed to drop the suit if I would donate a few thousand dollars to a charity of his choice. I was making no more than $30,000 to $35,000 a year at the time. My $10,000 investment in this company was gone, and now I had to come up with a couple of more thousand to put this behind me. You can be sure that I was not terribly unhappy a few months later to learn that Levin had sold the team to a real estate investor from Los Angeles. His name was Donald T. Sterling.

Sterling was simply incapable of understanding his role as owner of a professional sports team. These teams are a part of the fabric of a city, and the fans feel such a vested interest in them. Believe me, none of this ever occurred to the man who liked to be known as DTS, his adopted initials.

No professional sports team was longer suffering or so poorly run as the San Diego/Los Angeles Clippers under the tight-fisted supervision of Donald T. Sterling. The team did not have a winning season in the first ten years of Sterling ownership. In his first twenty-four years as an NBA owner, the Clippers had one winning season while burning through fifteen head coaches. The team had thirteen draft picks in the top four over the Sterling years and still, they could not come up with a consistently winning combination.

Sterling was infamously frugal. The NBA not only has a salary cap that limits the amount of money a team can have on its player payroll, they also have a seldom-discussed minimum that a team was mandated to have on its books. DTS was much more interested in the minimum figure than he was the maximum. I was told that he would pressure general manager Elgin Baylor and business boss Andy Roeser to get as close to that minimum as possible.

Sterling questioned the most minor expenses, from the reams of paper being used in the mimeograph machines in the Clipper offices to the adhesive tape to wrap players ankles ("Couldn't they reuse it?" he'd ask) and our legitimate need for trainers. No expense was safe. Credit cards would be denied when the team checked into hotels on the road; bus companies would not show to pick the team up at the airport because they had not been paid for the team's last visit. It was always a relief in those days to look out the airplane window after landing and see that a bus was actually waiting on the tarmac.

Sterling loved young players because they were less expensive. He always said he would happily pay top dollar for superstar players, but oh, he said a lot of things. In 1983, he suggested that his team needed to lose to improve its chances of getting the top pick in the draft, where Virginia's seven-foot-four center Ralph Sampson awaited. The league levied a heavy fine and started seeking a means of forcing Sterling out of the NBA. Undeterred, the owner flouted league rules further in 1984, when he defied all conventions by moving his team from San Diego to Los Angeles. He had tried to move in 1982 but was rebuffed by the NBA. This time, he did not ask. The league announced a $250 million fine for the unauthorized move. Sterling responded with a $100 million countersuit. His fine was soon reduced to $6 million, and the Los Angeles Clippers commenced playing in the L.A. Sports Arena in the fall of 1984.

San Diego did not miss the departed Clippers, and Los Angeles hardly noticed their arrival.

I have to be honest: from day one in San Diego, when his advertising blared a picture of him along with the promise "I will make you proud of the Clippers," Donald Sterling created a toxic work environment that was both offensive and unhealthy to virtually anybody who came in contact with it.

Not long after I arrived at the Sports Arena in Los Angeles, I remember his wife coming to the office, counting reams of mimeograph paper, and telling the staff that they were "going through too much paper." That's the kind of penny pinching that was going on all the time. One day at a hotel in Oakland, our trainer, Mike Shimensky, had to put everything on his personal credit card just to get room keys for the players because the team credit card was overextended. There was a time in New Jersey when the bus to pick up the team at the airport was a no-show because the team was past due on previous charters. Those were common logistical nightmares, and they happened all the time. Again, the cheapness and insane frugality gave new meaning to the term "penny wise and pound foolish."

But nothing could match the crassness and tastelessness of Sterling's more erotic interests. There were constant whispers about scandals, things concerning strippers and hookers. I remember in 1987, we brought Jo's young daughter to Sterling's home for the annual holiday party. It was a gorgeous place located just off Wilshire Boulevard in Beverly Hills. Cary Grant had reportedly once lived there with fellow actor Randolph Scott.

Attending the party was our number-one draft pick that year, a Midwestern boy from Wisconsin named Joe Wolf. He was very decent young man, shy and bashful. At one point, Sterling brought Wolf into the foyer and there was a knock at the door. Innocent Joe was asked to open the door, revealing a busty, topless woman in red shorts and a Santa hat. All Joe could muster was, "Mr. Sterling, I went to church this morning. I'm not sure I should be seeing this." Sterling just laughed his head off. I somehow drew the short straw to earn the misfortune of sitting next to DTS at dinner that night. I listened to him grouse about the woman he had *wanted* to appear as Santa's helper. Apparently, she had much bigger boobs than the one who had showed up.

Another low point I experienced working for Sterling happened when I was making the transition from radio to television with the Clippers in the late 1980s. It was not an awkward move, because I had done 76ers TV in Philadelphia before returning to the West Coast in 1978. At least, it wasn't "awkward" most nights. One morning in late November of 1987, I was packing for a quick trip to Portland when I received a phone call from Clippers top executive Andy Roeser. After lamenting the previous night's home court loss to Washington, he wanted to talk about our telecast the next night in Portland. They were a very good team, featuring Clyde Drexler, Terry Porter, Kiki Vandeweghe, Kevin Duckworth, and Jerome Kersey.

The Clippers had not won a game in the Rose City since moving to Los Angeles in 1984. The prospects for the L.A. team would not be good the next night. Roeser had a command for me: Don't mention the names of any of the Portland players during the broadcast; only talk about the Clippers. The demand had clearly come from Donald Sterling; Roeser was the messenger, but the message had Sterling written all over it. I didn't feel like getting into a debate after that absurd suggestion, so I just indicated that I had to get packed and get to the airport.

I received a phone call a short time later from the team beat writer for the *Los Angeles Times*. She had covered the Clippers since their days in San Diego, and we had played tennis together and become close friends, or so I thought. She asked me how things were going, and I blurted out the unbelievable call I had just had with Andy Roeser. This was not an "on the record" conversation—it was just two friends talking. We hung up, and within five minutes I had another call from Roeser. To paraphrase, he asked me if I knew what the team did with traitors. Let's just say the answer wasn't pretty. It made me wonder why I had left real estate.

Well, we went to Portland, where I broadcast the game in a conventional way. Clyde Drexler scored 27 points in leading the Blazers to a 97–87 win. I think I mentioned him—*a lot*. Happily, I never heard another word about it.

I seldom had teams try to influence my broadcasts. Irv Kaze always wanted to be sure I read all the season ticket drop-ins that he supplied me with during my days working San Diego Charger broadcasts. Pat Williams was the very supportive 76er general manager while I was in Philadelphia. I had a rotating cast of bosses in the San Diego Clipper days, and no one ever interfered. My only critique in that time frame came from Joe "Jellybean" Bryant. He was the father of a little toddler named Kobe Bryant, and a colorful player in his own right. One night on a road game, the lanky six-nine forward was dribbling the ball up-court and was goose-walking his dribble as he crossed mid-court. I said something about Bryant showboating his unique style at mid-court. That was it.

Jelly's wife, Pam, was listening to the radio broadcast at home in San Diego. Sure enough, the next day, the player confronted me at the team hotel. "Why did you say I was showboating last night?" he demanded. "Weren't you?" I retorted. "Yeah," he replied. We exchanged knowing smiles and the case was closed.

Oh, and there was Joe Barry Carroll of the Golden State Warriors. We had a moment in the 1986–1987 season. Carroll was a talented player who performed in a seemingly effortless style. He averaged 20 points a game while hardly breaking a sweat. His style earned him the dubious tag: "Joe Barely Cares." I made that mention in a game leading up to a meeting with the Warriors in Oakland, adding that "sometimes it seems he barely does." The night of the Clipper-Warrior game, I was at my courtside broadcast location well before the game when Carroll approached me at the press table. Towering over me, he said he'd heard what I said about him on the air and he did not like it at all.

I was a bit taken aback. Once I collected myself, I explained that the comment was just referring to how his easy style on the court belied his effort. He said he wished I had just said that, and I agreed that I probably should have. We wound up having a very interesting conversation. It was apparent that he was a very bright young man with eclectic interests. We would always find time to at least say hello each time our paths crossed along the NBA trail. He has had a wildly successful and multifaceted career since his retirement from basketball in 1991, and I'm not at all surprised.

You just never know what to expect when you go to an NBA game.

It could be a blowout win or a lopsided loss. It could be closely fought from start to finish, or it could even go into overtime. It could even be the unthinkable that happens; I've had a few of those over the years.

Working for Donald Sterling was our dirty little secret. Looking back on it, I feel a little sullied by it. We all told ourselves back then that we needed to work, we needed to support our families. And that's true. But we also helped enable DTS's behavior by showing up every single day. I know hindsight is 20/20, but today I really feel that we could have done things differently. He was so inappropriate on so many levels, it amazes me that it took so long for his basketball empire to crumble.

It wasn't as if he had a capable basketball mind. Quite the opposite. He had this incomprehensible habit of not just listening to, but taking advice from anybody who offered it, except his general manager and coach. He would ask the cab driver or an usher at the arena, "What do you think of the coach?" And if that person being questioned said something like, "I think his substitution patterns are awful!" Sterling would take it as fact. He wouldn't think about it. He wouldn't analyze. He would simply act on emotions and adopt anybody's point of view. Here one day and there the next.

DTS often called me into to his Sterling Towers office for a conversation about the just-completed season. He had a massive office with minimal Louis XVI furniture on a parquet floor. His desk was right in the middle of the room. It was like sitting at center court at the L.A. Sports Arena. He would ask about the coach and about key players. I would defer and remind him that I was just the team broadcaster. He would point out that I was with the team home and away. "Tell me what you think," he'd say. It was remarkably uncomfortable. There were a couple of occasions when he turned to the telephone to dial Patti Simmons in Del Mar. He would put her on the speakerphone so we could exchange hellos. That was the only pleasant part of these near-annual visits.

It has always been my opinion that Sterling copied the Lakers logo when he moved to Los Angeles. There was nothing original about him. In the end, he really got away with so much for so long because that's just how it was back then. In a pre-social media society, it was much easier to hide your bad behavior, and then he had all of us around him pretending like everything was semi-normal. It gave him cover—at least, for the time being.

Chapter 12

April 27, 2014:
A Day That Will Live in NBA Infamy

SOME DATES ARE JUST FOREVER ETCHED in your memory. On Saturday, April 26, 2014, we were in Oakland, and we were on top of the world. The Clippers had split the first two games of their opening-round playoff series in Los Angeles with the Golden State Warriors, and had just taken Game 3 on the road. This had returned home court advantage to the Clippers. All was good in Clipper Nation. At least, that's what I thought when I went to sleep that Saturday night before Game 4.

The Sunday game was in the afternoon, so I woke up extra early to start getting ready. Before getting out of bed, I was scrolling on my phone to check the news of the day when I saw the report.

"Holy shit," I said out loud.

"What?" Jo asked.

"Holy shit, this is awful."

"What?" Jo repeated.

"My God, this can't be."

"Ralph, what on earth is happening?"

I explained that the scandal-chasing website TMZ had published voice recordings of Donald Sterling making terribly racist statements to his mistress. Sterling could be heard saying: "In your lousy fucking Instagram, you don't have to have yourself walking with Black people. It bothers me a lot that you want to promote, broadcast that you're associating with Black people. Do you have to?"

And it only got worse from there.

I didn't know what to do. I wandered down to the hotel lobby to grab a cup of coffee and ran into team president Andy Roeser. "How bad is this?" I asked him. "It's bad," he said, "but it will blow over. It's not that big a deal." He thought there would be a hefty fine, but that would probably be it. I'll admit, that made me feel a little bit better. Maybe TMZ was blowing something out of proportion. I was searching for some way for this to not be true. But obviously, as I know now, Andy was spinning the story and things got crazy very fast.

This went beyond just basketball. The country went into an uproar over the story, and we had a game to play that day. I wasn't sure what I was going to do, so I just addressed the situation as calmly as I could on the air. I expressed how serious it was, and that the team was going to do whatever they could to not get distracted from the game at hand. But, of course, they lost. They wound up winning the series in seven, but I think the loss in the next round to Oklahoma City was the result of the chaos that Sterling's behavior had created.

All of a sudden, the cat was out of the bag. There was no more hiding anything. Other people began stepping forward with anecdotes and observations that spoke to Sterling's racist, offensive behavior. Many of us in the inside knew that this was how he rolled, but now the rest of the world was experiencing it, too. It was an unprecedented moment in the NBA.

The *L.A. Times* reported:

Clippers coach Doc Rivers said he told his players that they will have to deal with fallout from the NBA's banning Clippers owner Donald Sterling for as long as they are in the playoffs.

"We're not through this," Rivers said.

The Clippers on Tuesday night won Game 5 against the Golden State Warriors at Staples Center, after learning in the morning that NBA commissioner Adam Silver had banned Sterling for life from the game for remarks in recordings that were released in the last few days.

Sterling also was fined $2.5 million by the NBA, and Silver wants other NBA franchise owners to force Sterling to sell the team.

The Clippers, who didn't practice Wednesday, lead the

best-of-seven series 3–2 and can close it out by winning Game 6 on Thursday night in Oakland.

"Like I told my guys [Tuesday], this is going to be with us," Rivers said during a conference call Wednesday, referring to the Sterling ban. "'But let's just keep winning. Let's deal with it.' But it's not going anywhere. And you've just got to embrace that. That's just part of this year's playoffs for us.

"We don't have a manuscript or a rule book on how to deal with each issue that's going to come up. There will be more issues that we don't know about."

Of course there was no playbook. But Doc handled things like only he could, with a firm, cool grip on the situation and a dedication not just to his team, but the rest of the staff and the community large. I was shaken, and the coach would put an arm around my shoulder while offering assurances that we were going to get through this.

That Game 4 Sunday was the darkest day in franchise history. Sterling had insisted that he and his hardy traveling companions fly on the team charter to Oakland for Games 3 and 4. Coach Rivers really wanted to limit the traveling party to the regular season crew, but Sterling reminded Rivers that he was the team owner. So DTS, his wife, and three or four others piled onto the plane and chose prized seats that were used all season by assistant coaches and key staff members. It was uncomfortable, but it was nothing compared to what was coming.

Sterling actually wanted to attend Game 4 in the middle of all the storming controversy. Rivers did win that battle, and even convinced Sterling to not fly home with the team. His wife, Shelly, and Roeser's wife sat in the owner's front-row seats at the game, and Andy watched the game on television with his boss. None of us realized that Sterling had attended his last NBA game.

My wife did not fly with me on the team charter; it was over-crowded and she had to surrender her seat. Oh, but she was there. Jo grabbed a short fight to SFO for the two key games. She took a taxi to the airport after the team's distracted fourth game performance. She entered the airport lobby, where she was greeted by the owner. She told me later that her heart was in her throat. Sterling approached and said something about her knowing him for a long time. "Do you think I'm a racist?" he asked her.

Jo had never thought more quickly. "You have always been really good to Ralph and me," she replied, "and we really appreciate it."

On the flight to LAX, Sterling wound up sitting in first class with

---

TIME OUT NBA Commissioners

There have been only five commissioners in the league's seventy-five years, and each made significant contributions to the sport. The earliest league leaders were known by the title "president." That was changed to "commissioner" in 1967. It is easy to overlook the contributions of the commissioner in basketball or any other sport. It is a role typically filled by an old White guy who never played the game at a high level. How relevant can he possibly be? Let's see.

MAURICE PODOLOFF (1946–1963) was the league's first president. He served for seventeen formative seasons. A Russian-born attorney who had earned his law degree at Yale, Podoloff had no background in basketball. The entry on his resume that earned him the new top spot in the Basketball Association of America was his time as president of the American Hockey League.

Podoloff exercised uncanny skill in accomplishing tasks for which there was no template. He instituted the college player draft in 1947. He also merged with the rival National Basketball League in 1949, for what is now called the National Basketball Association. He signed the league's first national television contract in 1953, added the twenty-four-second shot clock in 1954, and oversaw the move west (to Los Angeles in 1960, and San Francisco in 1962).

That is an impressive and exhausting list of major accomplishments that define the league to this day. The NBA's Most Valuable Player trophy is aptly named after Maurice Podoloff.

J. WALTER KENNEDY (1963–1975) replaced Podoloff in 1963, and took on many serious challenges of the day. The early television contracts negotiated by his predecessor had expired and not been renewed. The league was down to nine teams, and by 1967, it faced the challenges of the rival American Basketball Association. Kennedy recovered nicely by negotiating a three-year, $27 million network television contract in 1973. It was the league's first major TV deal.

Kennedy helped the league double in size during his tenure;

a number of the players' wives. It gave new meaning to the term "awkward." The entire weekend was a terrible experience, but like many manmade catastrophes, it actually did lead to something positive: Sterling would soon be gone, and a new owner and new hope were on the horizon.

---

when he retired in 1975, there were eighteen teams in play. It was twelve years of work well done.

LARRY O'BRIEN (1975–1984) replaced Kennedy after a career in politics. He had been chair of the Democratic National Committee. O'Brien was born in Springfield, Massachusetts, the birthplace of basketball, so maybe his role was preordained. His plate would be full for an active nine years at the helm.

The league was going through growing pains in the 1970s. Still, six new cities were added to the league during O'Brien's tenure. The rival ABA was a troublesome pest. Oscar Robertson was challenging the league's cherished reserve clause in the courts. This all might have led him to miss his former life in the political forum. Undeterred, the commissioner marshaled the merger with the American Basketball Association in 1976 after the courts ruled against the league in the Robertson case. He battled on, adding cable television to a big television rights increase in 1982. A year later, he introduced a revolutionary salary cap that gave owners some peace of mind and a sense of what it would take to repair their red-soaked balance sheets. It was quite a decade for the commissioner whose name now adorns the league's championship trophy.

DAVID STERN (1984–2014) was widely regarded as the best commissioner in all of sports during his three decades on the job. He surely led the league into what would be regarded as its "golden era." Though an attorney by trade, Stern had the mind of a master marketer. He was the first commissioner to sense the value of promoting star players in ways none of his predecessors had ever imagined. He loved super stars and super teams. Once, when asked who he would want in his Dream NBA Finals, he responded: "The Lakers versus the Lakers."

Stern marketed both the star players and super teams brilliantly, and he had plenty of each during his thirty years in office. He was also a spirited negotiator and right smack in the middle of myriad tense and protracted labor negotiations with the NBA Players

Association. It was not always pretty, but he got the job done while protecting the interests of the owners and the integrity of the game. The feisty commissioner also led the globalization of the game and helped make the NBA a truly international sport.

The owners loved him because he kept putting money in their pockets. The riches began when he doubled the national TV rights package in 1986. Then he quadrupled it in 1990. All of that was simply the warm-up act for his parting gift to the owners: an unimaginable $24 billion television bonanza, signed in 2014. NBA owners mention Stern in their prayers each night.

ADAM SILVER (2014–present) had been Stern's right-hand man, and the mentoring he received served him well. However, he could hardly have been more different from Stern in substance as well as style.

While Silver embodies quiet self-efficacy, Stern wore his confidence on his sleeve. Silver is tall and angular, while Stern was short and feisty. But, like Stern, Silver knows how to get things done. He is more likely than Stern to think outside the box. Silver envisions the league as a futurist. He is willing to take chances, as evidenced by his approach to game rules, the long-sacrosanct eighty-two-game season, sports gambling, advertising on player uniforms, the draft lottery, the play-in format, and the controversial concept of an in-season tournament.

It did not take long for Silver's metal to be tested. When Los Angeles Clippers owner Donald Sterling was captured on a leaked audiotape making blatantly racist comments, the resulting furor put the commissioner in the hot seat hardly before he had time to *find* his seat. Silver's quick and decisive response in banning Sterling from the league for life defined his first year in office.

Silver would be tested again in 2020 by the worldwide coronavirus outbreak. The fast-moving epidemic struck home in the NBA when Utah Jazz center Rudy Gobert became the first player diagnosed with the disease. Silver was ready. Within twenty-four hours, he had suspended the NBA season with almost one-fourth of the schedule yet to be played. Like the lifetime ban of a team owner, the move was unprecedented, yet thoughtfully warranted.

The National Hockey League and Major League baseball followed with restrictions of their own. The NCAA cancelled its beloved March Madness. Professional golf moved all of its major tournaments out of harm's way. The Kentucky Derby and Indy 500 were casualties of the disease. But it was all a case of follow-the-leader, and the leaders were Adam Silver and the NBA. The league was ahead of state governments across the country as well as the federal government. This NBA commissioner embodies all that it takes to be an effective leader. ●

Chapter 13

My Journey to Overcome Racist Attitudes

I GREW UP IN PEORIA, ILLINOIS, in the '40s and '50s. It was a geographically segregated community. African Americans lived in one or two places in the city, and the remainder of the town was White. The exclusive country clubs in the city were all-White. They also did not accept Jews. That was the environment in which I was raised.

Our exposure to Black people was limited. I never had a Black classmate in grade school. We knew "Rochester" from the popular Jack Benny radio program. We knew Hattie McDaniel as the maid in the motion picture classic *Gone with the Wind*. We knew heavyweight boxing champion Joe Louis. But that was about it. It was a distorted view, but it was our only view.

Growing up, my singular experience with a Black person was with my parents' twice-weekly housekeeper, Dilly Lampkin. She was a delight and a close friend of my live-in maternal grandmother, who so looked forward to Dilly's day-long visits. Mom and Dad would pass along my clothing as I outgrew them to Dilly's son, who was younger than me. I have no idea what pittance they paid her, but she would take the bus and walk a couple of blocks to our house two times a week. I feel that she was treated well, but I don't think she ever entered through the front door of our home. It was always the side door. She would enter and go downstairs to change into her maid's outfit.

In high school, from 1952 to 1956, I had Black classmates for the first time—fifteen in my graduating class of 300—and I had Black teammates on the basketball court for the first time. My college class-mates were, again, largely White, with perhaps a similar ratio as I had experienced in high school. After I broke into broadcasting in my fourth year at Bradley U, I don't think I worked with one person of color at radio stations in Peoria, Riverside, or San Diego—a span of time encompassing the first fifteen years of my career. That seems in-comprehensible now, but those are the historical facts.

Finally, the move to Philadelphia in 1974 broadened the col-or chart. Thank God! WCAU radio had Black reporters in our large newsroom, and when I moved into television, I shared the set with African American news anchors. When I broadcast Temple University football games on the radio, I had three-time Super Bowl champion and Hall of Fame NFL star Herb Adderley as my color commentator, and we roomed together when the team was on the road. My dad met Herb, who was a very classy man, and he liked him immediately. However, he was a bit taken back when he learned that we shared a hotel room on the road. Dad could not help it. Born in 1903, he came from a different era.

I broke into television when a cable sports channel called PRISM debuted in Philly, and former star Hal Greer was my partner on home 76er telecasts. At my family's home in suburban Gulph Mills, our next-door neighbors were Black, and they had a son the same age as my son. The two went back and forth from one home to the next each day. It was great for young Ralph and for old Ralph, as well.

Slowly but surely, the old barriers were overcome. Old prejudices melted away. My full-time entry into the NBA in 1978 led to me de-veloping close and long associations with World B. Free, Randy Smith, Elgin Baylor, Derek Smith, Rory White, Norm Nixon, Marques Johnson, Danny Manning, Charles Smith, Don Chaney, Ron Harper, Quentin Richardson, Darius Miles, Dennis Johnson, Corey Maggette, Elton Brand, Cuttino Mobley, Kareem Abdul-Jabbar, James Donald-son, Sam Cassell, Mike Woodson, Eric Gordon, Chris Paul, Jamal Crawford, Doc Rivers, and many others who helped me see people as people rather than as Blacks or Whites. It was the great emancipation of my life's biases.

TIME OUT L.A. Riots

It was spring of 1992. The Clippers were in the NBA playoffs for the first time since their long-ago Buffalo Days in 1976. Fourteen fruitless years in California were behind them. Larry Brown was coaching the team, and Clipper fans finally had a reason to cheer.

Their first-round foe was the Utah Jazz; they had won fifty-five games to capture the Midwest division title. Jerry Sloan was the coach of a team led by Karl Malone, John Stockton, Jeff Malone, Thurl Bailey, and Mark Eaton. They were a legitimate championship contender against the underdog Clippers, who had won forty-five games and gone 23–12 since Brown had taken over for Mike Schuler in mid-season. I was thrilled to get a taste of the NBA playoffs for the first time since my experience with the 76ers in Philadelphia fifteen years earlier.

The Jazz won Games 1 and 2 in Salt Lake City, and each win was by double figures. The series moved to Los Angeles for Games 3 and 4 at the L.A. Sports Arena. The Clippers responded with a 10-point win to stay alive in Game 3 on April 28. Game 4 was scheduled two nights later.

However, the city erupted in riots the next day—a reaction to a not-guilty verdict for policemen accused of using excessive force in the arrest and beating of Rodney King. The city was ablaze by nightfall. Much of the rioting took place in South Central Los Angeles in the shadow of the L.A. Sports Arena, which was to become the chief staging area for law enforcement, including the National Guard. There was no way the Clipper-Jazz game could be held there on April 30.

I sat at home in my wooden matchbox of an apartment building in Marina Del Rey, watching the horror on television. The rioters moved to Beverly Hills and other posh spots in the city. I would jump when I heard any sound outside my channel-side apartment. It was frightening.

Game 3 was postponed, and the city was locked down in a tight curfew. We had no idea when the Clipper-Jazz series could resume. The Utah team was stranded at their Marina Del Rey hotel, and Coach Brown could not even gather his Clipper team to practice. This was a good team, featuring Danny Manning, Ron Harper, Charles Smith, Doc Rivers, Ken Norman, Gary Grant, Loy Vaught, and Olden Polynice.

Life was on hold as the rioting continued. The Lakers moved their playoff series against Portland to Las Vegas. The Clippers had waited so long to make the playoffs that they really wanted to play in Los Angeles.

The league and local governments finally allowed a return on Sunday, May 3, but not at the Sports Arena. The game would be moved to the Anaheim Convention Center on that Sunday afternoon. Clipper VP Carl Lahr arranged for the team's home basketball court to be shipped to and reassembled in the Orange County facility. The Clipper players were surprised, happy, and energized when they walked into the foreign building and saw that they would be playing this big Game 4 truly on their home court. Everyone in Southern California could breathe a sigh of relief with the worst of the rioting behind them.

A win would force a deciding Game 5 in Salt Lake City the next night. The players' bags were packed for the trip right after the game, and mine were, too. The Clipper-Jazz Game 4 in Anaheim was the first public event allowed since the rioting had begun four days earlier. The importance of this game far exceeded any meaning in the world of professional basketball. It was a welcome return to a semblance of normalcy.

I worked the telecast of the game with former Clipper star Marques Johnson. It was a joyous event, a celebration. The Clippers capped it off with a solid 115–107 win to force a Game 5 showdown. Unfortunately, the four-day delay interrupted the series every other night cadence. The league had run out of days for round one, and Game 5 was set for the next night in Utah. This was particularly difficult for star forward Charles Smith, who was playing on a very sore knee that benefited greatly when he didn't have to play on back-to-back days. This was no time to fret. The Clippers had evened the series at 2–2 and had a shot to advance with an upset win the next night in Salt Lake City.

We all rushed to the airport from Orange County to LAX. The Clips simply ran out of gas in Game 5 as they scored a series-low 89 points in a 98–89 series-ending loss to the Jazz, who would go on to reach the Western Conference Finals for the first time.

The Clippers gained far more than they lost in their first California playoff appearance. It was a win in the City of Angels. The team provided a much-needed distraction after days and nights of watching the ugly rioting that had people glued to their television sets for the better part of a sadly memorable week. The first happy memory for people, whether they were basketball fans or not, was that Sunday afternoon Clipper win in Anaheim. It is one of my most gratifying experiences in forty years with the team. ●

I was having dinner in Orange County in 1995 with Clipper general manager Elgin Baylor and his wife, Elaine. The topic of the O. J. Simpson trial was raised. Pretty much all of my White friends and family members thought that O. J. had gotten away with murder, and were dismayed by the not-guilty verdict in his televised trial. Here is where my eyes were focused more clearly. Elgin and Elaine knew O. J. and his wife, Nicole, well, and had socialized with them often. Both had reasonable doubts that he had murdered his wife and Ron Goldman on that fateful night of June 12, 1994.

I grew up trusting the police. That is the way I was raised. Elgin and Elaine had a very different experience. Elgin said he had been pulled over by police at least a hundred times, just because he was a Black man driving a nice car in a largely White neighborhood. Elaine chimed in that, likewise, she had been pulled over at least half that many times. They did not trust the police and felt it was very possible that they had planted the glove and other incriminating evidence at O. J.'s house. The White experience and the Black experience of law enforcement was as different as night and day—yes, as different as black and white.

This conversation with trusted friends has changed the way I look at the world around me. I do not have it perfected yet. But I continue to work on it. I am thrilled that our country has elected an African American president, and now an African American vice president who also happens to be a woman. Another barrier broken. There are still lessons to be learned. We must keep working on it.

Chapter 14

From the Sports Arena to
Staples Center to Inglewood

IN 1967, THE LOS ANGELES LAKERS fled the L.A. Sports Arena for the Fabulous Forum in Inglewood. Their former home was less than ten years old, but would be without an NBA tenant until the Clippers moved north from San Diego in 1984. The Forum was still the far superior venue; the Sports Arena had not aged well.

Ten years into their almost-unnoticed launch in the City of Angels, the Clippers experimented with a limited number of games each season at the flashy Arrowhead Pond of Anaheim. It was home to the NHL Ducks and hungry to attract an NBA tenant. The games were generally well-received there. I went with owner Sterling and team president Andy Roeser on an up-close inspection of the property in 1997. The locker rooms needed to be upgraded to NBA standards, but that was about it in this squeaky clean, five-year-old building.

I lived in Orange County at the time, and I was excitedly anticipating the possible move. It seemed almost inevitable in the months ahead; the team and the arena were in serious negotiations, and the NBA was very supportive of the move. Everybody wanted to see it happen. Except, in the end, Donald Sterling. Some believe he simply did not relish the commute from Beverly Hills. I think it was more simply that it was not Los Angeles. In any case, the Clippers crossed Anaheim off their wish list, and the club seemed destined to stay in the musty Sports Arena for the foreseeable future.

With that in mind, I made a detailed twenty-page proposal to the team to renovate the old building. It was a great place for fans to watch the game. I touted old-style wooden bleachers at one end of the court, with cheap seats for raucous fans. There would be a historic-style scoreboard and live music, and even the season tickets would have a 1950s look. If you've been to the Pacer's Fieldhouse in Indianapolis, you have an idea of where I was heading. It would feature spacious and sparkling new locker rooms for the Clippers, and a more antiquated space for the visitors. Everything would be done to make this a palace for the Clippers, but a dreaded dungeon for the opponents. Frankly, I thought it was rather brilliant. But team president Roeser saw nothing but dollar signs. I'm almost certain that the owner never saw or heard anything about it.

Meanwhile, early in 1998, the L.A. Kings of the National Hockey League were building a new arena in downtown Los Angeles. It would house the Kings and the Lakers in a gigantic, luxurious new facility. Before too long, it was announced that the Clippers would join the Lakers as Staples Center tenants. That would mean three winter sports teams in need of a total of 123 regular season dates for home games, plus pre- and post-season. It simply seemed unimaginable. Somehow, they figured it out, but it was often at the expense of the Clippers, who received third choice for the prime calendar dates.

Roeser called and asked me to join him on a visit to view the new building's construction. We went to the Civic Center to peer into a giant hole in the ground. Amazingly, the building opened in the fall of 1999, just eighteen months after breaking ground. The Clippers wound up playing the first NBA game at Staples Center. Sterling got a better financial deal with Staples than he'd been offered in Anaheim, and he kept his team in Los Angeles. Score another one for DTS.

The move to Staples Center did not pay immediate dividends for the Clippers, but it did add a layer of legitimacy to the franchise that had been languishing largely without notice in the City of Angels for fifteen years. The first season was a certifiable disaster under Chris Ford. They won only eleven of their first forty-five games before Ford was dismissed and replaced with assistant coach Jim Todd. The 15–67 final tally marked one of the worst seasons in franchise history.

Things started to look up when Alvin Gentry was named the team's new head coach. The free-spirited Gentry was the perfect coach

TIME OUT If You Build It, They Will Come

I love history, and the history of sports is as interesting as any.

Historic buildings have played host for mankind's greatest sporting events. The Olympic Games date back to the all-marble Panathenaic Stadium in Athens in 1896. Baseball's Fenway Park in Boston opened in 1912. The National Basketball Association prides itself on its shiny new state-of-the-art arenas that populate the land. Madison Square Garden in New York City is the only arena in the league that pre-dates the 1990s. It traces its birth to 1968.

In many ways, I miss the historic old buildings. MSG remains a magical place to play the game of basketball. I have broadcast NIT college tournament games there, along with decades of Clipper-Knick encounters. You feel the magic the minute you walk into the building. You know you are in the mecca of the sport. All eyes are on games in the Garden. Many New Yorkers tend to think that if it didn't happen in the Garden, it didn't really happen.

I have witnessed exhilarating wins and devastating defeats at MSG. The most thrilling win at the Garden took place on January 2, 1993. We had taken in New Year's Eve at Times Square two nights before. The Clippers' 98–97 overtime win over the Knicks provided a great way to open the New Year. Larry Brown was the Clipper coach against Pat Riley of the Knicks—one Hall of Fame coach against another.

The Clippers were trailing by 1, with time running out in the extra frame, when big John Williams hit Gary Grant with a pass along the right baseline. Gary rose and knocked down the game-winner as time expired. There is not a better place to win than at Madison Square Garden. That one was as good as it gets.

The other side of the coin is not as much fun. There was a game in the '80s that saw the Clippers down by 18 to the Knicks in the first quarter. An NBA representative stopped by the press table to tell me, "Thank God you guys only come here once a year." I was reminded of that a few years ago as the L.A. team swept the Knicks five straight years, winning one year at the Garden by 31 and the next year by 28. I so wanted to see that NBA representative again, so I could say, "Thank God we only have to see you guys here once a year." But it wouldn't have been true. The buzz of playing at the Garden was special every time I was there.

Interestingly, the buildings that stand out in my mind are those without corporate sponsorship names: Madison Square Garden, for the happy-go-lucky Clippers; he was in his early forties and had a good understanding of his young team's psyche. The Clippers began adding exciting young talent through the draft and deft trades. In came Darius Miles, who was nineteen years old. He was joined by a trio of twenty-year-olds: Corey Maggette, Quentin Richardson, and Keyon Dooling. They complemented a twenty-year-old holdover named Lamar Odom. These young players had all known each other since their AAU days, when they were in their early teens. The Clipper future had never looked brighter. Miles landed on the cover of *Sports Illustrated* with Kevin Garnett. He was the first Clipper player on the prestigious magazine's cover since Bill Walton in 1979.

The team was too young to win consistently, but they did more than double the previous season's win total. Miles made

---

Boston Garden, Chicago Stadium. These iconic old buildings added to the very character of the teams that called them home. Boston Garden was a one-of-a-kind masterpiece of home-court advantage; nobody knew how to make use of that better than Celtics architect Red Auerbach. The visiting dressing rooms were spartan at best, and it was amazing how often the visiting showers lacked hot water on the nights of big games. The picturesque parquet floor looked great on TV, but was unforgiving for visiting players. The court had dead spots where master defenders like Dennis Johnson would guide visiting ball handlers to help earn a key steal or deflection. Above all, the rows of championship banners and retired numbers hanging in the rafters reminded all challengers that this was the Celtics they were playing. The old Boston Garden is long gone, but never to be forgotten for any of us fortunate enough to have worked games there.

I have similar feelings for Chicago Stadium. The stadium served as home for the six-time champion Bulls from 1967 to 1995, and actually dated back to the 1920s as the longtime home of hockey's Blackhawks. It was a fixture in the illustrious Windy City sports scene. It also may have been the noisiest sports venue in NBA history. Its moniker, "Madhouse on Madison," was well-earned. The dramatic video and musical introduction before each game had the Bulls up by 10 points before the opening tip. I will admit, it was not quite as the all-rookie first team. Odom led the club in scoring and rebounding. The stage was set for a run at the NBA playoffs the next season. In 2001, general manager Elgin Baylor took a big step forward in a draft day trade for another young warrior, twenty-two-year-old Elton Brand. He was the perfect fit.

These guys were so much fun to be around. Despite the forty-year age gap between us, I had a great relationship with Darius and Q, who had also grown up in Illinois and were inseparable. They respectfully called me "The Man." The two pals now live near each other in Florida where they host a popular podcast called *Knuckleheads*.

The head-bumping pair was the focal point of that 2001–2002 Clipper team, and the nation was taking notice. ESPN developed a weekly reality television program called *Sidelines: L.A. Hoops*, and their camera crew and a producer had full access to the colorful young team.

effective a few years later across the street at the new United Center when, instead of Jordan, Pippen, and Rodman, the public address announcer introduced Toni Kukoc, Dickie Simpkins, and Mark Bryant.

Still, my memories of the old Chicago Stadium are rich. I remember doing a game there on radio one year. I asked their longtime public relations ace, Tim Hallam, if I could grab Michael Jordan for a pre-game radio interview. Hallam, doing his job, informed me that Michael did not do pre-game interviews. Undeterred, I walked into the Bulls' locker room and found Michael having his ankles taped. I asked if he could give me a couple of minutes for Clippers radio. He was totally accommodating, and I will never forget it. That is just another Chicago Stadium memory.

There's a reason why the new arenas are always tagged with the names of corporate sponsors. Chicago Stadium cost a reported $7 million to build in 1967. Madison Square Garden was built for less than $5 million, and the fabled old Boston Garden was built for only $4 million. The Golden State Warriors play in the NBA's newest arena, which cost a reported $1.4 billion to build. The Warriors play in the Chase Center after negotiating a twenty-year, $300 million naming rights deal; the glitzy hoop palace could not have been built without the corporate funds. So, it's little wonder that corporate sponsorship is needed. ●

They were with us at games and practices, and on team flights and bus rides. It was the first time that many fans became aware of the existence of L.A.'s "other" team, and they could not wait for the weekly program to air.

The cameras rolled almost nonstop. Miles's Number 21 jersey became one of the league's top sellers, which had been virtually unimaginable in years past. Darius and Q became the young darlings of the league, as fans became fascinated by their celebratory double-fisted head bumps after a made 3 or a thundering slam dunk. Kids were copying the act in high school gyms all around the country. Some fans were touting the Clippers as "America's team."

Brand had a brilliant All-Star season, and if Odom had not battled injuries and a five-game drug suspension (he missed fifty-three games), this team would have made the playoffs. As it was, they were three games over .500 in late March, and right in the middle of the playoff race. Sadly, they would drop ten of their final thirteen games to finish ninth, with the top 8 making up the playoff field. No matter—the joy was there. The Clippers sold out twenty-five games that year, a total that matched their prior five seasons combined. At last, the team was on the local map.

The final home game was one of the happiest nights in team history. The Clippers beat Memphis to finish 25–16 on their home court. At game's end, Lamar Odom jumped up on the press table in celebration. Miles went back to the locker room time and again to grab sneakers, wrist bands, and t-shirts to toss to the fans in the stands. Nobody wanted to leave the building, and I didn't want to leave the air; nobody wanted to let go of this exuberant young team. Little did we know that we would never see them together again. Four months later, the Clippers traded Miles to Cleveland for NBA assist leader Andre Miller. The magic vanished, and aside from the 2005–2006 near-MVP season by Elton Brand, the team had few bright spots until the drafting of Blake Griffin in 2009. That was the beginning of the team's rise to relevance in Los Angeles. We would soon learn the value of quality ownership.

In 2014, Steve Ballmer purchased the Clippers, and soon learned the perils of playing not second, but third fiddle when it came to scheduling at the Staples Center. Originally, he'd had no intention of building his own arena; Staples Center appeared to be one of the jewels of the NBA. I'm so thrilled that the team broke ground in 2021 for the Intuit Center in Inglewood. It will be right there next to the magnificent SoFi Stadium, and it's going to be the spectacular hub of sports and entertainment in the city, a true basketball arena.

Team president Gillian Zucker, who often joined us on the road in my final couple of years with the team, was also scouting arenas. She wanted to find out why the buildings in Salt Lake City and Oklahoma City were so loud. She wanted to see the new ideas displayed by recent buildings in Sacramento, Detroit, Milwaukee, and Brooklyn. They left no stone unturned. The new Clipper building will blow everybody away. Sound gets swallowed in the high ceiling at Staples Center, but that will not happen in the new Clipper home when it opens in 2024. It will be a beautiful place, but hellish for rivals. It will also be a magnet for free agent players.

The new arena is a true game-changer for the Clippers. It will be much like the Barclay's Center that has given the Brooklyn Nets new life in the Big Apple. The Clippers will have their own home court, and it will be the envy of teams throughout the land. And you know . . . it likely never would have happened if Sterling had moved the team to Anaheim. Ballmer probably would not have bought the team, and he certainly would not have paid $2 billion for it. I would say that things are turning out pretty well for the Clippers.

THIRD QUARTER

BANK SHOTS

Chapter 15

Era by Era:
The Greatest Players of All Time

TWENTY-FIVE YEARS AGO, THE NBA chose its fifty best players from its first fifty years. Now, it has named its seventy-five best players from its first seventy-five years.

The larger the package, the easier it is to choose. At least, until you get down to the final few and are forced to leave a handful of very good players just short of making your list. It is far more difficult to name the five best players in NBA history. I've seen them all—from George Mikan to Giannis Antetokounmpo—and I simply am not able to confidently name a top five.

Comparing the stars from 1950 to the stars of 2020 is absolute folly, truly comparing apples to oranges. Take Mikan, for example, the game's first dominant big man. He consistently led the league in scoring and carried the Minneapolis Lakers to five championships. He did all this before the advent of the twenty-four-second shot clock in 1954. He never led the league in scoring again, and the Lakers did not win another championship until 1972, long after their move to Los Angeles.

It is reasonable to wonder if Mikan would even make a roster in the current-day NBA. That is not to diminish his early superiority. Mikan would camp out close to the rim, and the free throw lane was only six-feet wide. The league increased it to twelve feet to move players like Mikan further from the goal. Wilt Chamberlain's presence a decade later saw the NBA stretch the lane to its present sixteen feet. Mikan would be playing on a very different basketball court today, and at an unforgiving pace for such a slow-footed plodder. In my mind, we need to compare players within their own eras. And that is what I have done here.

BEFORE THE SHOT CLOCK: 1946–1954

F. Ed Macauley – Boston/St. Louis (7-time All-Star; would be effective "Stretch 4" in today's NBA)

F. Dolph Schayes – Syracuse (12-time All-Star; later won an NBA championship)

C. George Mikan – Minneapolis (5 NBA titles before the shot clock that ended his dominance)

G. Max Zaslofsky – New York (4-time All-Star; 1947–1948 scoring champion)

G. Bob Davies – Rochester (the game's first great point guard; 1951 NBA champion)

Note: Other little-known early-league stars: Joe Fulks, Carl Braun, and Arnie Risen.

NEW-LOOK GAME: 1954–1960

F. Paul Arizin – Philadelphia (lost 1952–1954 years to the military in Korea; 2-time scoring champ)

F. Bob Pettit – Milwaukee/St. Louis (11-time All-Star; 2-time MVP; title 1958)

C. Neil Johnston – Philadelphia (six-foot-eight center; led league in scoring 3 times in the decade and won title)

G. Bill Sharman – Boston (one of the best shooters in league history—imagine if he'd had 3-point line)

G. Bob Cousy – Boston (early playmaking genius; led NBA in assists 8 years in a row)

Note: Shot clock ended Minneapolis title run; 4 different cities hosted NBA championships between 1955 and 1958.

THE NBA COMES WEST: 1960–1970

F. Elgin Baylor – Los Angeles (10-time All-NBA first team; averaged 38 points and 18 rebounds per game in 1961–62)

F. Jerry Lucas – Cincinnati (ROY 1964; All-Star 6 straight years in the '60s)

C. Wilt Chamberlain – Philadelphia (simply the greatest offensive force in hoop history)

G. Jerry West – Los Angeles (All-Star every year in the '60s; averaged over 30 points per game 4 different seasons)

G. Oscar Robertson – Cincinnati (ROY; led league in assists 6 times; All-Star every year)

Note: The Celtics won an amazing nine titles in this decade. Bill Russell and other Celts warrant attention in this top five.

NEW WAVE: 1970–1980

F. John Havlicek – Boston (8-time NBA champion; Celtics all-time leading scorer)

F. Elvin Hayes – San Diego/Houston/Washington (a scoring and rebounding machine)

C. Kareem Abdul-Jabbar – Milwaukee/Los Angeles (NBA's all-time scoring leader)

G. Walt Frazier – New York (led Knicks to their only 2 championships)

G. Nate Archibald – Cincinnati/KC (led NBA in scoring and assists 1972–1973)

Note: Others of special note in this decade: Bob McAdoo, Rick Barry, Pete Maravich, and Bob Lanier.

GROWTH YEARS: 1980–1990

F. Julius Erving – Philadelphia (a class act from the ABA; Dr. J helped save the NBA)

F. Larry Bird – Boston (competitive, super talented winner and All-Pro trash-talker)

C. Moses Malone – Houston/Philadelphia (he let his game do the talking)

G. Michael Jordan – Chicago (exploded onto the scene in 1984; averaged 37 points per game in year 3)

G. Magic Johnson – Los Angeles (a refreshing talent who put a happy face on the NBA)

Note: The '80s saved the day for the NBA, and were historically deep in talent: Isiah Thomas, George Gervin, Alex English, Kevin McHale, James Worthy, and Dominique Wilkins.

THAT WAS A LOT OF BULL: 1990–2000

F. Karl Malone – Utah (in the mix for greatest power forward of all time)

F. Charles Barkley – Philadelphia/Phoenix (colorful, provocative, talented)

C. Hakeem Olajuwon – Houston (one of the greatest all-around centers ever; 2 NBA titles)

G. Michael Jordan – Chicago (everybody wanted to be like Mike; 6 titles within the decade)

G. John Stockton – Utah (this late bloomer became the league's all-time assist leader)

Note: David Robinson, Gary Payton, Scottie Pippen, and Patrick Ewing just missed the cut on the second-best all-decade team.

THE NEW MILLENNIUM: 2000–2010

F. LeBron James – Cleveland (lifted the Cavaliers from laughing stock to NBA Finals)

F. Tim Duncan – San Antonio (took the Spurs to 3 NBA titles in the decade)

C. Shaq O'Neal – Los Angeles/Miami (won 4 championships with 2 teams in the '90s)

G. Kobe Bryant – Lakers (won 3 rings with Shaq and 2 without him)

G. Steve Nash – Dallas/Phoenix (2-time MVP; made everyone around him better)

Note: This five would beat the all-comers from any other decade.

THE PAST DECADE: 2010–2020

F. LeBron James – Miami/Cleveland/Los Angeles (Finals 9 years)

F. Giannis Antetokounmpo – Milwaukee (2-time MVP; 2021 title)

F. Kevin Durant – OKC/GSW/BRK (brilliant, nomadic superstar scoring machine)

G. James Harden – OKC/Houston/Brooklyn (one of the most lethal offensive weapons we've seen)

G. Stephen Curry – GSW (accurately regarded as the greatest shooter ever)

Note: Chris Paul and Kawhi Leonard just missed this top 5 list.

THE FUTURE OF THE NBA: 2020–2030

F. Jason Tatum – Boston (gets better each season; a superstar in the making)

F. Zion Williamson – New Orleans (only injuries can keep him from all-time greatness)

G. Ja Morant – Memphis (2020 Rookie of the Year; All-Star starter in his third season)

G. Luka Doncic – Dallas (could become one of the game's all-time best)

G. Trae Young – Atlanta (broke out in 2021 playoffs; superstardom awaits)

G. LaMello Ball – Charlotte (the youngest of this group, with unlimited potential)

Note: These stars, all under the age of twenty-five, will shine through the decade.

THE GREATEST OF ALL TIME

A difficult task, but here is my all-time top 5:

F. LeBron James (does more positive things on the court than any to ever play the game)

F. Tim Duncan (the most fundamentally sound player the sport has seen)

C. Kareem Abdul-Jabbar (his sky-hook was the game's most unstoppable weapon)

G. Michael Jordan (dominating 6-time champion who truly changed the game)

G. Magic Johnson (combined the size of a power forward with a point guard's skills)

Note: These five combined for 26 NBA Championships.

OVERTIME Most Memorable NBA Players and Coaches

RICK BARRY

Thinking about former NBA and ABA champion Rick Barry does not bring a smile to my face; he was one of the sport's most perplexing and underrated players. Trust me, Rick could play. He was an eight-time NBA All-Star and four-time ABA All-Star. But that hardly hints at how good he was. He was a smooth-as-silk, six-seven forward who could do it all. He's best remembered for his deadly accurate two-handed, underhand shooting style from the free throw line.

Off the court is another matter. It's difficult to find someone who will say they liked Rick Barry. He worked a few Clipper games with me on television, and he was a splendid basketball commentator. I frankly had no problem with him, but his stints as a network announcer were short-lived because he just could not get along with people. This extended even to his sons—three of whom played in the NBA—who had complicated relationships with their father.

There was something about Rick that I cannot quite put my finger on. He was always friendly, but in a rather guarded way. I would see him from time to time at Nugget games in Denver, near the home he shared with his second wife, Lynn. He really touted his son, Brent, when he joined the Clippers in 1995, convinced that he was a future NBA All-Star. That never happened, but Brent did win championships with the Spurs in San Antonio to match Rick's NBA ring, won with Golden State in 1975.

I last saw Rick in Springfield, Massachusetts, in the fall of 2019 at the Naismith Memorial Basketball Hall of Fame. He quietly congratulated me for my honor, but even then, there was a guarded nature in everything he said. There are some people you never hear a bad word about. And then there's Rick Barry.

HUBIE BROWN

Hubie Brown had an impressive coaching career. His accomplishments included winning an ABA championship with the Kentucky Colonels, and later earning two NBA Coach of the Year awards during his stops in Atlanta, New York, and Memphis. He would win over 500 games as an NBA coach, but was never able to advance his team beyond the second round of the playoffs. In fact, his teams lost more games than they won during his thirteen years as an NBA head coach.

The one constant during Brown's sixty-plus years in the sport was the high esteem his peers held him in. I've had dozens of coaches over the years rave about the Hubie Brown basketball clinics. Maybe more than anything else, we're talking about a man who has been a master-teacher of the game of basketball.

Coach Brown used those same skills to become one of the game's all-time great radio and television analysts. If you don't learn something about the game of basketball by listening to Hubie Brown, you simply are not paying attention. He was admitted into the Basketball Hall of Fame as a contributor in 2005, and much of that contribution was made as a broadcaster.

I was fortunate enough to work with Hubie on L.A. Clipper telecasts in the early 1990s. We would later work together on a dramatic TV series called *The Sentinel*. The UPN series was filmed in Vancouver, and the coach and I spent the week filming by day and talking basketball over dinner by night. I think I learned more about the hoop sport in that week than any other similar time period in my entire life. Happily, Brown is still teaching us about the game well into his eighties on ABC and ESPN. His second career has outlasted and outshone his first.

STEPHEN CURRY

Stephen Curry of the Golden State Warriors is widely regarded as the greatest shooter the game has ever seen. That puts him on top of an impressive list of contenders for the honor: Reggie Miller, Larry Bird, Ray Allen, Steve Nash, and Kevin Durant, among others.

When Steph entered the league in 2009, he wasn't deemed to be a future NBA superstar. Two point guards were chosen immediately ahead of him in the draft (Ricky Rubio and Johnny Flynn). Curry looks very little like an NBA player. He is generously listed at six-foot-three and 185 pounds. But his lethal shooting from just about anywhere on the basketball court sets him apart from all others. He has made over 40 percent of his 3-point shots in each of his full seasons in the league until last year. The guy made 402 3-pointers and connected at an impressive 45 percent clip during a record-shattering 2015–2016 season.

In 2020–2021, at the age of thirty-three, Curry produced maybe the best season of his spectacular NBA career. Somehow, he shoots with the same form and ease from thirty-five feet as he does from the fifteen-foot free throw line, where he is a 90-percent career marksman. He is also a low handicap golfer, and one heck of a classy young man.

My final regular season swing through Oakland as the Clipper announcer was in April of 2019. Each final visit before retirement was a little nostalgic, but I received an unexpected treat when Stephen broke out of the Warriors' pre-game warm-up line to come over to the press table, shake my hand, and congratulate me on my long career. I would have been surprised if he could pick me out of a line-up of Oracle Arena ushers. It was very special of him, and much appreciated to this day.

More importantly, Curry's success has changed the game, right down to middle school teams filled with Curry wannabes. It used to be that young players just longed for the time when they could first touch the bottom of the net, and then later maybe even dunk the basketball. The hoop sport was regarded as a big man's game. You would see a tall kid and ask, "Play basketball?" Curry has changed that. Kids now want to shoot threes. You can watch a game of twelve-year-old players today, and they will be hoisting up 3-pointers. Back when I was in high school, it was all about learning to shoot a jump shot. The virtually unknown shot had been popularized by Hank Luisetti, and came to replace the standing set shot that was commonly used by shooters at all levels in the early years of the sport.

Mikan, the game's first defining player, was six foot ten. Curry is the latest to fill that role, and he is over half a foot shorter. You no longer need to be six ten to play the game. Quickness, smarts, and the ability to make the long ball can carve out a spot for smaller players at any level. And the credit for that goes to Stephen Curry.

CHUCK DALY

I was in Philadelphia at the best possible time for a person in my profession. My introduction to Big 5 college basketball was a special treat. Philadelphia has five schools that boast a major college basketball program: Penn, LaSalle, Temple, St. Joseph's, and Villanova. The five competed annually for the unofficial, but critical, local basketball crown. The games were staged at the famed Palestra on the University of Pennsylvania campus. The basketball shrine was built in 1927, and is regarded as one of college basketball's greatest venues.

I don't think I ever had more fun broadcasting a basketball game than I did at the Palestra. A Penn-LaSalle game would give you chills that lasted a lifetime. The coaching roll call for the Big 5 schools was remarkable. Rollie Massimino was the head coach at Villanova. Mike Fratello was one of his young assistants. Paul Westhead coached at LaSalle, Don Casey at Temple, Jimmy Lynam at St. Joe's, and Chuck Daly was the head man at Penn. Amazingly, each one of those teams had future NBA head coaches on their bench. They accounted for three NBA championships. None were more successful in the pro game than Daly, and I'm not surprised; he impressed the heck out of me at Penn. He had a special bearing. He demanded respect and he got it.

Daly joined the pro game in the 1980s and dominated much of the decade during his years with the Detroit Pistons. His team went to the NBA Finals three times and won two championships. These were the Bad Boy Pistons, and they took on the personality of their taskmaster of a head coach. It wasn't a game for this group, it was a war.

I would stop by Daly's office in the Palace of Auburn Hills before a Clippers-Piston game. It was an education just hearing him talk about the game. I do not think I ever met a coach who better understood his role as a head coach. He saw the big picture. He excelled at dealing with the media, the front office, the league, and the players on his team. He just got it.

"HOT ROD" HUNDLEY

Few present-day basketball fans got to see Rod Hundley play basketball. That is their loss. His NBA career lasted only six seasons, as the sturdiness of his knees did not equal his unmatched flair for the game.

Rodney was the first overall pick in the 1957 draft after an outstanding three years at West Virginia University, where he preceded Jerry West as a Mountaineer hoop legend. He would be a two-time All-Star with the Minneapolis/Los Angeles Lakers, though he would average only 8 points a game over his career.

Those of us who were fortunate enough to see "Hot Rod" play will forever remember his razzle-dazzle style. He was among the rare early practitioners of the behind-the-back pass, as well as the behind-the-back-and-through-the-legs dribble. He would spin the ball on his finger mid-game. The fans adored him. He played with an unbridled sense of absolute joy.

After the premature end to his playing career, Rod became a broadcaster. He first worked as color announcer with Al McCoy in Phoenix, and then with Chick Hearn in Los Angeles. He carried the same colorful, no-holds-barred style to broadcasting that he had displayed on the court. By 1974, he had become the first play-by-play broadcast voice of the expansion New Orleans Jazz. Rod was also the first former player to become an NBA team's broadcast voice. He followed the Jazz in their move to Salt Lake City in 1979, and it was there that he would become one of the best known and most popular personalities in the entire state of Utah for the next thirty years.

Hundley unashamedly copied as much of Chick Hearn's style as possible when he graduated to the role of play-by-play man for the Jazz. It served him well. It was fun watching him play, fun listening to his broadcasts, fun being around him. In the early '90s, he had a restaurant and bar bearing his name in Salt Lake City. It was a hot spot for sports fans and was characterized by the waiters and waitresses, who wore striped referee-style shirts. I went there a few times to dine and sip with Rod, along with the late Jazz head coach Jerry Sloan and assistant coach Phil Johnson. Hundley was nothing but fun.

Rod was enshrined in the Basketball Hall of Fame as a broadcaster in 2003. He did simulcasts of the Jazz games for years until 2005, when he was given the choice to do one or the other—radio or TV. He told me he chose radio because his eyes were not too good anymore, and on radio the listener could not see his mistakes. That was pure Rod Hundley.

He announced his retirement in 2009. Rod was a hoot. I miss him. We lost him at the age of eighty in 2015.

LEBRON JAMES

LeBron James exploded onto the NBA scene in 2003. He came in just as Michael Jordan was bowing out for the final time. No player had or has ever entered the league under such bright spotlights.

James's high school career at St. Vincent-St. Mary High School in Akron, Ohio, was chronicled on national television seemingly game by game. LeBron was a young teen in a full-grown man's body, but he was mature both physically and emotionally well beyond his years. Despite being fresh out of high school, he was the first player chosen in the draft and fittingly, it was by his home state Cleveland Cavaliers. He would be Rookie of the Year, but it took three seasons for James to lead the Cavs into the playoffs. That began a string of thirteen straight years in the post season, highlighted by an extraordinary eight-straight trips to the NBA Finals that included three league championships. After a single miss, James was back in the finals for a fourth NBA title.

LeBron is a career 27-point-a-game scorer. He seems destined to pass Kareem Abdul-Jabbar to reign as the NBA's all-time leader in career points scored. It would be an amazing accomplishment for a player who never seemed focused on scoring in basketball. He won his only NBA scoring title during the 2007–2008 season, with an average of 30 points a game.

A couple of years later, the Clippers had a two-game pre-season set with LeBron's Miami Heat in China. I was standing behind LBJ in the buffet line at the teams' shared hotel. I mentioned something to the effect that, since he seemed to score so easily, it was a little surprising that he had won only that single scoring title. His response was defining: "I can't imagine not passing the ball to an open teammate." It provided clarifying insight into his greatness.

LeBron James brought new fans into the game, and truly became the face of the league in his stops in Cleveland, Miami, and Los Angeles. Long live the King!

MAGIC JOHNSON AND LARRY BIRD

The year 1979 will go down as one of the most important years in the history of the Association. Not only did Magic Johnson and Larry Bird debut in the league, but so did the 3-point shot that was reluctantly resuscitated from its days in the American Basketball Association.

Make no question, few NBA coaches or players knew what to do with the 3-point field goal. They had figured out that if you could make 33 percent of attempts counting 3 points, it was equal to making 50 percent of your 2-point shots. Trust me or do the math yourself. The problem was, nobody shot the ball very well from the prescribed distance of twenty-three feet and nine inches.

Chris Ford of the Boston Celtics made the NBA's first 3-pointer. San Diego Clipper guard Brian Taylor (who had played in the ABA) led the league with ninety "threes" made in the novel shots' first NBA season. It would be several years before the league, coaches, and players learned how to best utilize the long ball. Today's league sees individual players topping 300 and even 400 "threes" made in a season.

At the same time, the rivalry between Bird and Johnson brought never-before-seen attention to the pro game. The preamble saw them go head to head in college basketball's title game in 1979. Magic and Michigan State then prevailed against Bird and his Indiana State team. The serious-minded and media-shy Indiana country boy could not have been more different from the smiley-faced Johnson. Each had brilliant rookie seasons. Bird scored 21 points a game, winning Rookie of the Year honors. Johnson led the Lakers to a truly magical and title-clinching Game 6 win over the 76ers in Philadelphia for the NBA Championship.

Magic and Bird would meet three times in the finals; the Lakers won two of the three. Sports fans were riveted by the movie-like Magic vs. Larry drama. It is a safe bet to suggest that they and the three-ball saved the league and helped propel it to its current lofty status.

I broadcast Magic's first NBA game, which was against the Clippers in San Diego on October 12, 1979, at the San Diego Sports Arena. It was supposed to be a network TV match-up of former UCLA superstar centers Kareem Abdul-Jabbar of the Lakers and the newly signed Bill Walton of the Clippers. Some of the game's luster was diminished by Walton's absence (foot problems), but the game was a memorable classic nonetheless. Magic had an impressive debut, but the game was won by the Lakers due to a buzzer-beating sky hook by Kareem. I called it a fifteen-footer, Brent Musberger on CBS television envisioned a seventeen-footer, and the Lakers' Chick Hearn went with a twenty-one-footer. Whatever—it was dramatic, and first-timer Magic Johnson raced across the court to jump joyfully into the arms of a startled Abdul-Jabbar, as if he had just won another NCAA title after winning at Michigan State just six months earlier.

Kareem put the rookie down and exclaimed, "Settle down, rook—we still have another eighty-one games to play!" But neither that, nor anything else, could quell Magic Johnson's joy for the game and life itself.

MICHAEL JORDAN

Michael Jordan was a game-changer in so many ways. He set the bar high in the running for Greatest of All Time. Jordan punctuated his amazing career by leading the Chicago Bulls to six Windy City championships.

Beyond basketball, MJ changed the way millions of people look today when his receding hairline led him to start shaving his head. It was not long before players all over the league were having their domes shaved, and fans were quick to follow. Goodbye, Afro! Hello, baldy!

Jordan also changed the uniform look of the league early on, when he opted for longer, fuller shorts. Three reasons given here: One, when weary in a game, he tended to bend over slightly and rest his hands on his thighs while grabbing the bottom of his shorts. Two, he would habitually tug on the bottom of his shorts while playing defense. (Either way, it worked better to have the seam of his shorts closer to his knees.) Three, MJ liked to wear his old pow-der-blue University of North Carolina practice shorts underneath his NBA shorts as a good luck charm, so he ordered baggier shorts for his NBA uniform.

Almost immediately, players around the league followed suit. Everyone wanted to "Be like Mike." Well, almost everyone. Utah Jazz point guard John Stockton was the exception.

Stockton was not being defiant. He was simply comfortable with basketball's original mini shorts because he'd been wearing them that way ever since he began playing the game as a kid in Spokane, Washington. Today's NBA players would not be caught dead wear-ing the Stockton-style shorts in public. Jordan's stylistic tastes have lived on long after his retirement in 2003.

Even the original Jordan-style shorts would seem old-fashioned in today's NBA. A few facts for you here: The old Stockton-style shorts had a three-inch inseam. It would later become eleven inches or more, as some players got away with shorts that dropped three inches below their knees. League regulations state that the shorts should not fall below one-tenth of an inch above the kneecap. Some rules are simply made to be broken.

JASON KIDD
The Clippers limped toward the close of the 1994–1995 NBA sea-son with a final week encounter against the Mavericks in Dallas on April 14. It was to be loss number sixty-three in a largely forgettable season.

But this was not a forgettable night. Rory Markus was my radio broadcast partner at the time, and we kept our spirits up throughout the 13-point loss to the mediocre Mavs. A Dallas public relations aid checked with us late in the game to see who we wanted for a post-game interview. We quickly tabbed Rookie of the Year candidate Jason Kidd. At game's end, we were told, "Jason does not want to do visiting radio." At that time, the NBA post-season awards were determined by the vote of reporters covering the league, including team broadcasters and beat reporters. I had a vote, and Rory had a vote. I looked this Dallas PR guy squarely in the eye and asked him to tell Kidd that the two visiting radio announcers each had votes in the Rookie of the Year race. In what seemed like a nano-second, a smiling Kidd joined us at the press table. We had a solid interview that no doubt impacted our ballot inclinations.

If Kidd had snubbed us, I promise he would not have received a vote from either of us. It proved to be vital in the Rookie of the Year race; Kidd and Detroit Piston star Grant Hill each had forty-three first-place votes in a flat-footed tie for NBA Rookie of the Year in 1995. They were co-winners for the year. It all hinged on that post-game interview following a seemingly meaningless Game 5, days before the season's end. Our votes were pivotal.

I had the chance some years later to share the story with Grant Hill. He found it ironic and amusing. Grant was always one of the most cooperative and engaging players in the game. I felt a little bit bad that my vote for Kidd had cost him an outright win for the Rookie honor that season.

I was never comfortable with the power that was given to us in this NBA voting booth. Players often have incentive clauses in their contracts, and many get bonuses for being All-NBA or All-Defense or whatever. Happily, the league changed the voting method starting with the 2016–2017 season, and team broadcasters were no longer eligible to vote. It was always awkward when one of your team's players was a legitimate candidate for one of the post-season awards. I would try not to be biased, but team loyalty was not easy to ignore. The change was a welcome one, even though my memory of the impact we had on the 1995 Rookie of the Year race lingers on to this day.

"PISTOL" PETE MARAVICH

"Pistol" Pete Maravich was a tremendous player. He led the NBA in scoring in 1977, and he was a five-time All- Star in his ten years in the league. One thing was for sure—he was the greatest showman the NBA game has ever seen. His trademark floppy socks and hair gave him a distinctive look that perfectly matched his colorful game, from his college days at LSU through his NBA career.

Pete was drafted with the third pick in the 1970 draft by the Atlanta Hawks. He spent four years with the Hawks, only one of which included a winning season. Then, the 1974 trade to the New Orleans Jazz opened up a whole new world for Pete Maravich. It was a homecoming, and he was to be the featured player on an expansion team with very low expectations. The former LSU star loved being home and gave the fans a show. He told me late in his career that he always "played for the fans." As Pete's star rose, the Jazz moved their games from the cozy confines of the Loyola Fieldhouse to the massive Superdome. The Jazz set franchise attendance records that stand to this day. Four separate times, they attracted crowds in excess of 30,000 fans.

Maravich was part Bob Cousy and part Harlem Globetrotter. He had a flair that kept your eyes glued to the court for fear you would miss something. His ball handling, passing, and unorthodox shots just took your breath away. All but his final season pre-dated the debut of the 3-point line in 1979. He would have been something even more special if his unexpected, distant missiles to the goal had been worth 3 points rather than 2. For the record, he made 67 percent of his 3-point attempts in the single season he played with the tantalizing 3-point line.

Elgin Baylor was the Jazz coach on a night in 1978 when I was marveling at Pistol's play in the Superdome. Baylor's memory of Pete, voiced over forty years ago, is worth reviewing: "Oscar [Robertson] was the best guard I've ever played against. Jerry West was the best I've ever played with. And Pete Maravich was the best I've ever seen."

Pistol did nothing to discourage Elgin's opinion that night. It seemed as if all of his passes were of the no-look variety, and he was ready to shoot the instant he got across the mid-court line. He is the rare player in league history to have his number retired in three cities (Atlanta, New Orleans, and Salt Lake City). Suffice to say, I think I enjoyed watching the Pistol play as much as I did any player I have ever seen.

GREGG POPOVICH

I can't imagine ever enjoying or respecting an NBA head coach more than I do Gregg Popovich of the San Antonio Spurs. His acerbic answers to reporters' questions mid-game on network telecasts belie the true nature of the man. All NBA coaches hate the intrusion.

Pop makes his case by the way he handles the often-inane questions. The Spurs coach meets a gaggle of reporters before every game, home and away, and gives incisive answers to meaningful questions but buries the unfortunate lad or lass who dares to ask a poorly-thought-out question. Many are just afraid to ask anything. That never stopped my one-time broadcast partner Mike Smith. Mike dove right in one night at the AT&T Center on the outskirts of San Antonio. I don't recall the question, but I sure do remember the Popovich response: "With that question, it's no wonder you didn't last long as a player in this league."

One night, our TV producer asked if Pop would consent to a

pre-game TV interview with me. He graciously accepted, and we had a solid five-or-six-minute interview. We were to go out for his meeting with the full force of the media right after this. I told him that we had a young radio guy named Brian Sieman who, at the time, was totally intimidated by him. I suggested that the coach single Brian out for a question during the media gathering. Pop burst into a big grin and said, "Just point him out to me." He was all in.

We went out to the hallway where the reporters were gathered. Brian would have stood there for days without daring to ask Popovich a question. I stationed myself behind Sieman and the questions began. A few questions in, I rose my hand and pointed over Brian's head. Pop got the message. "Okay, Brian, you haven't asked anything. What do you want to know?" Brian's face turned beet-red. He turned, looked at me, and I think he made some reference to my mother. Popovich laughed a laugh most of those reporters had never heard.

I received a nice handwritten note from the coach when it was announced that I had received a star on the Hollywood Walk of Fame. The next time I saw him, he burst into "Hooray for Hollywood." He even invited my wife and I to visit a vineyard south of Portland where he is an investor. He later sent a bottle of his special wine, Rock & Hammer, in honor of my induction to the Basketball Hall of Fame. Sadly, Gregg lost his wife a few years ago. I wrote a heartfelt note of regret and condolences. A few weeks later, I received an unexpected response quoting something I had said about trying to find a new purpose in life. We clearly had built a special bond.

I was thrilled when Popovich coached the U.S. men to Olympic Gold in 2021. The door to the Basketball Hall of Fame is open and waiting for the winningest coach in NBA history.

JERRY SLOAN

There have been few people in sports who could match Jerry Sloan's competitive nature. I'm not sure how he developed it, coming from the tiny town of Gobbler's Knob in downstate Illinois. He was the youngest of ten Sloan kids who were raised by their single mother. Those roots somehow grew deep in the fertile Midwestern soil.

Jerry was a small-town boy who attended a small college in Indiana and became a major star on the national stage, as a player in Chicago and one of the game's all-time coaching greats with the Jazz in Salt Lake City, Utah. He made his reputation as a player with his physical and tenacious defense. Nobody wanted to be guarded by Jerry Sloan.

In 1988, he took over as head coach of the Jazz. He had no coaching pedigree that gave anyone reason to expect the brilliance that followed. Sloan's everyman personality off the court belied his fiery persona as a head coach. I was lucky enough to spend time with him and his longtime assistant coach, Phil Johnson, for drinks and bites throughout the years. He was just another small-town guy from Illinois on these occasions.

In 2004, Jerry lost his longtime wife and high school sweetheart Bobbye to cancer. It was devastating news. When the Jazz came to Staples Center early the following season to play the Clippers, the Fox Sports TV producer asked for a pre-game interview between the Jazz coach and me. Then I was told to ask about the passing of his wife. I objected, but the "ask" was more of a demand. We were standing in the hall outside the Utah locker room, conducting the interview, when I was reminded in my earpiece to ask about his wife. I did so in the most sympathetic way I could. Jerry stood silent for a moment and then excused himself with a tear on his cheek. He left me standing there with mic in hand.

Sloan was the last of the NBA head coaches to eat his pre-game dinner in the media dining room. I ran into him there fifteen or twenty minutes later. He came over to me to apologize for walking out on our interview, but I was the one who owed him an apology. But that's just who Jerry Sloan was.

I last saw the man who coached teams to 1,221 NBA wins in late February of 2019. It was my final swing through Salt Lake City during my farewell season. Jerry had not coached for eight years at that point, but he was still around for most home games and available as a trusted advisor. It was always so good to see him. He was in failing health; Jerry suffered from Parkinson's disease and Lewy body dementia. We shared a man hug after the game, and I think we both knew it was likely the final time we would see each other. It was. Jerry Sloan left us in May of 2020. But he left me a better man for having known him. ●

Chapter 16

On the Road Again:
Changes in NBA Travel and Lifestyle

PEOPLE OFTEN SUGGEST TO ME that one of the greatest joys of my retirement must be not having to deal with the rigors of NBA travel. But the travel is one of the things I miss the most, and countless retired coaches and players have told me the same thing over the years. The camaraderie shared with your fellow travelers is unique and virtually impossible to match in any other endeavor.

I also had an advantage shared by few others in the league: my wife, Jo, was allowed to travel with me. She has been the biggest Clipper fan in the land since the earliest days in San Diego in 1978. There are no NBA wives who have seen as many pro games as my sweet Jo. All that said, there is a special rhythm to a road warrior's life, and we both reveled in it. As soon as the schedule was released, you knew exactly where you were going to be each day for the next seven months of your life. You were pretty much always either packing or unpacking.

Fans cannot possibly compare their personal travel to that of the modern-day NBA. There's no question that travel in the league today is the best it's ever been. First-class, custom-configured charter jets have been widespread in the league for thirty years. Teams leave home from private charter terminals well-removed from the hustle, bustle, traffic, and parking hassles involved at crowded commercial airport terminals. Upon landing, two buses meet the airplane on the tarmac. One bus is for players, coaches, and basketball staff. The other is for local television, radio, public relations, and guests. Both buses carry security personnel. Your bags are picked up at your car, and you don't need to think about them again until you arrive at your destination, where the luggage is brought to your room at the team's 4- to 5-star hotel (think Four Seasons or Ritz Carlton).

Each player and member of the traveling party receives something like $135 per diem. On top of that, the team provides three quality meals a day at the hotel, a catered buffet in the locker room after the game, and catered meals on the flight out of town. It's a far cry from typical airline food. Pizza and burgers used to be the menu of choice on flights, but the food on today's charters is approved by a team nutritionist. Forget the cheese and cracker appetizers; try the carrots and hummus.

Players and coaches carefully eye the NBA schedule the moment it becomes available. Today, they see a limited number of back-to-back games—that is, games on consecutive nights. There may be a few instances of three games in four nights. However, teams no longer face four games in five nights, and never, ever the old curse of three games in three nights. Coaches and players now fret over the limited number of games on consecutive nights, the dreaded "back-to-backs." They warily eye a week with five games in seven nights. Oh, how times have changed.

The Clippers' first year on the West Coast was in San Diego in 1978. They opened the season in October with three games in three nights in three different cities. The newly formed team opened 0–3. A few weeks later, they started the month of November with three in three nights again, and it was another 0–3. By the end of the season's second month, they had played four sets of three games in three nights. That accounted for twelve of their first twenty-five games. As cruel as that seems by today's scheduling standards, it was pretty much par for the course for teams of the era.

The other thing that needed to be factored in was travel before the advent of charter flights. Keep in mind those three games in three nights in three different cities. Teams did not race to the airport after a road game to catch a flight to their next stop because there were only very limited scheduled flights available, at 11:30 PM or midnight. So, it was back to the hotel to unwind, find a place for a late-night bite or a drink, and then brace yourself for a 5:30 or 6:00 AM wake-up call. The league mandated that teams take the first available flight out if they had a game that night. There was a heavy fine if a team was either late or a no-show if they had not been booked on the earliest possible flight.

The travel party was much smaller in those days: ten to twelve players, a head coach, an assistant, a trainer, and a broadcaster. It was fifteen people, tops. Teams limited the traveling party largely because of the cost of airfare. Now, the sky is literally the limit. Most NBA charters are Boeing 757s, custom-configured for fifty-ish people, and there is seldom an empty seat.

The most extravagant charter service for the Clippers was provided by a service called MGM Grand Air. The Larry Brown-era Clippers led to the affiliation with the ultra-first-class flying service. Three 727s were custom-configured to carry thirty-five passengers in plush surroundings, which included four private state rooms and a bar. They offered service to rock groups, movie stars, politicians, and, of course, NBA teams. The Clippers used this service for four or five memorable seasons. It is safe to say that the flight crew got to know their passengers very well. It was so memorable that one of the flight attendants memorialized the charter service in a racy book. Oh me, oh my.

A couple of memories stand out from those MGM Grand Air days. The Clippers went to the playoffs in each of Larry Brown's two seasons with the team. The coach had a relationship with comedy star Billy Crystal from their days in New York. Billy was, and is, a big-time Clipper fan. Larry invited him to join the team on a flight to Houston for the 1993 playoffs. The three of us were comfortably seated in one of the plane's four state rooms, talking about basketball, movies, and life. I was thrilled to be involved in this trio: Hall of Fame coach Larry Brown, movie star Billy Crystal, and a star-struck announcer from Peoria. Billy would soon be heading to the Cannes Film Festival and said they had room on the plane if we wanted to join him. I had never traveled internationally and did not even have a passport. The offer was out of my league, and of course the nomadic coach Brown was busy plotting his next career move. It remains a very memorable flight.

Another MGM Grand Air moment that I will never forget was the time I was in a state room with cerebral Clippers point guard Pooh Richardson and lumbering center Stanley Roberts. The big man was regaling us with the story of how he had lost $1 million in an

TIME OUT Do You Know the Way to Peoria?

October 12, 1991, remains etched in my mind because the Clippers met the Philadelphia 76ers in a pre-season game in downtown Peoria, Illinois. I would get to announce an NBA game in my hometown! I was very excited. The Clippers bused down from Chicago for the game at the Civic Center Arena that served as the home court for Bradley University. It was a Sixers home game because the city wanted to host a game featuring former Bradley star Hersey Hawkins, who was entering his third season in Philadelphia.

We boarded a bus in Chicago early in the afternoon for the game. I was seated on the team bus directly behind Clippers head coach Mike Schuler. It had been over twenty-five years since I'd left Peoria to live out my broadcast career dreams. I had made the trip from Chicago to Peoria many times, but there were new expressways and other new changes to the area, so for the first hour and a half of the bus ride, I didn't notice anything unusual. Then I noticed a sign pointing out that we were closing in on Rock Island, Illinois. I knew that was due west of Chicago, while Peoria was due South. I mentioned to the coach that I thought we were going the wrong way.

Mike leaned up to the driver and asked if this was the best way to Peoria. Rather indignantly, the driver said, "I knows the way to Peoria!"

So we continued westward on Interstate 80. I was now sure that we were a good two hours out of our way. Suddenly, so did the driver. He quickly veered left on what is now Interstate 74, and we sped south through Galesburg and then back east toward Peoria. It was now clear that we were going to be late getting to the game site. Trainer Keith Jones was busy on the phone, communicating with the 76ers and the game officials. They moved the start time back thirty minutes, which would just give the Clipper players time to get dressed before a brief on-court warm-up. It also cut into my reunion time with friends and former classmates, who had planned to welcome me home.

Finally, we made it to the one lone NBA game in my dear hometown. The drive back to Chicago was a breeze. The driver may not have known the way to Peoria, but he did know the way to Chicago. ●

investment gone bad. He thought it was hilarious. But then, Stanley owned twenty-two cars, and "Excessive" was his middle name. Pooh, who treasured every dollar he ever made, almost jumped out of the plane at 35,000 feet. He could not believe that Roberts didn't think this was a big deal. He scolded his younger teammate with the admonishment that he would never get that money back. It was gone forever! He warned Stanley that the day would come when he'd wish he had that million back.

That day came sooner than we thought. Roberts went through $35 million in career earnings through drug and alcohol abuse, an NBA suspension, one bad investment after another, and the inability to say no to friends and distant relatives who asked for money.

It is salient to note that Stanley Roberts was a better pro prospect than Shaquille O'Neal when the two were teammates at LSU during the 1989–1990 season. I heard that from more than one NBA scout. He was lovable, but he just never loved the game. I ran into big Stanley in the lobby of the Fess Parker Resort Hotel in Santa Barbara, California, during a Clipper training camp. The big guy was never in shape and was constantly injured. He had not taken part in any work on the court with his team at Santa Barbara City College. Lightheartedly, I asked, "Hey, Stan, are you out for the season, or what?" His response was telling: "I wish."

But I digress. Charter flying was not always quite as comfortably plush as it was on the MGM flights. The Clippers' first-ever charter flight was in the pre-season of 1987. Somehow, the team played an exhibition game against the Utah Jazz in Cedar City, Utah, one night and were slated to face Golden State the next night in Santa Barbara. That is a separation of over 500 miles. The good news was that the tight-fisted Clipper management arranged for a charter flight between the two small-town airports. The bad news? They booked us on an old World War II transport plane to get us to the SoCal city.

This was not a jet aircraft. I'm talking about a Douglas C-47. It was a twin-engine prop intended to transport troops during the war more than forty years earlier. Now, it was transporting fifteen basketball players, a trainer, a couple of coaches, and broadcaster Ralph off into the wild blue yonder. I was sitting in the back row with head coach Gene Shue as we took off. We were trying to digest the 38-point loss the team had just suffered to the Jazz. David Thirdkill, a veteran player trying to keep his five-year NBA career alive by earning a spot on the Clipper roster, was seated a few rows in front of and across the aisle from us. Moments into our flight, Thirdkill screamed in terror while looking out the window, "We're on *fire!*"

That tends to get your attention when you are in flight. Sure enough, the right wing of the plane was engulfed in flames. The pilot made a quick turn and was able to safely land back at the Cedar City regional airport. We all breathed a big sigh of relief. The pilot announced that it was really nothing to worry about, just some excess fuel burning off the wing. They took a little while to make sure it was as benign as he suggested, and then we took off a second time.

Minutes later, Thirdkill screeched, "We're on fire again!" It was not quite as unsettling as the first brush with flames at 5,000 feet. The pilot quickly cautioned that we had no reason to be concerned because the fire would soon burn itself out. "Hopefully before the wing falls off," I thought to myself.

That was the team's first experience with charter flights. It was a crazy one for sure, but even that flaming arrow darting across the night sky was better than the challenging task the teams faced in playing back-to-back-to-back games on the road and flying commercial each morning to reach their next destination. Those occasions would have teams at the airport by 6:30 am, having played a game the prior night and due to play again that very night. You prayed for good weather and no flight delays. Sometimes those prayers were answered, but sometimes not.

I painfully recall a big Clipper loss in 1988 to the Sonics in Seattle. Not just a loss—a 154–104 annihilation. It stood for thirty-two years as the most lopsided defeat in franchise history. The players licked their wounds and returned to their hotel downtown in the Emerald City. The wake-up call arrived, predictably, at 5:30 am. We were booked on the first commercial flight to Phoenix, where the schedule called for a game against the Suns that night.

The groggy group made it to SeaTac airport to find it shrouded in fog. The outbound flight would be delayed until the fog lifted. Breakfast ate up an hour or so, but still the fog lingered. The long and tall players fidgeted uncomfortably on the rock-hard airport lobby seats. Eight o'clock rolled around, then nine, ten, eleven, and noon. The fog persisted. It was mid-afternoon before we were airborne. The team had been marooned at the airport for the better part of nine hours.

Upon landing in Phoenix, we raced straight to the old Fairgrounds Arena for the date with the well-rested and well-tanned Suns. The Clipper players barely had the energy to get through their pre-game warm-ups, but somehow they did and then even wound up forcing the Suns into—can you believe it?—overtime! It was an exhausting but courageous effort in a 114–102 loss. Moral victories were often that team's only victories.

This was not an isolated event. Every team of the era could recount similar stories. The point is, that's the way it was in the NBA three or four decades back. Naps, cards, and video games in more recent years were the most popular means of passing the time. Originally, Hearts was the game of choice before being replaced by Booray. The players typically anted $10 to $100 a hand, and thousands of dollars were on the line each long flight. If you hear rumors of a couple of players on your favorite team not getting along, do not be surprised if a bad night of losing at cards had something to do with it. I've seen times where you could hardly get the Clipper players off the team plane after landing at home because they were so involved in their card game, with $100 bills littered all over the table. I was invited to sit in a few times over the years, but my Daddy wisely told me a long time ago to never gamble with somebody who has more money than you do.

The NBA players of the 1940s, '50s, and '60s deserve our admiration. They competed nightly without many of the advantages enjoyed by today's players. They were simply a different breed. Much of the difference, I think, can be attributed to guaranteed salaries. Television has provided unthinkable funds to the league. Half that money is passed on to the players, and almost all of it is guaranteed. No matter what. Once I encountered Chris Kaman in the locker room before a game. He was out of the Clipper line-up for a while with a bad back during the 2004–2005 season. "Hey," I said, "are you ever going to play again?" I'm chilled by his response to this day: "Great thing about the NBA— guaranteed contracts!"

I never had a guaranteed contract. My deals with Fox Sports West/ Prime Ticket outlined what they would pay me each game for a set number of years. However, the fine print showed that they would decide, game by game, whether or not they would use me; if they decided to, they'd pay me X amount of money. That's the way it was for years.

They would tell me they had never exercised that "easy out." I thought, "Good—should be no problem to delete it from the contract." That ran us into "company policy." It was still, miss a game and you miss a paycheck.

The NBA's player policy is much different. Some of today's NBA players are signing contracts for $30 million or $40 million a year, with the knowledge that they are unlikely to play a minute in year one of the deal (see: Kevin Durant, Kawhi Leonard). Think about that money for a minute. A player making $40 million a year collects $769,230.77 per week!

It was not always that way. My long-ago broadcast partner Kevin Loughery used to tell me about playing in the NBA in 1960s, and there was no such thing as guaranteed contracts then. It was much more like my contract with Fox. Kevin told me how players would hide an ankle sprain or knee sprain from the coach and just play through the pain. The very real fear was that if you sat out a game, your spot on the roster just might get replaced. Loughery would regale me with stories about rooming with Bobby "Slick" Leonard. Oh, the fun they had. Everybody smoked too much, drank too much, caroused too much, and then went out and played forty minutes a night, rarely missing a game. Their methods of travel were medieval by today's standards. They remain my biggest NBA heroes.

Chapter 17

The Show Must Go On

MY FATHER AND MOTHER GAVE ME SO MUCH. Among their greatest gifts was an abiding work ethic.

From my earliest days as a disc jockey in Peoria, I just did not miss work. I'm proud to say that I only missed a couple of games in my long career. One was due to horrible traffic driving in from the desert. A tractor-trailer rig had crashed and shut down the 10 Freeway between Palm Springs and Los Angeles. There was no alternative route. We progressed six miles in six hours. Obviously, we did not make it to the game. That incident was what inspired us to move to Marina del Rey, to avoid any future traffic jams of that level.

The other time was after my kidney stone operation. The Clippers were in Charlotte to play the Hornets on November 24, 2014. While preparing for that night's telecast at our hotel, I started suffering dramatic pain in my lower back. It got to the point that my sweet Jo joined me for a walk across the street to a drugstore in hopes of finding some relief. I went back to the hotel to complete my game prep and showed up for the team's short bus ride to the Spectrum Center, where the two teams had a 7:00 PM date. I was not comfortable as I went through rehearsal with our crew. The pain in my lower back worsened as the 7:00 PM airtime approached. Mark Rogondino, who was ably working our pre-game show from the game site, said he had some super pain pills with him if I needed them. I sure did need one. I gulped down a pill a few moments before air time. I was poised to go on the air, with microphone in hand, as the producer was counting down in my ear: "Five, four, three, two, one."

At "three," I suddenly cried out in pain. Fortunately, my yelp reached completion by the time the producer got to "one." I smiled, looked at the camera, and said, "From Charlotte, North Carolina, welcome to Los Angeles Clippers Basketball." I was the most comfortable I had been all day. The first half of the game transpired before the pain returned. I knew from past experiences that I was trying mightily to pass a kidney stone. Mark graciously gave me a second one of his Super Pills, and I was able to complete the telecast.

I suffered no further discomfort, but tests revealed a large stone that had no chance to pass naturally. I had to get it removed before suffering another debilitating attack. My urologist and I agreed on a very early morning ureteroscopy on Saturday, December 6. The plan was that the early surgery would give me sufficient time to recover so that I could broadcast that night's Clipper game against New Orleans at Staples Center.

We arrived at the UC Irvine Medical Center in the pre-dawn hours. I'd had the last couple of off-days to complete my prep for the Saturday night game. The surgery went well, except that I apparently had some trouble breathing at one point. The doctors placed a tube down my throat to aid my breathing. When I awoke from the anesthesia, I was very raspy-voiced, but my doctor said it would clear up naturally in time.

By the time Jo drove me to our Marina Del Rey apartment at midday, I could hardly speak. I remembered a Laker game years ago, when Chick Hearn wanted to keep his consecutive-games streak alive and showed up even though he had very little voice left while battling a bad cold or the flu. It was painful to listen to him. The Lakers sent him home at halftime, and his partner, Stu Lantz, handled the play-by-play in the second half.

Those thoughts were in my mind as we headed north on the 405. I had been mentoring Brian Sieman, who was doing a great job on Clippers radio. It was my hope that he would get the call to replace me once I retired. I sensed that it was best to sit this game out, and it could provide Brian with a great opportunity. I called Christian Howard of the Clippers and explained my situation. He was the team's vice president in charge of marketing and broadcasting. I said I wanted to be assured that Brian would get the call to work the telecast in my absence. He seemed very unsure about that. I told him if it was not Brian, it would be me. I insisted that he was the only alternative.

Brian did a great job. Now in hindsight, I think the evening helped boost Brian's stature several notches in the eyes of both the Clippers and Fox Sports West. I would never want to go through that surgery again, but it may have been worth it if it played any role in the eventual decision to have Brian Sieman replace me at the start of the 2019–2020 season.

Another incredibly painful night in an NBA arena took place at the Smoothie King Center in New Orleans, early in Doc River's tenure as Clipper head coach. Brian Sieman and I would meet with Doc an hour and forty-five minutes before each game, home and away. I would record my TV interview with Doc, and then Brian would record his radio interview with the coach. We would usually sit in to hear each other's interview because we might learn something.

On this night, we convened in a glass-walled office at about 5:15, just blocks away from Bourbon Street. It was always a great time to visit with the engaging Clipper coach. Suddenly, the stage manager for the telecast came rushing in to tell me I was needed immediately for our television rehearsal. I excused myself and hurried out of the room. The clear glass office door was closed and I hit it with a loud thud, dropping to the floor in a daze. The New Orleans team doctor was called. They put me through some concussion protocol tests, iced the swelling above my right eye, and bandaged my wounds. There would be no rehearsal that night. Once I was eventually able to make my way to the court, it was clear that I was in no shape to go on camera.

We decided to perform the game opening off-camera. I wore sunglasses to our first game at home; I just did not want to subject people to the swollen and blackened mess that was my face. Even though we worked strictly off-camera, viewers could spot me on the sidelines as the play passed my courtside location at the press table. The NBA contacted the Clippers: "What is Lawler doing wearing sunglasses?" I think they feared that I had "gone Hollywood." It was four or five games before the wonders of makeup allowed me to appear on-camera again. Happily, I did not miss a game, but each morning the mirror gave me a frightful reminder of what had happened.

One time, while I was courtside for a Clipper telecast at the TD Garden in Boston twenty or so years ago, an odd smell was permeating the press table area before the game. Security people were rushing around during our pre-game telecast, and me and my broadcast partner, Mike Smith, were startled for sure. We were warned that we might be forced to evacuate. The cause was discovered quickly, and the source was diluted. No harm, no foul. Nobody in the crowd was aware that the game had been in jeopardy.

Then there was the frightening night on March 19, 2001, at Staples Center in Los Angeles—the Clippers versus the Cleveland Cavaliers. We arrived at the arena early, as always, and there were only a few people in the lower bowl of the building about two hours before game time. I was at the press table while Jo was seated alone in the stands, reading a book. There were three or four players on the court, getting in some early warm-ups. Suddenly, I heard shouts from above the right end of the court. Some deranged guy was storming down the steps through the empty stands, brandishing a long knife. He wound up at center court, where he struck a menacing pose. The players jumped over chairs and the press table to escape, and I raced to Jo in the stands. We felt safe five or six rows removed from the court. However, arena security quickly came up to advise us to head to a backstage location near the Clipper locker room. The police had been called, and before long they were circling the hardwood with this knife-wielding man still poised at center court for God knows what reason.

We set up camp in the hallway outside the locker room, watching the drama play out on a closed-circuit TV monitor. Clipper star Blake Griffin was a few feet away, trying to stay sharp and dribbling a basketball. After a stand-off of a little over half an hour, the police stormed the court and tackled the perpetrator near the Cavalier bench. He was apprehended and taken to jail. The court was then cleared, and the game went on without a hitch. I'm not sure we ever learned the guy's true motivation. There were reports that he was after Clipper guard Baron Davis for reasons unknown. Like I said, you never know what to expect when you get to the arena.

You *do* expect to have your dress clothes ready for the game. However, one afternoon in Memphis in 2012, I realized that I had not packed a sports coat for that night's playoff game telecast. I scampered over to Lansky's famed clothing store at the nearby Peabody Hotel. Lansky had been the clothier for rock music icon Elvis Presley. Time was growing short as I asked for whatever they had in 42 Long. They had only one option: a garish, multicolored checked item that looked like it was straight out of Craig Sager's TNT closet. So I took it and wore it to the game. Referee Monty McCutcheon was also known for his colorful attire; you would look forward to seeing what he was wearing each time he came into the arena. Monty was working that night's Clippers-Grizzlies game, and he spotted me on the court before our TV opening. He came over and said, "Nice jacket."

Another bizarre and frightening experience at a game also took place in Memphis. The Clippers were playing great basketball behind what might have been Baron Davis's best game ever for the team in 2010. He was well on his way to a big triple-double. The Clippers were up by 12 points late in the third quarter, with Baron at the free throw line. Things were looking good for Mike Dunleavy's Clipper team. Davis had the ball in hand at the line when a startling siren blared though the FedExForum. It was loud, and it was frightening. The public address announcer calmly advised fans to leave the arena in an orderly fashion. Mike Smith and I were soon the only people still seated at our end of the press table. The producer in the TV truck was advising us to stay the course for a few minutes until it was clear what was happening. My immediate fear was a bomb threat or a terrorist attack. Jo was among the crowd ushered out of the arena. When the building was nearly empty, I said to Mike, "Let's get the hell out of here." I grabbed my precious broadcast folder and briefcase and headed for the exit, where I frantically searched for my wife. I found her over near the press entrance on the back side of the building.

We waited outside in the cold for about twenty minutes before we were told it was safe to return to the building. We walked past the Clipper team bus, which was filled with players and coaches from both teams. They were cautiously exiting the bus one by one. Word began to circulate that a broken water line in the arena sprinkler system had triggered the alarm. I would say that about half of the crowd returned to the arena to watch the balance of the game. They missed a heck of a finish by the local team; the Clippers did not recover from the unusual interruption, but the Grizzlies did. They quickly erased the 12-point deficit in the final quarter and scored a 104–102 win. The Clippers had been flirting with .500 at the time, but this would begin a run during which they lost fifteen of nineteen games to drop out of contention. Dunleavy did not make it that far. The coach was fired after forty-nine games, with a record of twenty-one wins and twenty-eight losses. That wacky game in Memphis had a lasting impact on that Clipper season.

Certainly, the most controversial game that I missed was over a couple of comments made by myself and my broadcast partner, Mike Smith, on the air during a game. To this day, I'm still not quite sure how this all happened, and it haunts me because it's a blot on my record that I don't feel I deserve. It was November of 2009, and we were in Memphis broadcasting a game against the Grizzlies. Here's the exact transcript of what was said on air:

SMITH: "Look who's in."

LAWLER: "Hamed Haddadi. Where's he from?"

SMITH: "He's the first Iranian to play in the NBA." [Smith pronounced "Iranian" as "Eye-ranian," which offended the single viewer who complained.]

LAWLER: "There aren't any Iranian players in the NBA?" [Repeating Smith's mispronunciation.]

SMITH: "He's the only one."

LAWLER: "He's from Iran?"

SMITH: "I guess so."

LAWLER: "*That* Iran?"

SMITH: "Yes."

LAWLER: "The real Iran?"

SMITH: "Yes."

LAWLER: "Wow. Haddadi, that's H-A-D-D-A-D-I."

SMITH: "You're sure it's not Borat's older brother? If they ever make a movie about Haddadi, I'm going to get Sacha Baron Cohen to play the part."

LAWLER: "Here's Haddadi. Nice little back-door pass. I guess those Iranians can pass the ball."

SMITH: "Especially the post players.

LAWLER: "I don't know about their guards."

And here's how the *Los Angeles Times* reported what happened afterwards:

> Ralph Lawler hadn't missed a Clippers broadcast in twenty-five years. Not for a cold or flu or even a kidney stone attack. He's been at the microphone for every dreary Clippers loss and the occasional uplifting victory.
>
> Until this Friday night.
>
> Fox yanked Lawler and analyst Michael Smith from Friday's Prime Ticket broadcast of the game against the Denver Nuggets after Clippers season-ticket holder Arya Towfighi objected to an on-air exchange between the announcers toward the end of Wednesday's 106–91 Clippers loss at Memphis.
>
> A source with knowledge of Fox's decision but who was not authorized to speak publicly said Lawler and Smith had "been suspended." They are expected to be back on the air for Monday's game against the Minnesota Timberwolves.

When I drove to Staples Center to broadcast the game against Denver, I was told to stop first at the Fox Sports offices for a meeting with the manager and executive producer. I had spent the entire day preparing for the broadcast; I'd showered, shaved, and put on a suit and tie before driving two hours in from La Quinta. When I arrived, they told me about the season ticket holder who had complained. Originally, Fox was fighting for a two- or three-game suspension. Thankfully, the Clippers public relations VP, Joe Safety, was able to get it knocked down to one game. I thought it was crazy, and I was really sick over it. Everybody around me, from fans to staff, thought it was nuts.

The Fox brass kept saying our comments were "inappropriate." It may not have been our finest moment on the air, but everyone I knew felt that it was worthy of no more than a cautionary reprimand. My statement that "I guess those Iranians can pass the ball," was in line with dozens of my past comments, like, "Those Bradley Braves can sure shoot the ball" after a player from my old school knocked down a jump shot.

They kept saying it was no big deal, that it would blow over in no time. I disagreed and suggested that the suspension would be a bigger story in tomorrow's newspaper than the game itself. They thought that was nonsense, but sure enough, the headline about the suspension topped the smaller story about the game. T. J. Simers and Mark Heisler of the *L.A. Times* both wrote weekend columns in our defense, but it didn't matter; we were still docked our pay for that game. For years, anybody Googling my name would see the news about the suspension pop up first. Those links still exist today.

A few weeks later, when Memphis came to town, it was suggested that Michael and I get together with the gentleman who had filed the complaint, as well as with Haddadi. I think both men were a bit embarrassed and felt like the punishment had been too harsh. In fact, the season ticket holder who started the whole thing even asked for my autograph! Haddadi's agent was there, too, and he asked me to pose for a picture with him. Oddly, the agent pronounced Haddadi's country as "Eye-ran," yet, when the complaining viewer had heard Mike and I pronounce it that way, he had gotten so upset that he had his young son leave the room.

I can hardly believe this story to this day.

Chapter 18

The Business of Basketball

THE NBA'S SEVENTY-FIVE-YEAR RUN has hit a few road-blocks along the way. It was certainly not a straight-line ascent. We watched the fans' attention slowly evolve from college basketball to the pro game. It took more than a few years; it took decades, and continues to grow to this very day. The players of the future owe a huge debt to those who spent years paving the way.

Early on, basketball players earned small salaries, and even those were not guaranteed. Players disguised injuries for fear that they would wind up out on the street if they missed a few games, and they had good reason to be concerned. Many of them took off-season jobs to supplement their basketball income. They might be selling insurance in the summer, and playing hoops in the winter. Even the advent of improved salaries, benefits, and conditions were not enough to assure a player's long-term financial security. A *Sports Illustrated* story in 2009 estimated that 60 percent of NBA players would go broke within five years of retirement. The average player salary at the time was $2.5 million a season.

The league does a better job today at educating players about the sometimes-confusing confluence of youth, fame, and big dollars. Those dollars have grown almost absurdly. NBA players now average over $7.7 million a year. Break that down into twenty-four equal, twice-a-month payments, and each paycheck would be over $300,000!

The old timers can only dream of what it would be like to play in the present-day financial environment. A $6,000 annual salary in 1946 or 1947 computes in the present day to $70,000, adjusted for inflation. Even then, the early NBA players did make more money than most fans; the median family income when the league began was only $3,000 a year. However, players were making nothing close to the movie star dollars made today.

Much of the credit goes to a superstar player from the 1960s and '70s named Oscar Robertson. Known as the "Big O," Oscar came into the league as a highly touted player side by side with Jerry West in 1960. He joined the Cincinnati Royals after three spectacular seasons at the University of Cincinnati. West and Robertson quickly replaced Boston's Bob Cousy and Detroit's Gene Shue as the best guards in the league.

Robertson grew up in Indianapolis before his college and pro days a state away in Ohio. West likely had the bigger transition, going from college stardom at his home-state West Virginia U to the newly re-minted Lakers across the country in Los Angeles. Jerry went on to have his profile serve as the league logo. Robertson's impact was even greater, though less heralded.

Few present-day fans have any idea how good Oscar was as a player. Standing six foot five and weighing 200-plus pounds, he was an unmatched physical presence in his point guard position. He was bigger and stronger than just about any player he faced. He dominated NBA games with his physicality sixty years ago, much like LeBron James has been doing since 2003. Through his first five years in the league, Oscar essentially averaged a triple-double (double figures in points, rebounds, and assists). He established seasons unmatched until Russell Westbrook's triple-double explosions between 2017 and 2019. However, Westbrook is quick to add, "I'm not even close to the things Oscar was able to do." Still, Robertson's twelve All-Star appearances, three All-Star game MVP awards, amazing league MVP season, and late-career NBA championship pale in comparison to the lasting impact he has had on the NBA and, really, all professional team sports.

In 1954, the NBA Players Association was founded by another point guard of note—the Celtics' Bob Cousy, who led the fast break to collective bargaining. Early on, progress for the players was painfully slow. They had no health plan, no minimum wage, no guaranteed salaries, no pension plan, and not even per diem when traveling with their teams. What they were certain of was a belief that things could be better. The players knew they had a very brief window in which they could get paid for playing a game they had happily played for free in their youth (the average length of an NBA player's career is a scant five years).

Tom Heinsohn succeeded Cousy as NBAPA president, and by 1960, the average annual salary in the league had reached $12,000. That was more than double the nation's median annual family income of $5,600. Such was the setting when Oscar Robertson entered the National Basketball Association in 1960. Change was in the offing.

Ten years later, the firmly established "Big O" was one of the top earners and biggest stars in the game. The average salary in the league had ballooned to $35,000, or the equivalent of $225,000 in today's dollars. He was now the player rep for the Cincinnati Royals and president of the Player's Association.

There was a rival league competing for fans' attention and, more importantly, competing for players. It was the American Basketball Association. The ABA never really got the full attention of the American sporting public, but they sure received the attention of the now-fourteen-team NBA. The new league was drafting charismatic young stars, while also raiding the established league for the likes of Billy Cunningham and Rick Barry. Uh-oh.

Professional sports had been incubated by something called the reserve clause. In essence, it gave teams the absolute rights to a player. Courts ruled variously that team rights were forever, or for at least one year after the completion of their contract. Either way, it severely limited a player's rights of self-determination. Even if a player could gain free agency by sitting out one season, that represented possibly 10 to 20 percent of a limited career, in a profession where athletes start hearing they were getting old when they approached thirty.

With this in mind, let us take a closer look at what Oscar Robertson accomplished. He had spent ten years in Cincinnati with the Royals. They had missed the playoffs three seasons in a row, and Robertson feared that the Royals would own his basketball rights for life. This was not just a great basketball player, but a very bright and business-savvy young man. Oscar had an almost unheard-of "no trade" clause in his contract. That gave him the right to decide where he was interested in playing if he were to approve a trade. The previously powerless player now had some limited control over his destiny. Despite the team's struggles, Cincinnati was home for Oscar Robertson. He had spent three years there in college, and then ten more with the Royals. He had no reason to want to play elsewhere. Or did he?

Bob Cousy was named head coach of the Royals in the summer of 1969. Cousy had been the best point guard in the NBA before Oscar. Both had won the league MVP award. Both had strong personalities and ample egos. It was not going to be a match made in heaven.

I attended a Royals game at Cincinnati Gardens in 1969, while in town for a job interview at radio station WLW. I was thirty-one years old at the time. It was a treat to see Oscar as a pro after seeing him many times in college, and also to see the forty-one-year-old Cousy, who was somehow determined to be a player-coach, though he had retired from the Celtics as a player six years earlier. Boston waived their rights to Cousy, but it was apparent as I watched the game from the cheap seats that the one thing the Royals did not need was another point guard. Robertson was ten years younger than Cousy and still a 25-point-a-game scorer, while playing over forty minutes a game. Cousy would play only seven games, but the friction between the two all-time greats was exacerbated by Cousy's desire to play in an effort to show the pace at which he expected Oscar to play. By season's end, their rift was impossible to overcome; Cousy wanted Robertson gone. But if Oscar were to go, he would pick the spot, thanks to his "no trade" clause.

The Milwaukee Bucks had drafted UCLA's superlative center Lew Alcindor (Kareem Abdul-Jabbar) the prior summer. Oscar knew an opportunity to win the elusive championship when he saw one. The Royals went to work to make a trade happen, and they did it. The Bucks' intention was to gut the team, shed some salary, and build around Alcindor and Robertson. They looked to trade their top established role players, Jon McGlocklin and Bob Dandridge. Robertson got wind of this and again exercised his hard-earned power by saying he would not approve the trade to the Bucks if McGlocklin or Dandridge were traded. Some power plays work, and some do not. This one resulted in McGlocklin and Dandridge staying in Milwaukee, and the Robertson trade was consummated. It also led to the NBA title for the

Bucks and Oscar in 1971.

Robertson was in the autumn of his career at the time of the trade, but he was not one to hide in the shadows. Just six days before approving his move from Cincinnati to Milwaukee, Robertson filed an unprecedented anti-trust suit against the NBA and its fourteen teams. The player representatives of the other thirteen teams were listed as co-plaintiffs.

There were multiple reasons for the suit. The NBA was working hard to accomplish a merger with the rival ABA to cease the costly bidding war for players between the two leagues. The anti-trust suit meant that such a merger would be on hold until the suit was settled. The ABA kept the pressure on the established league, year by year. In this interim, they drafted and signed the likes of Hall of Famers-to-be Dan Issel, Artis Gilmore, and David Thompson. Behind the scenes, the upstart league was going after college basketball's greatest players.

While Bill Walton was on the way to leading UCLA to back-to-back NCAA titles, the ABA felt that signing Walton in 1973 would be the straw that could break the NBA's back. After the Bruins won in the Big Redhead's junior year, he was confronted with an unexpected opportunity. The night UCLA won the NCAA championship in St. Louis, the American Basketball Association requested and received a meeting with Walton. They brought with them the most unbelievable offer in the history of professional sports. If Walton would leave school a year early, they would create a team in Los Angeles and give Walton a significant piece of ownership, allowing him to select the coach and general manager and also pick his teammates from all the existing ABA rosters (excluding Julius Erving, who they wanted to keep with the New York Nets). He could have teamed with Billy Cunningham, David Thompson, and/or Dan Issel. Whoever. It was his choice. Oh, and there was that briefcase one of the ABA suits was carrying. They opened it to reveal a breathtaking cache of cash. Walton was assured that all the money he had ever dreamed of would be his.

The big center did not ask for a chance to think about it. He wanted to play another year under the legendary John Wooden at UCLA. "Thanks, but no thanks" was the essential sentiment.

That does illustrate how intent the young league was to challenge the NBA, and it is why the older league was so frantic to come up with a merger to ward off further unforeseen and expensive challenges. It took six full years for the NBA to reach a game-changing class action settlement.

Oscar's greatest "assist" actually came two years after his 1974 retirement as a player. What became known as the "Oscar Robertson Rule" essentially eliminated the dreaded reserve clause that had bound players to their teams at the sole option of the team. It also led to the almost immediate merger that saw four ABA teams graduate to the NBA.

I saw that reserve clause play out up close and personal in San Diego in 1973. The NBA had fled the Southern California city when the Rockets moved to Houston in 1971. The American Basketball Association swooped in a year later by establishing the San Diego Conquistadors. The Conquistadors played a season at the cracker-box Peterson Gym on the San Diego State campus. It held only 3,200 seats, but that was more than enough as the team averaged roughly 1,800 fans a game. The team's owner was a local dentist named Leonard Bloom. Give him

TIME OUT **Wilt Chamberlain**

Wilt Chamberlain entered the NBA in 1959 after a year of touring with the Harlem Globetrotters. He was seven foot one, boasted a seven-seven wingspan, and weighed 250 pounds. Wilt was more than big; he was an athletic marvel. Basketball had never seen anything like him. He would average 37.6 points and 27 rebounds a game as a twenty-three-year-old rookie. In his early years, he had an unimaginable and never-duplicated 100-point game and, almost as impressively, a 55-rebound game. There were no newspaper reporters at Wilt's historic 100-point outburst in Hershey, Pennsylvania. Afterwards, Warriors statistical maven Harvey Pollack grabbed a piece of paper and wrote "100" on it while asking the lone photographer there to snap a photo commemorating the amazing feat. It stands today as one of the NBA's most iconic photos.

Wilt's dominance was beyond comprehension. The league tried to level the playing field a little in 1964 by further widening the free throw lane from twelve to sixteen feet. Nice try. Wilt averaged about 35 points a game over each of the first three years of the widened lane. No player has ever dominated the league to the extent accomplished by Wilt Chamberlain. ●

credit for thinking big. In the summer of 1973, he signed possibly the greatest big man to ever play the game: Wilt Chamberlain, the NBA's all-time scoring champion. He had won titles in Philadelphia and in Los Angeles, where he had played for the Lakers for five years. Bloom announced that he had signed the thirty-seven-year-old big man to be his team's player-coach.

I was at the introductory news conference in downtown San Diego. Wilt quickly emphasized that he was there to be a "PLAYER-coach." The event was seemingly better attended than many of the team's games the previous season. It looked like pro basketball would suddenly have a chance in what many perceived as just a sleepy Navy town.

The optimism was short-lived. The Lakers cited the reserve or option clause and claimed that if Wilt wanted to play professional basketball, it would be with the Lakers or nobody. Certainly not for a team in a rival league just 120 miles away. I had been excited at the prospect of watching Wilt play. It was a big disappointment for me and the anticipatory fans in the area. So, Wilt was left to coach. The big man had little-to-no real interest in coaching. He would miss games for book signings, and miss practices because, well, he never liked them that much as a player. He had his able assistant, Stan Albeck, do all the real work. The rigors of coaching were of mild interest to the towering giant of a man, who seemingly only tolerated practices when he could take the court for a scrimmage with his team. I witnessed some of those scrimmages, and they were fun to watch. Wilt would score at will against his ABA players. He was in his element.

However, once the big man was prohibited from playing, the dentist's team needed more than a root canal. Let us do the math. They were paying Wilt $600,000. According to a March 21, 1976, story in the *New York Times*, the combined salaries of his eleven players totaled $469,000, and the team's gate receipts for the season were just $241,551.50. Whoops. It could not and did not work. The Conquistadors were forgotten about in San Diego the next summer, and Wilt Chamberlain had sadly closed the final chapter of his life in professional basketball. This scenario is a classic example of the restrictive power of the reserve clause.

Oscar Robertson observed all of this as he was finishing his playing career, while the courts were dealing with his anti-trust suit. There was a tremendous sense of relief once the favorable verdict was reached. "When you look at the Oscar Robertson Rule, it was like throwing a raft into the water for the guys whose boat was sinking," Robertson said at the time.

There is no way I can over-state Robertson's impact on professional sports. He alone seemed to have the vision that players should receive movie star or rock star-caliber money. Once they did, he felt, fans would put them on a pedestal. Big money would put them on a par with the film stars of the day: Burt Reynolds, Steve McQueen, and Paul Newman. Nobody else at the time saw this with Oscar's pristine clairvoyance.

Nobody, that is, until David Stern became commissioner in the mid-1980s. Even the NBA owners were off the mark on this one. The court verdict looked like terrible news for the league. However, the fans' stargazing served everyone well. It got network television's attention, and that piqued fan interest still more. The NBA pie had gotten much bigger. And while that led to some contentious bouts of wrangling between the owners and the players in the years ahead, the end result of the Oscar Robertson Rule was that it was a win for the players, the teams, and the league. All have thrived.

The resulting addition of four teams from the ABA in 1976 was a rousing success, as it shut down the competing league and brought bright new stars such as Julius Erving, George Gervin, Artis Gilmore, Moses Malone, Bobby Jones, and David Thompson into the NBA's expanded tent. The pro game was ripe for renewed growth.

It would not be fair to talk about NBA labor issues without mentioning the coaches. When Red Auerbach took over as coach of the Boston Celtics in 1950, he was given a salary of $10,000 a year. No NBA coach signed a $100,000-a-year contract until Gene Shue with the Philadelphia 76ers in the 1970s. By the mid '80s, coaching salaries had topped $200,000 a year, and by the end of the decade, the league saw the best of the best taking home salaries in the range of $500,000 a season. That pales in comparison to the $10-million-a-year stipends offered to the crème de la crème of the coaching fraternity today.

Let me rewind just a bit. The early league coaches had no clout. They had no pension. They had no significant list of benefits. That began to change in 1976, with the establishment of the National

Basketball Coaches Association. Former Celtic great Tommy Heinsohn was the early leader of the move to get the coaching fraternity
some of the perks he had helped the players attain almost twenty years
earlier. Four years later, the legendary Michael Goldberg took over the
helm of the NBCA, a post he held until his passing in 2017. He holds
near-sainthood status with the league's head and assistant coaches to
this day. David Fogel has ably filled the post in Goldberg's absence.

The NBCA now presents three prestigious awards to coaches
present and past. Their Coach of the Year honor is given in advance
of the league's official award to the season's top coach. They also offer
the Chuck Daily Lifetime Achievement Award to a coach with ten or
more years of service, and then the Tex Winter Award to an all-time
top NBA assistant coach. The annual honors have given the NBCA
a higher platform. But it is clear that the group's service behind the
scenes has served the coaching fraternity very well.

Slowly, but surely, even NBA announcers began to see their salaries elevated by the growing popularity of the game. I think I received
just a couple of hundred dollars a game working local 76er telecasts
in the 1970s. At about that time I heard that Andy Musser was getting $1,000 a game announcing Bulls TV games in Chicago. It was
a stunning reminder that I really wanted to be the voice of an NBA
team. I had the desire and the connections to make it happen, though
the money part would take a while. I moved to San Diego with the
founding of the Clippers in 1978, and received a whopping $25,000 a
year to broadcast their games on radio. I soon had to supplement my
income by selling real estate in the off-season. The Clippers' move to
Los Angeles six years later was heaven-sent—television and comforting dollars would follow.

Meanwhile, the network talent had ridden a true gravy train. Sev-
en-figure contracts are now common. They often make more in a game
than I used to in a season! I write that without a hint of rancor; I loved
being a part of a team, and caring whether it won or lost. I worked
next to a variety of freelance color commentators over the years, and
they really had no vested interest in the outcome of the games. I did,
and that was a large part of what made those forty years so rich and
enjoyable. The money was good enough that Jo and I can now live
comfortably in retirement. Thanks, Dr. Naismith.

Chapter 19

The NBA and Drugs

LIKE A DEMON, DRUGS HAUNTED THE NBA in the 1970s and '80s. Critics claimed that the league was overrun with narcotics. Television ratings were down. Attendance was a fraction of today's SRO venues.

In the mid-'80s, the league made giant strides with a precedent-setting drug policy. Players are now randomly tested four times a year. I recall a Clipper training camp a few years ago during which I left my courtside seat to take a bathroom break. There were a couple of rookies in the men's room, along with NBA representative and former Clipper Darnell Valentine. He looked at me and said, "Don't worry, Ralph, we aren't testing for Viagra."

I was aware of Clipper players who smoked marijuana over the years. Teams and the league had generally looked the other way. Some, like Lamar Odom of the L.A. Clippers, was twice suspended for it. The enlightened league no longer tests for THC, the hallucinatory substance in marijuana.

John Lucas, the number-one overall draft pick out of the University of Maryland in 1976 by the Houston Rockets, has spent much of his life helping young players deal with their addiction issues. He has saved numerous careers and likely a few lives. He knows the topic from first-hand experience—Lucas began failing league-mandated drug tests a decade into his pro career. His downward spiral began as he bounced from one team to another. His talent was never questioned.

Washington took a flyer on him in 1982.

Coach Gene Shue told me about a time before a Bullets game in Landover, Maryland, when Lucas was not on the court for early pre-game warm-ups. He was spotted wandering aimlessly in the upper regions of the empty stands. He was lost in whatever fog it was that enveloped his life at the time. He would somehow play for five more NBA teams before retiring in 1990. He went into drug rehabilitation, and is now the poster boy for the program's success. He was back in the league as an assistant coach within two seasons, and was soon named head coach of the San Antonio Spurs after their failed experiment with former college coach Jerry Tarkanian.

Lucas used the success of his own rehab to apply it to others in need. He worked a season as a Clipper assistant under Mike Dunleavy, and it was such a pleasure to get to know him. I can tell you that he is now one of the most respected people in the sport. He still serves a vital role as a player development coach with the Houston Rockets, and is always there for a player in need.

My most personal brush with a player whose career was constrained by drug use was John Drew of the Atlanta Hawks. I loved watching John play. I have seen and admired players like George Gervin and Alex English, who seemed to score with uncanny ease, and Drew had that knack as well. You would hardly notice him in the game, and then you would look down at your score sheet to see he had scored 25 points! Drew was a consistent 20-points-a-game scorer through eight often-troubled seasons with the Hawks.

John was variously burdened with drug issues, followed by recoveries and pledges that he was through with drugs. I interviewed him on the radio once in Atlanta before a game against the Clippers. I simply asked how he was doing. With his brown eyes riveted on mine, Drew explained, very directly, that he had been forced to avoid all of his former associates. He had cut ties with every one of his friends. His exact words to me were: "If you go to the barber shop often enough, pretty soon you are going to get a haircut."

Drew had surrounded himself with a supportive group of new friends. Everyone who knew him cautiously hoped that the troubled player was over the hump. I really liked him and pulled for him. I knew he faced a challenging time. But the challenges proved to be too much. After pleading guilty to selling drugs to an undercover agent, Drew was ultimately banned from the NBA for life, sentenced to six months in jail in 1987, and ordered to undergo drug therapy. He must have gotten one haircut too many. So was life in the NBA in the 1970s and '80s.

Basketball life used to seem so simple to me. Players smoked cigarettes and drank beer. So did I. I have a clear vision of Hall of Famer-to-be George McInnis after he had defected to the Philadelphia 76ers from the ABA Indiana Pacers in 1975. Big George was one of the top stars in the upstart league, and acquiring him was a major coup for the Sixers. I was at one of his first practices, and during some running drills, he needed to take a break. McInnis lumbered off the court, took a seat on the bench, and reached down into his socks to remove a package of cigarettes. Sure enough, he lit one up while sitting right there on the sidelines.

Vlade Divac was one of the first European stars to enter the NBA. He joined the Los Angeles Lakers in 1989 and smoked regularly throughout his sixteen-year career. Divac reportedly even smoked during halftime.

Superstar Michael Jordan's primary vice was cigars, but he enjoyed cigarettes as well. As recently as a couple of years ago, Euro superstar Melos Teodosic joined the L.A. Clippers at the age of thirty, as an addicted smoker. He could get away with it in Europe, where they play just once a week. The savvy Serbian star and former Euro League MVP never was able to get in true NBA basketball condition, and his U.S. career lasted only a season and a half. He returned to Europe, where he quickly excelled again while being named MVP of Euro Cups regular season. Melos is still smoking, literally and figuratively.

My most memorable NBA sniff of something stronger than cigarette smoke came in December of 1980, when the San Diego Clippers bused up to Los Angeles for a meeting with the Lakers. The Clips shocked the Lakers at the Forum, 120–114. There were some happy players on the team bus for the two-hour ride home after the game, but a couple of the players were a little too happy. I was seated on the bus directly behind Clipper first-year coach Paul Silas when I noticed the sweet scent of illegal smoke coming from the rear reaches of the bus. I leaned up to Coach Silas and whispered, "Paul, somebody is smoking grass back there." Silas looked back, sniffed, and said he didn't smell anything. He did a few minutes later, though, and got up to confront two players in the back of the bus who were sharing a joint in apparent celebration of their rare win over the Lakers.

Smoking was hardly the only vice practiced by players over the years. A big cooler of iced beer used to be available in virtually every NBA locker room after each game. It is hard to believe in today's NBA; yet, through the '80s and into the '90s, there it was. Everybody wanted to grab a cold one, including this broadcaster. General manager Elgin Baylor and I shared more than a few of them over the years, often taking a brew onto the team bus. By and large, it was not a problem.

That changed in 1988, when Chris Mullin of the Golden State Warriors checked himself into a rehab facility in Los Angeles at the insistence of head coach Don Nelson. The former St. John's star picked up his love of the suds while playing for coach Lou Carnesecca in college. Beer and wine were pretty much an accepted part of daily life on the school campus. Mullin brought that mentality into the pro game after being drafted by Golden State in 1985. I would be standing by his locker after a game with my trusty tape recorder in hand while the southpaw shooter would suck down one can of beer after another. His weight would take wild swings up and down, and by his third season, Nelson had seen enough.

Nellie sent the player to a rehabilitation facility. It certainly saved Mullin's career, and may well have saved his life. Chris Mullin was a new man once he dealt with the demon that led him to drinking. His scoring average soared; he averaged over 25 points a game for five straight seasons. The rehabilitation salvaged a career and led to his induction into the Basketball Hall of Fame in 2011.

The path of the NBA was sometimes the road less traveled, and sometimes not.

Chapter 20

Load Management

I AM ASTOUNDED AT WHAT IS GOING ON in pro sports today. Today's athlete has a bevy of supporting partners, and star players are pampered like infants in the cradle. It is getting worse year by year. The typical NBA team carries not just a trainer, but an assistant trainer, a strength and conditioning coach, an assistant strength and conditioning coach, one or two massage therapists, at least one chiropractor, a team chef and assistant team chef, a team nutritionist, a director of performance, a performance therapist, and, of course, a performance scientist and biomedical analyst. That is just the list for the L.A. Clippers during my final 2018–2019 season.

When the Clippers were born in San Diego in 1978, the list above was limited to just one: team trainer, who also doubled as the travel coordinator. Today, there are more members of the current support staff than there were players on that first Clipper team.

Oh yes, I know . . . this is a new day. Times have changed. But the changes should be making today's players stronger and more durable. They also have immense travel advantages, which began with the advent of charter flying thirty years ago. No more three games in three nights, or even five games in five nights. That is all long gone, and even the number of games on back-to-back nights has been dramatically reduced in recent seasons.

I flew with the Clippers on commercial airlines from 1978 into the early 1990s. It was a far more taxing experience. The wear and tear on those players is foreign to the current-day athletes. Yet, the old-timers played more games and more minutes. An NBA player hasn't logged an average of forty minutes a game since guard Monte Ellis, with Golden State in the 2010–2011 season. Twenty or thirty years ago, you had to drag players off the court. Now, few players play all eighty-two games, and they rarely ever play even forty minutes in a game.

A. C. Green of the Lakers is the league's all-time iron man, playing in 1,192 games in a row (14-plus seasons). Former Clipper guard Randy Smith played in 906 consecutive games (11-plus seasons). Those feats are unthinkable in today's NBA culture. Prior to the 2014–2015 season, star Clipper guard Chris Paul vowed to play all eighty-two games. He was able to do that, but wasn't able to keep it alive in the playoffs; he missed the first two games of the semi-final series against Houston, with a strained hamstring suffered in the Game 7 clincher against San Antonio. The Clippers lost one of those first two games without CP3, and that loss was the difference between winning and losing the series. Was he paying the price for playing all eight-two games in the regular season? Just asking.

The popular concept today is "load management," popularized by San Antonio Spur coach Gregg Popovich. He would create nights off for aging stars like Tim Duncan, Manu Ginobili, and Tony Parker. It created new issues for a league that tries to stay ahead of the curve wherever possible. The official league policy is stated: "NBA teams are not permitted to rest healthy players during games broadcast on national TV, or during road games when there are not 'unusual circumstances.'"

I guess that means a team can short-change its home season ticket holders, but not the fans on the road. The idea is that if LeBron James is going to make only one appearance a year in Chicago, the Bulls fans better get a chance to see him play. It is a thorny issue. A coach is expected to coach a team to win. Yet, he may look at a stretch of schedule where he feels the long-term interests of the team would best be served by resting certain players on a given night.

I do not have an answer to the dilemma, just utter amazement at how the players were treated so differently back when I came into the league in the mid-'70s, and especially when I first started following the NBA in the 1940s and '50s. I can tell you that I would not have lasted

forty years with the Clippers were it not for the convenience of charter
air travel. We never set foot in an airline terminal in the forty-eight
contiguous states. Our team bus would simply pull up on the tarmac,
leaving us with a ten-yard walk to and from the airplane.

It is as painless as travel can possibly be. Yet, NBA players' minutes are monitored like an expiring parking meter. This issue is not
limited to the National Basketball Association. The NFL finds many
teams playing few, if any, of their starting offensive or defensive players
during their very brief three-game, pre-season schedule. Teams played
six pre-season games back when I was broadcasting San Diego Charger games in the 1970s. The starters might only play a quarter or a half
in the early games, but by Games 5 or 6 they would play all four quarters. It worked out just fine for the likes of Joe Namath, Dan Marino,
and Steve Young. But not today for Patrick Mahomes, Tom Brady, or
Aaron Rodgers. Why?

Then there is Major League baseball. I have followed the sport
closely since 1945. My family and I would motor to Chicago from
Peoria once a summer to watch the Cubs play at Wrigley Field. I
would have been distraught in the 1950s if we had traveled 150 miles
to find that Ernie Banks was out for reasons of "load management."

Major league pitchers make present-day NBA players seem super-
human. Managers now just hope to get six or seven innings from their
starting pitchers. No MLB pitcher has pitched as many as 300 innings
since Steve Carlton of the Phillies in 1980. I was in Philadelphia in
the 1970s, and spent a couple of seasons broadcasting Phillies games.
I knew their manager, Danny Ozark, well and I can tell you he would
have been taking his life in his hands if he tried to take Carlton out of
a game in the seventh inning because he had reached the 100-pitch
threshold. In today's game, pitchers rarely log 200 innings in a season.

Three hundred innings used to be what was expected from a team's
ace. Back in the day, the game had pitchers routinely throwing 400 innings. Believe it or not, in the truly olden days there were pitchers who
threw 500 innings, and—fasten your seatbelts—even in excess of 600
innings, which is more than three times as many innings on the mound
as today's most active pampered hurlers. I've looked, but have not
found one case where these hardworking pitching warriors had their
arms fall off. Astonishingly, no American League pitcher has thrown

as many as ten complete games in a season since the hard-throwing Randy Johnson completed twelve games for Arizona in 1999.

What is going on? Fernando Valenzuela finished what he started twenty times for the Los Angeles Dodgers in 1986. The standard for quality starters was once twenty-five to thirty complete games. I'm talking about some of the game's all-time greats: Robin Roberts, Juan Marichal, Catfish Hunter, Bob Feller, and Steve Carlton. They each had thirty or more compete games thrown in a season. They were still strong in innings 8 and 9. Today's game sees maybe two or three complete games a season in both leagues. It is about as rare as the triple-play.

My dad ingrained in me the belief that "the show must go on." As I described in another chapter, I broadcast two different games while passing kidney stones, got through another one in Sacramento with a bad case of food poisoning, and did many more with a sore throat or a fever.

I am perplexed by today's athletes. It was unheard of even twenty-five or thirty years ago for a player to miss a game because his wife was having a baby. They had paid you money to play the game, so you played the game. Basketball players, as an example, are pampered beginning with their AAU days, and it continues throughout high school and college. They are given such nurturing treatment that they think they deserve it and even need it. But they are stronger than that. They can run faster and jump higher than their olden-day counterparts.

But are they as tough? They just do not seem to have the same staying power. Or maybe they do, but the money at stake seems to make teams and coaches overly cautious. As is so often the case, it might just come down to the dollars.

I feel bad for the fans who pay ever-increasing prices for tickets, or sponsors who foot the bill for just about everything. We are seeing less and less of our star players. It is a problem that may become worse before it gets better. I did not like it when I was a team broadcaster, and I like it even less now in my role as a devoted sports fan.

Chapter 21

No Business Like Show Business

DURING MY THIRD AND FOURTH YEARS at Bradley University, I discovered a love of performing. The theater department was under the direction of Dr. Bob Cagle, a fittingly theatrical and flamboyant personality who helped me discover a passion I did not know existed in myself. He cast me as Doc in the university production of *Mr. Roberts*. It was one of several productions I worked on in my final two years in college. I enjoyed it enough that I seriously considered going to New York City after graduation, with hopes of breaking onto the Broadway stage.

Fortunately, I came to my senses and found my niche in radio, but my love for performing remained. I would appear in local community theater in Peoria and again in Riverside, California. I loved appearing in front of a live audience. It was a thrill to hear applause. My thirst for stardom as a show biz performer was never fully quenched, but I did get a sip every now and then.

When I moved to Los Angeles to join the relocated Clippers in 1985, I received a surprising phone call midway through the first season that offered a new opportunity. Mary Tyler Moore had launched a new sitcom on CBS, an attempt to recreate the magic of her original mega-hit from the 1970s, *The Mary Tyler Moore Show*. David Isaacs and Ken Levine were the show's creators and producers, and they were fans of the recently arrived Los Angeles Clippers. I received the call a couple of months into the season, asking me if I would like to appear in one of the episodes of *Mary*. They had written an episode that needed some basketball play-by-play in the background. I thought being in Mary Tyler Moore's background sounded pretty great.

Hello, Hollywood! I sat down for a table read with Mary and her co-stars, James Farentino and John Astin. My lines were first intended to describe an NBA game. However, the league did not give approval for us to use the NBA team or player names. So it became a very awkward, generic play-by-play, but I would be on the air in prime time from coast to coast.

The show was performed in front of a live audience at CBS Television City. The taping went well. It was a thrill. Sadly, the episode did not air as *Mary* was cancelled after a thirteen-week run.

During the 1991–1992 season, I was working with Mike Fratello on our KTLA Clipper telecasts when we received a request from one of the producers of a movie called *White Men Can't Jump*. They wanted to use some audio from one of our telecasts in the movie. They sent a detailed Screen Actors Guild contract that Mike and I happily signed. Unfortunately, we wound up on the cutting room floor, but we did get paid for our non-appearance.

Hollywood came calling again in 1997. They just could not leave me alone. The UPN network had a four-year run with a dramatic series called The Sentinel. They had a two-parter titled "Three Point Shot" in season three, and it was all about a basketball-related murder. They asked me and Hubie Brown to play ourselves in an on-camera play-by-play sequence. We had a ball! Hubie and I were in Vancouver for a week or so to film, and we had our own trailers and felt like movie stars. Each night we had dinner together and talked hoops from the appetizer through the dessert. It was a memorable week for this small-town radio announcer from Peoria.

I was then asked to record play-by-play for the Nintendo NBA Courtside 2002 GameCube. They originally wanted Bill Walton and me, but Bill's new deal with ABC/ESPN would not allow it. It was still a hoot, though it wound up being exhausting work. You had to record *everything*—every score possible, all the game times, and the names of all the teams and players in the league. It took three long recording sessions to get my part completed. Once released, I gained new stature with players around the league. These guys spent countless hours playing NBA Courtside 2002. Lamar Odom of the Clippers was amazed and impressed when he heard my voice on the game. It was interesting to see how important this was to these young men. I would have players from around the league come over to the press table to ask, "Are you the guy on Courtside 2002?" Fame comes in many different forms. I'm happy to have done a project like that once, but once was enough.

My next taste of show biz came in 2011. The producer of the movie *Drive*, starring Ryan Gosling, was a Clippers fan and wanted to use a simulated broadcast of a Clipper game as a key part of the opening of the movie. Sounded cool to me.

I went to the Sony Picture Studios on West Washington in Culver City for the recording session. I was hooked up with an audio link with the movie's director, Nicolas Refn, and we went to work. They gave me an outline to follow and I was asked to describe the fictional game action. The director would chime in to be sure I gave the key game times: "Four minutes to go," "One minute thirty remaining," and "That's it— Clippers win." That was the cue to start the action in the movie, with Gosling, the driver, listening on the car radio before heading out of the arena parking lot as fans were leaving Staples Center. It was fun and especially nice to see that the Clippers and not the Lakers were being featured in the film. The long, slow process toward respectability was taking place. It was also rewarding to receive residual checks for several years after the film's release.

The Clippers' president of business operations, Gillian Zucker, was a great supporter over the years and the perfect choice by owner Steve Ballmer to take over the business side of the team after his $2 billion purchase of the ball club in 2014. She made a few changes that left some in the organization uncomfortable, but she knew what she was doing. Ballmer had given her a vision, and it was her job to keep it in focus. That included enhanced community involvement, game operations, plans for the new arena in Inglewood, and the purchase of the Forum, among other things. It is a big, multi-faceted job, and she sees and hears everything.

A few years ago, Gillian asked me to work with the immensely talented Funny or Die people on a video piece inspired by Will Ferrell. We spent the day at their West Hollywood studios, rehearsing and filming some fun called "A Day in the Office with Ralph Lawler." It was a series of vignettes that were shown online and on the big board at Clipper games. I was working with some hugely talented people. We had a ball.

I was talking with some of the crew during a break, and the subject of the Broadway Theater was under discussion. Someone in the group had just seen *Hamilton* on Broadway with Lin-Manuel Miranda. I mentioned how much my wife and I longed to see it during the Clipper visit to New York that season, but I had learned that tickets were going for something like $750. I was assured that it was worth it, and the conversation shifted to something else.

A couple of nights later, Jo and I showed up for a Clipper game

---

OVERTIME Most Memorable Celebrities and Other Athletes

STEVE CARLTON

Steve Carlton was one of baseball's best left-handed pitchers in the 1970s and on into the 1980s. He pitched 346 innings one year, while throwing thirty complete games. Run those numbers by any of today's carefully coddled Major League hurlers. Carlton pitched every fourth day for the Phillies as opposed to every fifth day, which is the routine in today's game. Oh, and he pitched until he was for-ty-three years old.

Steve had Tim McCarver as his designated catcher during the bulk of his time in Philadelphia. They were an odd couple. McCa-rver was lighthearted and outgoing, while Carlton was somber and introspective. Steve did not like the media. He clammed up when he saw a guy with a microphone or a notepad. After a Philly victory at the Vet in Philadelphia, I went over to him with a mic in hand and a cameraman at my side. This was not a welcome sight for Steve Carlton, who was set to pitch the next day. I said something like, "Nice win tonight Steve—you get these guys tomorrow. What special problems do they pose?"

Steve snarled, "I didn't play tonight. Go talk to the guys who did!"

That was one of my better exchanges with Steve Carlton. What-ever—it worked for him to the tune of 329 career victories.

at Staples Center. We were greeted by Gillian in the media dining room, who handed me an envelope containing two center orchestra tickets to *Hamilton* for the night before the Clippers were scheduled to play the Knicks at Madison Square Garden. She had been eavesdropping at the Funny or Die studios, and somehow landed those two prized tickets. I had been totally unaware of her presence at the time, but, like I said, she hears and sees everything. We went to see the amazing musical and found it mesmerizing. We've seen it twice since, and hope to see it again. As great as it is, it can never be the same after enjoying the original Broadway cast headed by Miranda himself. Thanks, Gillian Zucker.

JOE FRAZIER

"Smokin'" Joe Frazier was one of the greatest heavyweight boxing champions of all time. I was fortunate to get to know the Champ at the peak of his career during my years in Philadelphia. We did a one-hour radio interview in our WCAU studios one Monday night, and we just hit it off. Trainer Eddie Futch was there, and he became a valued ally as well.

They both invited me to Frazier's gym, so I took a film crew from Channel 10 down there with me. I am so glad it was film rather than videotape. The colors were rich, deep, and glorious. It was a setting that could have been out of one of the future *Rocky* movies.

Here was the man who'd had those three bruising fights with Muhammad Ali and two more with George Foreman, and he came across as almost gentle. He was not a big man; I was two or three inches taller, and I'm sure I had longer reach. Despite those advantages, I am thankful for never stepping in the ring with Joe.

Rocky Marciano was my first boxing hero, and Joe Frazier's style reminded me of the Brockton boxer. That is a compliment to both fighters. We lost the Champ too soon when he succumbed to liver cancer in 2011. I am grateful for my hours in his presence.

BOB HOPE

My father spent the better part of forty-five years in the movie business. He started as an usher at a theater in Galesburg, Illinois, at the age of fourteen. He was hooked before the first reel was over.

Dad grew to management positions and eventually became the owner of a small chain of drive-in movie theaters. It was during the war years that Ralph W. Lawler met many show business stars during the money-making war bond drives. Fred Astaire, Roy Rogers, James Cagney, Mae West, Roddy McDowell, Jerry Colonna, and Bob Hope were among the generous stars who lent their time to help raise money to support our fighting troops. Hope made several visits to Peoria and Toledo, Ohio, during the war. Dad would call him in California, and he would show up in the Midwestern city of choice.

In 1946, we took a family vacation. The war was over, we had a sparkling new car, and we were westward-bound. Bob Hope had invited Dad to visit Paramount Studios on Melrose Avenue in Hollywood. He was filming one of his famed *Road* shows with Bing Crosby and Dorothy Lamour. My family had never been west of Iowa. Hollywood, here we come!

The cross-country trip was a joyful adventure for Mom, Dad, my sister Jean, and me. We pulled up in front of the gates of the famed movie studio with our hearts in our throats. They had our names at the guard gate, and we were waved in with directions to the soundstage where Hope's movie was being filmed. We were then ushered in quietly to witness Miss Lamour playing the piano. In fact, she could not play a note, but someone who could was seated at a keyboard opposite her, playing away. Ah, a taste of movie magic.

Hope was in a nearby dressing room. We entered, and the clearly tired comedic actor brightened at the sight of my father. He warmly greeted the rest of the family with the kind, if not true, verse that he had heard so much about us. We were all on top of the world as the actor and my dad reminisced about their war bond drive experiences.

Bob suggested that we go over to the commissary to grab a bite to eat while he got back to work. We did that, and my mother almost passed out when she saw mega-star Cary Grant seated only a few feet away. That was my first taste of Hollywood, and I liked it. I never dreamed that I would spend almost thirty-five years working in and around the famed movie capital.

Most people today have no grasp of how popular a star like Bob Hope was. His career, which lasted close to eighty years, spanned everything from vaudeville and Broadway to network radio, television, and motion pictures. He was one of the most famous people in the world at the time.

My brush with Hope helped shape my goals and desires. One day in the 1960s, as I was coming through Corona on the way back home to Riverside after a basketball game, I spotted a large housing development looming to the left of the freeway. House lights were visible as far as the eye could see. "You know," I said to my pal, who was driving, "every single one of those people in all those houses has heard of Bob Hope. I'd like to be like that someday." It just popped out.

I saw Bob Hope one more time after that. Starting in the mid-'60s, he began hosting a very popular golf tournament in the Palm Springs area called the Bob Hope Desert Golf Classic. Hope was a devoted golfer and a lover of the Southern California desert sun. Anybody who was anybody in show biz was around for this colorful annual event, played over four different area golf courses. It was a unique ninety-hole tournament, rather than the customary seventy-two holes. Hollywood stars were matched up with the game's greatest players in the opening round. The list of stars to take part made up a virtual who's who of the business: Bing Crosby, Burt Lancaster, Fred Astaire, Phil Harris, Desi Arnaz, and even former President Dwight D. Eisenhower were there to tee 'em up. The parties around the tournament were as much fun as the star-studded games themselves.

In 1966, my great friend and co-worker Bob Steinbrinck had just purchased a new Plymouth convertible. We had press credentials for the tournament and motel reservations in the desert. The fun was about to begin. The short one-hour drive from Riverside to Palm Springs dropped us off on Palm Canyon Drive. We had the top down on Bob's hot new convertible. We looked around the crowded streets and saw nothing but Cadillacs, Mercedes, and limos. We positively looked like the hired help, rather than the hotshots we had thought we were.

We were there for the opening of the tournament the next day, and followed several favorites around the course. When I saw Bob Hope, the tournament's host, seated in his golf cart on the fairway, I ambled over to re-introduce myself. He was as gracious as could be. He certainly did not remember my visit to his dressing room at Paramount Studios, but he absolutely did remember the original Ralph Lawler during the World War II bond drives. It was nice, and my dad was very pleased to hear of it.

There is no question that Bob Hope was an inspiration to a young lad just getting his career going in Riverside, California.

JOHNNY UNITAS

The best player in the National Football League in the 1950s and 1960s was unquestionably Baltimore Colt quarterback Johnny Unitas, who re-wrote the NFL record book during his brilliant eighteen-year career. I caught Johnny at the absolute tail-end of that career.

Harland Svare had taken over for the legendary Sid Gillman as coach of the San Diego Chargers in 1971, and he had very limited success in his first year. He brought in veteran defensive lineman Deacon Jones and Lionel Aldridge to shore up the defense one year, and longtime superstar quarterback Johnny Unitas the next to run the offense. The problem was, Unitas was forty years old, Jones was thirty-five, and Aldridge was a beat-up thirty-two. It would have been a great move in 1968 that was not so great in 1973.

I must admit, it was exciting just being around Unitas. He still bore that special aura. We would see it at times on the field, when he would engineer a two-minute drill to perfection in closing out a half. Jones was still the occasional head-slapping, pass-rushing genius who had terrorized opponents in his heyday with the Los Angeles Rams. I was thirty-five at the time, and I never felt old around this 1973 Charger team.

Unitas had signed a two-year deal, and Svare believed he could lead the Chargers into the NFL playoffs. Johnny was friendly and never gave a hint that he knew how great he had been. He was unanimously known as the greatest quarterback the game had ever known. He had a young rookie named Dan Fouts behind him, preparing for his time to come. Then there was young veteran Wayne Clark, who was ready and available for whatever crumbs came his way.

The Chargers were buried in the Unitas debut, but he recovered nicely in a Game 2 win over O. J. Simpson and the Buffalo Bills in San Diego. The local fans felt that this old guy could still get the job done. Johnny passed for only 175 yards, but was very efficient in compiling a credible passer rating of 125.9. "Here we go Chargers, here we go!" Well, that was it. He was intercepted twice and sacked six times in a loss the following Sunday to the Cincinnati Bengals. The writing was on the wall. The amazing thing was, Unitas was just the same after a crushing humiliation as he was after a win. (Well, I only saw one of those.)

I learned a lot about pro football talking to veterans like Johnny and All-Pro offensive guard Walt Sweeney. Unitas would soon have a much more important pupil to worry about than me: Fouts came in to replace him after a faltering start in Game 4 in Pittsburgh against the Steelers.

A couple of weeks later, the team was in Cleveland for a date with the Browns. Unitas had gone from savior to mentor. Fouts was about to make his third start, and his first on the road. We were on the team bus heading to Cleveland Municipal Stadium. I was seated directly behind Unitas on the right side of the bus, and Fouts was directly across the aisle from the veteran football legend. Johnny turned to Dan, who was eighteen years his junior, and said, "Anything I can do for you today, just let me know."

The rookie looked squarely into Johnny's steel-blue eyes and nonchalantly replied, "No problem, I'm good." And he was. Not so much that day or that year, but down the line he would amass more total career passing yardage than Unitas. I knew from that instant on the team bus that Fouts was headed for greatness. He had a confident air that earned the confidence of those around him. I asked Johnny about the kid's response to his offer for help. I thought he might be a little offended. Not at all—Unitas said Fouts was going to be really good.

I was surrounded by two Hall of Fame quarterbacks. It was a very bad team, but still a privilege to be around those two. I broadcast the last game for Johnny Unitas and the first for Dan Fouts.

DEACON JONES

There were other memorable personalities on that woebegone Charger team. Svare had coached the Los Angeles Rams in the 1960s and was very familiar with All-Pro tight end Deacon Jones, who one year had sacked the quarterback twenty-two times under the young coach. The problem was, that was eight or nine years ago. Unitas had not completed 100 passes a season in either of his final two years in Baltimore. It would have been great to have all these guys together in 1968, but this was 1973.

Deacon had not lost his charismatic personality; he lit up any room the minute he entered it. I was on an elevator with him during a Charger road trip, headed down to the lobby. The elevator became crowded. Deacon and I were at the very back of the downward-moving boxcar. We arrived at the lobby level, and Deacon shouted, "Excuse me, lady with a baby coming through!" The crowd stepped aside as the smiling six-foot-five, 275-pound defensive end exited first.

If Deacon was in the room (or the elevator), you knew it. You certainly knew it if you were lined up opposite him on the football field. He was no longer the sideline-to-sideline menace he had been earlier in his career, but he still used that stunning head slap to distract blockers just long enough to give him a step and a shot at the opposing quarterback. I smile just thinking about Deacon Jones.

ARNOLD PALMER

Arnold Palmer burst onto the pro golf scene in the 1950s with much of the same gusto as Tiger Woods did forty years later. Like Woods, he went from U.S. Amateur Champion to Masters Champ, and on to reign as the game's greatest golfer before being challenged by Jack Nicklaus and then by Woods.

Arnold came to Peoria to put on an exhibition in July of 1960, having just won another Masters and the U.S Open. I was active with the local golf association, and they asked me to emcee the breakfast with Palmer before he put on a dazzling demonstration of his golfing skills. We sat together at the breakfast gathering, and it was clear that he was just like any other golfer there on that warm summer morning. I have never met a less pretentious person of fame.

Once we went out on the Peoria Country Club course, it was clear that he wasn't just any golfer. He hit every imaginable golf shot over the period of a thirty-minute demonstration. He did tricks with the golf club and the ball. He hit right-handed and even left-handed with his right-handed clubs. He would hit an amazing shot to the delight of the fans in the gathering and then look over at me with a sly, satisfied grin. I became a captain in Arnie's army on that day in Peoria.

PETE ROSE

There are few athletes that I enjoyed watching and covering more than baseball's Pete Rose. He was the spiritual and driving force for the Big Red Machine that led the Cincinnati Reds to back-to-back World Series Championships in the mid-'70s. I was covering the Phillies in Philadelphia at the time, and Rose and the Reds always seemed to be in the way of the Phillies' efforts to win the baseball title.

I was in the Reds' locker room night after night in awe of Pete Rose's handling of the media, who camped out at his locker knowing full well that some prized quotes would be coming their way. What amazed me was that Pete would sit there for forty-five minutes or an hour, giving a young pup reporter for a local weekly newspaper the same time and attention as the Major League beat reporters. He was always gracious, attentive, and absolutely fascinating.

There was not a whole lot that I enjoyed about working nightly television sports at WCAU Channel 10, but the highlight that stands out revolves around Pete and his attention-getting forty-four-game hitting streak in the summer of 1978. About the time he had hits in thirty-straight games, the media started paying attention to his possible assault on Joe DiMaggio's thirty-seven-year-old, and seemingly unassailable, fifty-four-game hitting streak. Once Rose reached forty games, the attention became intense. I had the TV station techs record each Cincinnati game. When Pete got a hit, I would show it on the 11:00 PM news. He had won me over, and I was rooting like mad for him.

He ended up ten games short of Joltin' Joe, but it was even more exciting than Hank Aaron's inevitable passing of Babe Ruth's 714 home run total. I'm hopeful this will open the doors of the Hall of Fame to the greatest baseball player I ever saw play the game: Pete Rose.

MIKE SCHMIDT

I went to the Phillies' spring training camp in Clearwater, Florida, for two or three years. It was such a treat to escape the Pennsylvania snow and cold in February to bask in the Florida sun.

Mike Schmidt was a promising young third baseman when I arrived in town in 1974. I was a little skeptical because he struck out so often; he whiffed 180 times one of those early years. He also smashed home runs at an alarming rate, while fielding his position with extraordinary skill.

Mike was baseball's best third baseman during my four years in the city. He was also an unspoiled superstar, just a down-home young man who loved talking about fishing as much as he did baseball. I enjoyed every exchange I ever had with him. One year, we played in an exhibition basketball game at the Spectrum, and I accidentally committed a hard foul on Schmidt. When I apologized in the locker room after the game, he looked at me funny and politely assured me that he was okay. I'm sure he was wondering how this middle-aged TV guy thought he could possibly hurt him.

The Phillies were becoming a very good team, and Mike Schmidt was rising from young prospect to superstar—but you would never know it, being around him.

ARNOLD SCHWARZENEGGER

WCAU-TV in Philadelphia produced a daily morning talk show in the mid-'70s that was hosted by my morning radio partner, Joel A. Spivak. The program aired each weekday morning from 10:00 AM to 11:00 AM. It was a popular stop for national and local personalities who had books, movies, or public appearances to sell. I had the privilege of filling in for Joel as program host when other commitments limited his availability.

Our guest one morning was bodybuilder Arnold Schwarzenegger. He was a six-time Mr. Olympia, the top title among the world's body builders and strongmen. Arnold's movie career was just getting underway, and he was on the program to promote his most noted acting role to date in the film *Stay Hungry*.

I was the guest-host for the day. It was clear from the minute we went on the air that our burly guest would rather be anyplace on earth than our Channel 10 studio. We struggled through the opening segment, with his responses curt and his heavy accent making what he did say difficult to understand. I thought, "Oh my God, we still have forty-five minutes to fill. No wonder Joel chose not to work today."

Luckily, things changed significantly after that first commercial break. The champion bodybuilder was from Austria, and when I mentioned to him that my mother was born in Austria, Arnold lit up like a Christmas tree. He asked where she was from, and I replied, "Timisoara." He had been there and knew the area well. We had a lively conversation for the remainder of the hour. It was amazing how that connection to his homeland changed the course of the interview.

I watched with great interest as his movie career blossomed. The interest grew further as he moved into politics, as governor of the great state of California.

BILL VEECK

The years have flown by, and each one has been filled with exciting, rewarding, and memorable experiences. Writing this book has brought back many long-forgotten exchanges with the famous and near-famous.

My first memorable encounter with fame was with Chicago White Sox owner Bill Veeck, who was an amazingly creative promoter. Veeck is probably best known for his stunt of sending the three-foot-seven-inch Eddie Gaedel to pinch-hit in a game for the St.

Louis Browns when he owned that American League Baseball team in 1951. Veeck had Gaedel wear the number "1/8." Not surprisingly, Gaedel walked in four pitches in his only Major League at bat, but Veeck received the publicity he was seeking in his battle with the St. Louis Cardinals for attention in the Gateway City.

When Veeck later became the owner of the White Sox, he faced a more popular city rival: the Cubs. He introduced a scoreboard that "exploded" each time a White Sox player hit a home run. He also was the first to put his players' names on the back of their uniforms. Attendance soared, and the team won their first pennant in forty years.

I was working for radio station WAAP in Peoria at the time, and we carried the White Sox broadcasts with the venerable Bob Elson calling the games. It was exciting for me to sit at the control console in Peoria to insert our local commercials into the game broadcasts (it did not take a whole lot to excite this broadcast newbie in those days).

The White Sox made a tour to their affiliate cities before each season, and Veeck himself was the team's principal personality. He hosted a luncheon in downtown Peoria for our radio station and our sponsors. I was thrilled to meet and interview him. I received a personal letter from the White Sox owner only days later, thanking me for my hospitality and gracious handling of our interview. He wished me well and hoped to see me at a White Sox game that season. I was thrilled speechless.

That summer, the radio station took a group of sponsors to Chicago for a Sox game. I was a part of the giddy traveling party on the trip to Comiskey Park. We arrived a couple of hours before the first pitch. I was walking along the nearly vacant concourse when I saw Bill Veeck approaching. He smiled broadly and shouted, "Ralph! Welcome to Chicago. How are things in Peoria?" I had seen the man just one time, and that had been two or three months earlier. Plus, we were one of twenty or thirty affiliate stations that he had visited. How he recognized me is a tribute to a man who remains one of the more unforgettable characters I have ever met.

Happily, Veeck was elected into the Baseball Hall of Fame in Cooperstown, New York, in 1991. ●

Chapter 22

Not for the Honors

WHEN I BROKE INTO BROADCASTING IN 1959 at a series of radio stations in my hometown of Peoria, Illinois, it seemed like I never went to work. Right from day one, I was just having fun, and I felt the same way in year sixty.

If that small-town Peoria boy dared to dream, it may have been about working in Chicago at a radio station like WGN. I certainly fantasized about calling Ernie Banks' Chicago Cub games; God knows I listened to enough of them in the late 1940s through the '50s.

Banks was my very first professional sports hero. I actually met him in the early 1970s, when we both appeared at a sports luncheon in San Diego. I sat across the table from him and was in such awe that I could barely speak. I would see Ernie again years later, while working for the Clippers in Los Angeles. He had moved to Marina Del Rey after a split with the Cubs organization, and had become a Clipper fan. I saw him at many games and remained a great fan of Number 14 right up until his death in 2015.

I idolized not only the Chicago Cub broadcasters, but also the trio of Peoria radio-talkers who described the basketball games of my Bradley University Braves. Hank Fisher, Tom Kelly, and Chick Hearn called the games home and away on three different radio stations. Hearn was the most popular of the trio, and he led the caravan west; Kelly, Bill King, Bob Starr, and I followed not many years behind.

Chick Hearn made an indelible impression on me. He had

broadcast some of my high school basketball games, and would serve as speaker at our annual Letterman's awards ceremony. He was a big fish in the small Peoria pond, on nightly TV on the local NBC affiliate. He went west in 1956 to broadcast USC football and basketball games in Los Angeles. No way did I dream that I would someday follow his trail. I just never thought much about life outside of Peoria. It was home, and I loved it there. Thinking back, if I had landed a job calling Bradley basketball games, I likely would never have left the Central Illinois city. It is a job that Dave Snell has excelled at on WMBD in Peoria since 1979. I've occasionally felt that I would happily exchange careers with Snell. That speaks to my love of Bradley as well as my hometown. The point is, winning national honors or being named to this Hall of Fame or that one was never a goal.

When I passed the thirty-five-year mark with the Clippers, people started using the word "legend" to describe me. I came to realize that what that really meant was "old." In 2011 or 2012, the acerbic *L.A. Times* columnist T. J. Simers asked me why I was not in the Basketball Hall of Fame in Springfield, Massachusetts. The thought had never entered my head. He felt I belonged there, and expressed that notion in a couple of columns. It frankly embarrassed me. He asked me how the process worked, and who chose the recipients of the Curt Gowdy Media Award. Again—no idea. I didn't even want to think about it.

One night before a game, team president Gillian Zucker pulled me aside in the media room at Staples Center and said she needed my signature on a document. I was flabbergasted to see that it was a nomination for a star on the Hollywood Walk of Fame. The team needed my permission to present it to the Hollywood Chamber of Commerce. That was the first time that I thought, "Hey, this is pretty cool." After all, those requests for a star on the Walk of Fame are not just rubber-stamped by the Chamber. I talked to one star recipient later who told me it took three tries to garner his spot among the almost 3,000 show biz luminaries who had been honored. I was amazed when I was granted a coveted spot in March of 2016. I think it was the greatest moment of my career.

I stood there at 1708 Vine Street, just a few feet away from the iconic corner of Hollywood and Vine where I had stood with my mother, father, and sister seventy years earlier on our family visit from

Peoria. I wished my parents could have been there with me on that special day. My sister was able to watch the ceremonies from her home in Bend, Oregon, as they were live-streamed from Hollywood. We had family who had come from as far away as London to share the memorable moment. Clipper coach Doc Rivers was also there, along with star player Chris Paul and a great collection of former Clipper players and coaches. Add some dear family friends, and it was a perfect day. We chartered a bus from the Marina to bring our family group to the event, and retreated afterwards to Lawry's Prime Rib on La Cienega for a special luncheon.

The floodgates had opened. I was named to the Peoria High School Sports Hall of Fame, the Bradley University Sports Hall of Fame, the Southern California Sports Broadcasters Hall of Fame, and the California Sports Hall of Fame. I was named California Sportscaster of the Year for 2018 and Los Angeles TV Play-by-Play Man of the Year for 2019, and I received the Vin Scully Lifetime Achievement Award in 2020. Wow. It was quite a whirlwind. I never saw any of it coming.

I had decided in the summer of 2017 that I would like to work two more years and then retire. The math just made too much sense. It would give me forty years with the Clippers, sixty years in broadcasting, and eighty years on earth thus far. The symmetry was irresistible. The Clippers and Fox Sports West were in on the plan, and we agreed to not reveal it until the following summer.

Early in that final season, Gillian Zucker made an unusual appearance at our broadcast location on game night as I was preparing for our telecast. She asked if I had a minute, and I knew it was always a good idea to have a minute when your boss asks for one. She informed me that a longtime season ticket holder was a big fan of mine. He wanted to honor me by working as my partner on a future Clipper telecast.

"The whole game?" I gasped. I asked if it was important to the team, and she affirmed that it was. I reluctantly agreed. Then Gillian asked if I wanted to know who it was. Of course I did. "Billy Crystal!" she exclaimed.

I went from dismayed to thrilled. Billy wanted to partner with me to honor my long tenure with the team. He spent a considerable amount of time preparing; he was taking this seriously. Fox Sports expressed some mild concern, but I said, "Hey, this man has hosted the

Academy Awards nine times and he's been coming to Clipper games since 1985. I think he can handle it."

Billy went on *Jimmy Kimmel Live* and said he had a major announcement: He would be working the Clipper-Laker telecast on January 31 with Ralph Lawler. "Oh me, oh my!" Kimmel said. It set the stage for a memorable night of television.

Meanwhile, Clipper communications chief Chris Wallace was busy preparing a case for my induction into the Naismith Memorial Basketball Hall of Fame. Recipients of the annual Curt Gowdy Media Award are not picked out of a hat; a campaign is launched behind the scenes with competing candidates being touted for the greatest basketball honor in sports media. I knew Chris was making an impressive presentation, but I refused to think about it too much for fear of setting myself up for a disappointment. Al McCoy, the Hall of Fame broadcaster for the Phoenix Suns, told me that the winner gets a phone call from Hall president John Doleva. When he got his call in 2007, the phone number calling wasn't familiar, so Al didn't answer the first couple of calls. He finally answered and received word that he was in the Hall of Fame.

Fast-forward to February 9, 2019. Jo and I were in our hotel room in Boston, prepping for that night's Clipper game against the Celtics. My cell phone rang and I checked it, noting that the number was from an unidentified caller in Springfield, Massachusetts. I told Jo that I thought I'd better take this call. Sure enough, it was John Doleva with word that I was the 2019 winner.

John asked that we not reveal the news right away—it would be announced the following weekend in Charlotte before the NBA All-Star game. We were invited to be there for the announcement ceremonies, and the award itself would be presented in September at the HOF in Springfield.

It was not easy to concentrate on my game prep the rest of the afternoon. The Clippers had just completed some major trades and would have a jumbled lineup against the Celtics that night. Almost predictably, Doc River's team was down 43–20 after the first quarter. Before long, they were 28 in the hole. They faced a 21-point deficit at the half. Newcomer Landry Shamet was making his debut after arriving from Philadelphia. He hammered down 4 dazzling 3-pointers to help the Clippers launch an amazing comeback. Final tally: the Clippers 123, the stunned Celtics 112. I would say it was the perfect end to a perfect day. The team still had two more games before the All-Star break.

Jo and I made our plans to fly from L.A. to Charlotte on February 14—happy Valentine's Day, sweetheart. We learned that our longtime friend, Marc Stein of the *New York Times*, was to be presented with the corresponding award for print media. Marc had long ago covered the Clippers' beat in Los Angeles for the *Daily News*. We were happy to share the honors with him on that special day. It was humbling to be on the stage with such a great cast of Hall of Famers.

The season was a blur from that point on. Teams and people around the league made a fuss on my final visit to each city. The honors came in many forms.

Philly general manager Elton Brand presented me with a signed Dr. J sneaker.

A 76er fan took the time to craft a remarkable bobblehead in my likeness, and the Clippers gave away "talking" bobbleheads to fans attending my final regular season game.

Clipper sixth man extraordinaire Montrezl Harrell amazed us time and again. Jo and I would always be among the first to board the Clipper charter flight. We would be seated in our comfortable first-class seats in the second to the last row of the customized aircraft. Trez had been making a series of shirts honoring old Ralph, and he would proudly come back to our seats before take-off to show us his latest creation. It amazes me to this day that he went to such trouble three or four times with a different photo on his shirt each time. I am sorry to see him bouncing around the league now. I wish he could have been a Clipper for life.

Miami coach Eric Spoelstra sent along a prized box of Cuban Cigars.

Coach Pop in San Antonio offered a precious bottle of his private reserve wine, Rock & Hammer. The pinot noir is from a winery in Oregon where it is made for him and him alone, and the only way to get it is to have him give a bottle to you.

Former Clipper ace marketeer Mitch Huberman honored me with a special bottle of my favorite bourbon.

The Los Angeles Chargers invited Jo and me to a game as a re-membrance of my long-ago work for the team. On the field before the game, we were presented with a Charger Jersey, and then brunched in the owners' suite before making a brief appearance on the radio cast of the game. They invited me to call a few plays. I politely declined. I only work when I am totally prepared.

The Fontana Motor Speedway invited us to attend a major NA-SCAR event during my final season. I had broadcast similar events fifty years earlier and loved my association with the motor sport. I had the honor of introducing the drivers to the massive crowd. It was a wonderful feeling to touch base with a treasured time from my past. They even provided us with a police escort to get to the speedway. Time was precious, in as much as we had a Clipper game at Staples Center that night.

It was just one special moment after another, and it was even more special being able to share it with Jo.

In late March, Doc Rivers arranged for a surprise dinner for us in Minneapolis. The entire team was there, lying in wait. Brian Sie-man got us to the restaurant on some ruse. When we arrived, we were guided through a doorway and found the entire Clipper team waiting there. Each player made his way up to us to congratulate me on the career that began way before any of them were born. Wow.

The team played its final road game of the regular season on Sun-day, April 7, in Oakland against the Warriors. On the flight home, another surprise awaited us. Doc was by our seats in the back of the plane, talking to Jo and me as he often did during flights. Suddenly, we looked up to see all the players coming toward us down the aisle in a line. The rookies were pushing a cart that carried a large "Happy Retirement" cake. This was such a caring group of players. They over-achieved not only on the court, but off the court, as well.

There were many melancholy moments in that final year. I had enjoyed the decade or so of working with Brian, the Clipper radio voice. He was a close friend. Jo and I considered him and his family as a part of our own extended family. Our final times together made my heart ache. I had pushed hard to have him named as my replace-ment on television simultaneous with my retirement announcement, but the team was not ready to do that. It frustrated me at the time. I think owner Ballmer had a process that he wanted to go through to be certain that the choice was the right one. The longer it went, the more I feared Brian would not get the job.

Brian and his wife, Amy, invited us out to dinner a few nights before we packed up for our move to Oregon in June 2019. At dinner, Brian told us that he'd gotten the job! It brought tears to my eyes then and still gives me goosebumps now as I write these words. I will always treasure the hours we spent together on and off the air.

The final game of the regular season was held on April 10: Clippers versus the Utah Jazz. I was poised to spend that night on the air with Bill Walton. I was so hoping that both teams would be secure in their playoff standing so that the game itself would have little meaning aside from offering some entertainment. Happily, it worked out just that way. It was so nice looking across the court during the game and seeing our three kids, Dawn, Ralph, and David, seated in our seats in section 119. It was a glorious night, indeed.

There were so many people with whom we wanted to share that night. The Clippers were very generous in providing a special luxury box for our gang, as well as offering to host a private party in a large room at Staples Center after the game. It was just fun, fun, and more fun.

The fact of retirement did not really hit us until we made the permanent move from Marina Del Rey to Bend, Oregon. It seemed like things were just as they had been for years: a basketball season in L.A. and a summer in Oregon. We had the Hall of Fame induction to attend in September, and that would be my final appearance as a professional broadcaster. The thought was a little daunting. I spent some time that summer preparing my acceptance speech. They wanted it carefully timed and read from a teleprompter.

We flew to Boston and drove a rental car the ninety miles to Springfield on the eve of my induction into the hallowed Hall. Our three kids were there as well, along with assorted family and friends. Bill Walton and his wife Lori came, of course. Bill hosted us for lunch just before my midday rehearsal for the night's event. God love him, Bill was always there when needed.

At that evening's gala, my speech went off without a hitch. I was happy to have it behind me, as it was a more emotional experience than I had anticipated. I thought of my old high school basketball coach, Dawdy Hawkins, as I spoke before the large assemblage of basketball royalty that night. He had seemed to dislike me as a player because he thought I was a "rich kid." The old coach passed some years ago, but I could not help but wonder what he would have thought if he could see me now.

That was the ultimate chapter to close my sixty-year career in broadcasting. Except for the day my sweet Jo agreed to marry me and the day my son was born, it was the proudest moment of my life.

Chapter 23

It's All About the Fans

FANS OFTEN ASKED ME how I could withstand working for Donald T. Sterling during his nearly thirty years as owner of the Clippers. I will admit that it had its challenges. I persevered with the firm belief that I was not working for the team owner or even for the team. I was working for the fans. I carried that belief through my fortieth year as the team's broadcaster.

Hall of Fame NBA coach Don Nelson told me years ago that the secret to coaching success was that a coach must love his players. I applied that belief to my role as a team broadcaster. I had an abiding love affair with the Los Angeles Clipper fan base. They are a special breed. This faithful group endured eight seasons during which the team won fewer than twenty games. The low ebb occurred during the 1986–1987 season, when the team won only twelve games and lost seventy. Those numbers will test the resolve of even the most ardent of fans. It would be so quiet some nights at the old L.A. Sports Arena that I found myself using almost a golf announcer voice for fear of disturbing the players or the referees. There was just nothing to cheer about. The team would urge fans to come out to see Dominique Wilkins, Michael Jordan, and Larry Bird. They, of course, played for the visiting teams, but it was more attractive than asking fans to buy tickets to see Benoit Benjamin.

There were some nights when I would sit there in my courtside press row seat and wonder why on earth even the 5,000 to 7,000 fans in attendance were in the stands. God love 'em, they cared. It was easy being a Laker fan. Like in Florida, where it was easy to be an NFL fan of the Tampa Bay Buccaneers—but not so easy following the Jacksonville Jaguars—it took a special resolve to hang in there year after year with the Clippers, who spent thirteen years on the West Coast before finally reaching the NBA playoffs. They averaged less than twenty-eight wins a season over that dreadful span. And yet, the loyal fans kept coming back for more. They would believe in Norm Nixon and then Mike Woodson, Loy Vaught, Bo Kimble, Reggie Williams, Benoit Benjamin, Gary Grant, Danny Manning, and/or Ron Harper.

Los Angeles is a unique sports marketplace where everything comes in twos: two Major League baseball teams, two National Hockey League teams, two NBA teams, two pro soccer teams, and now two National Football League teams. Add in the historic collegiate sports programs at UCLA and USC, and you can get a taste of the ferocious nature of the local sports landscape. There is no other marketplace like it. The battle for the local sports dollar is intense. The Lakers had a head start of almost twenty-five years when the Clippers sailed into the City of Angels in 1984. The ball club was hardly noticed. We would rejoice when the team got a rare mention in Allan Malamud's Notes on a Scorecard column in the *Herald Examiner*, or a reference from Jim Healy on his wildly popular daily sports report on the radio. Somehow, people found the Clippers.

Malcolm in the Middle star Frankie Muniz was a stalwart at the games early in the Clippers re-birth in Los Angeles. I think the team's first season ticket holder after the move from San Diego in 1984 was famed Academy Award filmmaker James L. Brooks. He recalled driving on the freeway when he heard the announcement on his car radio that the Clippers were moving from San Diego to Los Angeles. He pulled off the freeway, found a phone booth, called the Clipper office, and ordered his season tickets. He has been courtside ever since. We still stay in touch. He wrote me: "I read your tweets as if they were religious beads." Settle down, James.

Comedic genius Billy Crystal joined up in 1985 on the opposite side of the court from Brooks, first at the L.A. Sports Arena and then at Staples Center. I am sure that both will be front and center when the team moves into the grand, new Intuit Dome in 2024. Billy really gets into it during the playoffs. We will exchange a half-dozen messages a night some games.

Actress, director, and producer Penny Marshall was a huge NBA fan who first fell in love with the Lakers and then the Clippers. When the two teams played games on the same day at Staples Center, she would see both games. I suspect that she would have been there for a third game if one had been played. We have missed the *Laverne and Shirley* star since her passing in 2018. She was truly one of a kind.

James Goldstein is another fan who loves to double-dip when the Clippers and Lakers play a day-night double-header at Staples Center. Fashion and architecture are his business interests, but his life's passion is NBA basketball. He not only attends virtually every Clipper and Laker home game, he also bounces around the country to catch key NBA playoff games wherever they may be played. Fans will see the distinctively clad Goldstein in a front row seat at game after game. He typically attends over a hundred games a year.

Darrell Bailey, aka Clipper Darrell, has made the Los Angeles Clippers his life's purpose. There have been many nights when the Clipper team plane would arrive at the charter terminal on the south side of LAX and Darrell would be there at 2:00 in the morning to welcome the team home. I can hear him even now, leading cheers at Staples Center: "Let's go, Clippers!"

There have been famous fans around the league over the years. Robin Ficker was a menace to teams playing the Washington Bullets/Wizards in Landover, Maryland, before their move to the MCI Center in the nation's capital. The Maryland attorney was seated right behind the visiting team bench, and he would berate the visiting team coach and players unmercifully during every time-out. It was often hilariously funny but sometimes brutally personal. I can tell you that visiting players were often listening more to Ficker than to their coach during critical time-outs.

Leon the Barber was a presence at Detroit Piston games from their days at Cobo Hall, to the Pontiac Dome, and then for years at the Palace of Auburn Hills, where he became an institution. He hurled vile invective at visiting teams that got the fans fired up. He was very much a part of the Bad Boy Pistons who won back-to back NBA titles in 1989 and 1990. They just do not make them like Ficker or the Barber anymore. Players and coaches of the era remember both of them very well, if not fondly.

When I talk about loving and working for the fans, these are not the fans I have in mind. I am not talking about the stars in the court-side seats or the luxury boxes. I am still amazed by the Clipper fans and their devotion. As Jo and I walked through Staples Center during that fortieth and final season, and fans shouted out: "We love you, Ralph." I turned to Jo and pointed out that a year from now, nobody would even notice us if we walked through the stands.

Members of the media have pointed out that my record over forty seasons was whatever number of wins and way more losses. I respond that I have never lost a game. Winning and losing was never my job. I was there to connect with the fans. That was my focus each time that I went on the air for 3,200-and-some games. The game was the thing. Sometimes they were good, and sometimes they were bad. I mean, really bad. But my job was the same. I was to keep the fans in-formed and, as best I could, keep them entertained. I loved those loyal Clipper fans and NBA fans throughout the country and all over the world. NBA League Pass extended the reach of a team's local telecast literally around the world. But it was those local fans who patiently sat through twelve-win, fifteen-win, and seventeen-win seasons and came back year after year thinking, hoping, praying that better times were just beyond the next jump ball. I miss those insanely loyal fans more than anything else when it comes to my long career in the game of basketball. I firmly believe that their reward is just around the corner. They were *my* reward.

FOURTH QUARTER

MY FAVORITE PICK-AND-ROLL DUO

Chapter 24

The Big Redhead (Part Two)

SADLY, WHEN ABC/ESPN WON THE NBA broadcast rights in 2002, they prohibited Bill Walton from working our local broadcasts. It would never be the same again. I went from the free-spirited Bill Walton to Michael Smith, which could be compared to going from the Grateful Dead to the Book of Mormon.

Bill and I stayed in touch in the ensuing years, but I missed our game-to-game camaraderie. I missed everything about Bill.

Jo and I will never forget a quiet off-night at home during the 2003–2004 season. The phone rang. It was Bill, calling to invite us on an all-expense-paid white water rafting trip down the Colorado River through the majestic depths of the Grand Canyon. It would span eighteen days and seventeen nights, with no electricity, no cell phones, and no restrooms. We would sleep out on the banks of the river in tents each night.

I was thrilled, but said I had to check with my wife. I had done some camping in years gone by, but Jo thought roughing it was a hotel room with a faulty TV remote. I went down the hall and told Jo about the trip. "Great," she exclaimed, to my surprise. God love her, she was all for it, but with one caveat: since there would be no electricity, she would need a butane-powered curling iron for her hair. I raced to call Bill with our grateful acceptance. He wanted to know about our alcohol of choice. Vodka with cranberry juice was the response, and he promised we would never run dry. Now Jo was really getting into it.

We bought new hiking shoes and clothes to wear in variable weather, from warm and dry to cold and wet. I found a butane hair curler. Truth be known, when Jo woke up the first day in our tent, she dutifully curled her hair that morning—but never again for the next two and a half weeks.

It was a life-changing experience. Bill's guests were wildly eclectic: we had a mail carrier, a massage therapist, and the longtime drummer from the Grateful Dead. Bill and his wife, Lori, were the only two people we had known previously, but by the end of the trip we were one tight, close-knit family. There were tears aplenty as we bid our fondest farewells in Flagstaff, Arizona. This was yet another symbol of Bill Walton's unending generosity. He paid for it all. There's no way to repay him for what was truly the experience of a lifetime.

In May of 2007, I underwent prostate cancer surgery. It was a total success, but the recovery was slow and cumbersome. Our first visitors at our home in Laguna Niguel were Bill and Lori Walton. They were also our second visitors. It was a genuine show of concern and deep friendship, and it meant the world to me. As we settled down together in our living room, Bill jumped up and raced to his car in the driveway. He was out there for a good fifteen minutes before returning. Turns out, he had spent the hour-plus drive from San Diego to Orange County rolling joints for me. He figured I would be in some pain from the surgery and hoped this might help. He had put his twenty or so carefully rolled "presents" in a blue plastic container, and then misplaced it. He was out there looking under and between the car seats, inside the glove compartment, everywhere. He finally found it and gleefully presented me with the container. I can assure you, it was appreciated and put to good use.

A week or two later, the Waltons returned. I was now able to join the group at a nearby dinner spot in Dana Point. It was really my first time out since the surgery, and we had a delightful time. Bill asked Jo what she was up to this off-season, and she said she wanted to get back to some bicycle riding. Now, Bill is a prolific bicycle rider. He has fused ankles and fused vertebrae in his back, and before each surgery he would ask if he'd still be able to ride his bike. I enjoy going out on a casual bike ride; Bill enjoys riding his beautiful, ultra-lightweight custom bike from San Francisco to San Diego, or through the length of Death Valley.

Well, when Jo mentioned that she was going to purchase a new bike that very week, Bill said he had a place in San Diego that would take great care of her. "Don't worry about it," he said. He gave us an address and said we should be there next week to pick up Jo's new two-wheeler. When we made the trip to purchase and pick up the bicycle, the salesman informed us that Bill had taken care of it. It was yet another display of the big man's big heart and endless generosity.

Bill and I both became very busy in the years ahead. He was all over the place with his burgeoning broadcast career. He was a successful motivational speaker who was in great demand, and he had ever-broadening business interests and did a massive amount of little-publicized charity work. Meanwhile, Jo and I were busily looking for new horizons, first in the La Quinta area and then in Bend, Oregon. We spent as much time as possible with our family, which had grown to three kids, seven grandkids, and eventually two great-grandchildren. Bill and Lori Walton hosted our family at their home for one of my birthdays; we hosted them in our family Christmas celebration. They were family.

Bill would get busier and busier over the years. He had another date with physical misfortune as he suffered from debilitating back pain in 2009, born out of an injury during his college days. His pain was insufferable. He wrote about it in his best-selling book, *Back from the Dead: Searching for the Sound, Shining the Light, and Throwing It Down*. Bill's recovery from the surgery was slow and painstaking, and Jo and I were among the first to see him after the procedure. It was such a pleasure to be there for him, as he had been for me two years earlier after my own surgery.

We had many a great time together. The four of us shared a balmy New Year's Eve at Times Square in New York in the '90s. One evening, sometime after the glorious years of working together on the Clipper broadcasts, the Waltons were visiting us at our home in Orange County. I told Bill I was reading this great book about Bevo Francis. "Who?" Bill replied. I was surprised; Walton was an avid student of basketball history, and Bevo was one of the game's first high-scoring big men. He once scored 113 points in a game for the tiny Rio Grande College in Ohio in the 1950s.

Bill confessed to have never heard of Bevo. I teased that his master mentor, John Wooden, would be very disappointed by his lack of historical hoop knowledge. Bill said, "Let's find out." He grabbed his phone and dialed a number he had called almost daily since leaving the Westwood UCLA campus in 1974. He was calling Coach Wooden while seated in our backyard in Laguna Niguel.

As usual, the query to the old coach about Bevo Francis went to the answering machine. Bill left a message: "Have you ever heard of some guy named Bevo Francis?" Bill assured me that he would have a return call from the coach sometime tomorrow. Sure enough, he called me the next day and excitedly played Coach Wooden's recorded response. In essence, Wooden said he was shocked that Bill did not know about Bevo, the six-foot-nine scoring phenom from Rio Grande College in Ohio. He had been one of the most famous basketball players of the 1950s. Had Bill not learned anything in his years at UCLA? It was delicious.

I believe I only beat Bill to a check one time. Jo and I planned an afterparty following by 2,500th Clipper game. Bill was at the game to take part in the halftime ceremonies commemorating the event at Staples Center. We invited family and friends to join us after the game at the nearby Palm in downtown Los Angeles. We rushed to get there before Bill and Lori, and I spoke directly with the restaurant manager—the dinner bill was to be given to *us* at the evening's end. I told the manager that Bill Walton would try to find a way to pay, but under no circumstances should he be allowed to. The manager understood and passed the word to all the appropriate people. Sure enough, Bill insisted that he was paying for the dinner and drinks for the twenty or twenty-five people in attendance, but he was rebuffed. Thank you, Palm Restaurant! We finally were able to treat Bill and Lori Walton.

I think Bill believes I am somehow responsible for his long and successful broadcast career. That is certainly not the case, but he seems determined to pay me back again and again and again. He was there to offer an impassioned hyperbolic introduction when I was inducted into the California Sports Hall of Fame in 2016. The event was at a casino in the Palm Springs area, and Bill didn't realize that he was going to be asked to introduce me. It made no matter; he extolled on and on for no less than forty-five fascinating minutes. It left me time for little more than: "Thanks, Bill." He was also there for my Naismith Memorial Basketball Hall of Fame induction in 2019. He would be there in an instant if I needed him today, tonight, or tomorrow. I hope he knows the same is true if the roles were reversed.

Big Bill was truly honored in October of 2018, when a Boys and Girls Club basketball court was named in his honor. His generosity in his hometown of La Mesa had made it possible. Jo and I flew back from Hawaii in time to share the prized moment with him and his family. This was right at the beginning of my fortieth and final year with the Clippers. It was a melancholy year, for sure; Jo and I would make our final visit to New York's Madison Square Garden, not to mention Boston, Chicago, Washington, Philadelphia, Indianapolis, San Antonio, Miami, and all of our favorite stops along the NBA trail.

The Clippers were extremely supportive and determined to make it a special year for Jo and me. I really had only one serious request: I wanted to work one more game with Bill Walton. It worked out that we broadcast my final regular season game on April 10, 2019. Bill was totally prepared—he had a different outfit each time we came back from a time-out. He also had a long series of gifts to present me with. The dearest one was a painting he'd had a friend produce that was basically the story of my life. To this day, I don't know how Bill found out some of the details, but they are all there in that priceless painting.

Words are inadequate to describe what the Big Redhead has meant to my life. Bill wrote an impassioned letter to the Basketball Hall of Fame in the late 1990s that validates his standing as the greatest friend a man could ever hope to have. Here it is, word for word:

TO: The Naismith Memorial Basketball Hall of Fame
FROM: Bill Walton, member of your Hall of Fame since 1993

It is the greatest honor and proudest privilege of my life to nominate, by means of this letter, Ralph Lawler for enshrine-ment into the Naismith Memorial Basketball Hall of Fame as the surefire winner of this year's Curt Gowdy Award . . .

I have known Ralph for literally my entire tenure as a member of the NBA Family—dating back thirty-three years now . . . When I first joined the NBA as a player for the Port-land Trail Blazers in 1974, Ralph was the broadcaster for

"the enemy"—our dreaded rival, the Philadelphia 76ers . . .
Ralph called some of the biggest games of my career, and even
though he was working the game from the angle of his team,
we developed an instant rapport and bond based on trust, dig-
nity, civility, human decency, and professionalism—all quali-
ties that Ralph has in abundance and that I'm still seeking to
acquire . . .

Little did I know then the simple twists of fate that would
soon bring Ralph and I closer together than any relationship
that I have ever forged through the game that is my life . . .
I joined the San Diego Clippers in 1979; and by then Ralph
was that team's broadcaster . . . The rest is history as my career
disintegrated and Ralph's blossomed . . . Yet through all the
trials and tribulations of my failed venture with the Clippers,
Ralph remained the beacon of light and hope that allowed
me to survive . . . Our relationship soon came to cover every
aspect of our lives—professional, social and personal . . .

When my playing days were sadly over due to crippling
injuries, it was a chance encounter at the local convenience
store on the beach in San Diego that forever changed my life
. . . I was a dazed and confused ex-athlete, disabled and dis-
tanced from the love of my life . . . When I stumbled up behind Ralph in the checkout line, I could not have been a more
pathetic or pitiful figure . . . Ralph, as he has so often, took
solace on this rudderless soul and guided me step by step to-
wards a new life and an unheard-of career in broadcasting that
has now lasted seventeen years . . . Ralph and I did thirteen
years of Clipper basketball together . . . Because of Ralph, it
was the best thirteen years of my life . . .

Today, Ralph's career as a broadcaster has now spanned
more than fifty years . . . In that time he has done everything;
including but not limited to being one of only a handful of
broadcasters who have called the action in all four of our major
sports; duties with the NCAA and ABA; long-running forays
in golf, tennis, track and field, auto racing, boxing, and college
football overfill his resume . . . But it is Ralph's twenty-eight
years—and counting—and nearly 2,200 NBA games—and

counting—as the voice of the Clippers, the public face and persona of the franchise, that brings me to you today . . .

Ralph Lawler is the greatest broadcaster, human being, and friend that I have ever known . . . Over the past thirty-three years he has taught me more about everything (particularly life itself) than I ever learned from anyone else . . . Ralph has always done this, not as a favor to me or for his own self-interest, but because this is the kind of man Ralph Lawler truly is—humble, selfless, honorable, faithful, dedicated, loyal, caring, trustworthy, concerned, involved, and honest . . .

Ralph is the most unique of media personalities . . . He is constantly able to perfectly capture all the action, the whole time clearly and concisely transmitting the real story to his audience in a bright, joyful, hopeful, positive, dramatic, information-filled, and entertaining fashion that never draws attention to himself . . . With Ralph, it's always about the game and what he can do to make this more enjoyable—so that other people can have the time of their life . . .

With his incredible talent, Ralph has fused an unparalleled work ethic and determination, a razor-sharp wit, a computer-like mind, and a passion for creativity and excellence that makes every night out with Ralph seem like a glorious religious experience . . . He is the smartest, quickest, funniest, most thoughtful, most compassionate, most articulate, most insightful, entertaining, innovative, and intriguing broadcaster that I have ever heard . . . He is also my best friend . . .

Ralph Lawler has given his life to make this world and our game of basketball a better place . . . Ralph has never asked for anything in return . . . Instead, I am here, insisting on justice and accountability in the scorebook of life . . . Ralph would be embarrassed and ashamed if he even knew I was submitting him for this ultimate honor . . . The Naismith Memorial Basketball Hall of Fame is a most special place reserved for the select few who have actually changed and made history . . . No one that I know of fits this description better than Ralph Lawler . . .

If he doesn't qualify for enshrinement here at the Naismith

Memorial Basketball Hall of Fame right now, then we should all act forthrightly to disband this association and affiliation immediately . . .

Bill Walton
Hall of Fame, 1993

Fortunately, the Hall did not disband. A dozen years later, the call came and I joined some of my life's greatest heroes in the Basketball Hall of Fame in Springfield, Massachusetts, where our beloved game was born.

Chapter 25

My Sweet Jo

AS I STATED IN MY BASKETBALL HALL OF FAME induction speech in September of 2019, my wife, Jo, is the "oxygen in every breath I take." There is no way I would have or could have had the career I've had without her support and inspiration.

I met the beautiful young Jo Parent in San Diego in the fall of 1979, at a fast-start training class offered by regional realtor Forest E. Olson. Jo was a former beauty queen from a small town in Indiana—emphasis on "beauty" and not on "former." I'm talking about a curvaceous, green-eyed enchantress whose smile turned cloudy skies clear and blue.

Jo laughed at my jokes and shared my passion for life. On top of all that, she was a die-hard San Diego Clipper fan. So, there we were, two aspiring real estate students who were, by a fateful coincidence, assigned to work in the same office in suburban La Mesa. I had enjoyed my first year with the San Diego Clippers, but quickly realized it was not going to be easy living on $25,000 a year in this pricey Southern California paradise. The idea was that I would augment my meager basketball income by listing and selling houses in the summer, while hopefully picking up some valuable buyers and sellers during the NBA season through the coming and going of players and coaches through the Clippers revolving door.

At the time, Jo and I were both married, but neither of us was happy. Our respective marriages were train wrecks waiting to happen.

It was October of 1979 when we started working together; less than two years later, we were both separated from our spouses and falling more in love by the day.

My real estate concept was working well. I had success dealing with Clippers players and coaches. Jo branched out into new home sales as I continued balancing my dual careers. It did not take long to get out of balance. When Donald Sterling bought the Clippers on May 24, 1981, I received a phone call from the manager of the team's new radio station about a month later. I was probably making about $30,000 a year by that time, and I imagined that he was going to sweeten my deal. Well, not exactly. He felt that I sounded like a non-partisan network announcer, and he wanted a more zealous Clipper advocate. He was going to use veteran NBA announcer Jerry Gross to call the Clipper games. So be it.

Jo was there immediately to rescue my bruised ego. I was lucky that I had a back-up career in real estate. Forest E. Olson had been purchased by real estate mega-giant Coldwell Banker, and it advanced our stock as realtors. The regional head of the company was an old friend named Tom Williams. He was a former basketball coach at Ramona High School in Riverside. I had broadcast many of his team's games two decades earlier. It really is a small world, isn't it?

Tom was quick to sense that my skills were better utilized in management. He set me up as assistant manager at the CB office in Encinitas. I assumed that my broadcasting career was over.

Jo applauded my every step. We would spend as much time together as our busy schedules would allow. She had a teenage daughter and a teenage son, and my son had just graduated from high school when I moved on from my marriage of almost twenty years. It was not an easy time for any of us. A wise old friend had told me years earlier that divorce stains your soul for life. He seems wiser to me now than he did then. Nonetheless, we all moved on. I was so in love with Jo that it was easy to care for and love young Dawn and David as if they were my own flesh and blood. It was a little more awkward with my eighteen-year-old son, Ralph. He still lived with his embittered mother, and that made the changes in his life more cumbersome.

One day, Jo and I accidentally ran into Donald Sterling and his assistant general manager, Patti Simmons, while walking the warm sand beach in Del Mar. My real estate office had listed a spectacular beach-front home nearby, and I'd abandoned my spartan studio apartment to serve as a house sitter while we endeavored to sell this prestigious property amid a tight money environment that included 19 percent mortgage rates. So there we were, walking in the bright summertime sunshine, when we bumped into Sterling and his friend. It was a per-plexing happenstance. The uneasiness diminished when I invited them to join us for a glass of wine in the jacuzzi back at this home on the beach. They seemed delighted. I did not know what in the hell we were doing, but figured it would be interesting. It certainly was that, and more.

We were having a grand old time when Sterling suddenly asked, "Why aren't you broadcasting our games, anymore?" I thought, "What?" I explained that the team had changed radio stations and the manager there hadn't wanted me back. Sterling said he could change that, and instructed me to call his new general manager, Ted Podleski, the next day to remedy the error.

They left, and Jo and I were dumbfounded and in utter disbelief over the unlikely events of the day. The circumstances had to fall in perfect alignment for this to have happened. What if we had walked north on the beach instead of south? What if we had jumped in the pool instead of walking on the beach at all? My Clipper career would never have resumed. Instead of forty years, it would have totaled three. However, there were still plenty of potholes in the road ahead.

Jo and I continued our whirlwind romance. We would sneak off for weekends in Mexico or head up to the mountains. She was having great success selling new homes, and I was back where I belonged as the voice of the San Diego Clippers. I was very happy with my life. The road ahead looked straight and smooth—and it was, for two basketball seasons. Jo and I would often join Sterling and Patti for a drink or a bite after games at the San Diego Sports Arena. It was Don and Ralph, Patti and Jo. I would talk openly about trying to coax Jo into marrying me, and Sterling would exclaim, "Why would you want to do that?" It was the most normal relationship I had with the Clipper owner.

Things were relatively normal on the basketball side of things, too. Paul Silas lasted just one more year, and then Jim Lynam replaced him. I had known Jimmy from his days coaching at St. Joseph's College in

Philly, and I sold him a home that had belonged to former San Diego Charger quarterback John Hadl. I became close to his entire family. His wife Kay and my sweet Jo got along famously. Their daughter, Dei, wound up attending UCLA, and kept stats for me on our Clipper broadcasts in the early 1990s. She went on to a highly successful career in radio and television in Philadelphia.

When Sterling moved the Clippers from San Diego to Los Angeles in 1984, I did not accompany the team on its journey north, and I lost the Clipper job for the second time in four years. Enough was enough—I was through with the Clippers and the NBA. Coldwell Banker promoted me to branch manager at their thriving office in the North San Diego community of Poway. Jo was selling new homes nearby. Our new life looked very promising.

Early in the Clippers' first season in L.A., general manager Carl Scheer called to ask me to work a series of games on the radio while my replacement, Eddie Doucette, switched over to television. It would total ten to twelve games. At first, I considered it a chance to augment my income, but it became more than that by season's end, when the team asked me to come back full-time—again. I was conflicted this time around. I was enjoying having a real estate office of my own, and I had been promised a promotion to vice president by Coldwell Banker. A very clear career path was laid out for me. I was not sure I wanted to go through this Clipper thing again, and I was certain I did not like the idea of moving 120 miles away from my dear Jo. She knew my heart was tied more to basketball than to real estate, and strongly urged me to give my dream one more chance. She is the reason I made the move back to the Clippers full-time in 1985, and she is the reason my six-year Clipper career advanced to forty years.

It was not easy maintaining our relationship from afar. Jo would come up to visit weekly at first. We would talk on the phone daily, often for hours at a time. Time flew by, and her daughter was soon married and pregnant with twins. I would speed down to Rancho Bernardo to babysit as needed. I became "Grandpa Ralph," and loved it. However, I was having less success keeping the sparks alive in my relationship with Jo. Her outgoing personality and innate beauty was attracting other suitors in San Diego. We had devolved into an off and on relationship. I would try to find female companionship in L.A., but it did not take long for other women to realize that my heart was not available.

After the Rodney King riots in 1992, I moved from Los Angeles to Laguna Niguel, cutting the distance between us in half. Jo made a big career shift in 1993 by taking a management position with a growing home builder in Newport Beach, but she kept her home in San Diego. It was a daunting commute, and she often opted to spend the night at my home, which was only fifteen minutes away from her new office. There had been a method to my madness when I showed her the want ad describing the job in the *Orange County Register*.

Jo wound up moving in with me full-time in the late '90s. I was thrilled, even though she said she had no interest in getting married again. That suddenly changed one night in the summer of 2000, as we sailed on an NBA-sponsored cruise of the Caribbean.

Everybody in the L.A. Clipper organization knew how daffy I was over Jo, but no one knew she had agreed to marry me. One day on the team bus on an early-season road trip in Phoenix, Johnny Doyle, the team's strength and conditioning coach, announced that he was getting married in the spring to a former Clipper dancer. "Oh Johnny," I teased, "that good-looking girl is not going to marry you. I'll be married before you will." Johnny knew how long I had sought Jo's hand, and he retorted, "Yeah right, I've got fifty dollars that says that won't happen." Jo and I had not set a date, and no one outside of our family knew we were engaged, but I took the bet.

In the days and weeks ahead, the bet doubled to $100, then $200, then $400, and then $800 before finally settling in at $1,000. There was one problem: Johnny had not announced his wedding date yet, and Jo was anxious to firm up our plans. I kept saying we couldn't set a date until we knew when our betting foe was getting married. I asked everyone in our traveling party if they had heard any details about the Doyle wedding plans. Not a whisper. Jo had dragged her feet for years, and now she was getting frustrated by the delays in planning.

Finally, a trusted source whispered to me that Johnny was to be married the first weekend in June. There went Jo's hopes of a June wedding. We decided on May 26, 2001, instead. Still, nobody with the team knew. When Donald Sterling held a team Christmas party on the penthouse/rooftop of his cherished Sterling Towers on Wilshire Boulevard in Beverly Hills, Jo and I sidled up to Johnny and his fiancée, and I said Jo had something she wanted to say. She told them she wanted them to be the first to know that we are getting married. Johnny's jaw fell to the floor. Once he collected himself, he asked, "When?" We told him we'd set May 26 as the date, and I would give anything to have a photograph of that moment. Neither Johnny nor I could afford a $1,000 loss, so I gave him immediate relief by exposing the ruse: he had been set up from day one. It was like a big Christmas present for the Doyles. I should have also bet that our marriage would last longer. I would have won that one, too.

It has been dream-like ever since. The twenty years I waited for Jo's hand were so worthwhile. We had a dazzling honeymoon in the South Pacific Islands of Moorea, Vahini, and Bora Bora before returning home to face life's realities. Tragic and joyous events exploded all around us; 9/11 hit less than four months after our wedding. Jo was in the car on her short drive to work when she heard the news, and I was home when my son called from San Diego. "Turn on the television," he said. "It's really bad." The incident took on a meaning that would haunt us all for the rest of our lives.

Jo and I shared life's joys as well as its inevitable tragedies. We were together to grieve the deaths of both of our mothers and fathers, but we have also been together for the births of our seven grandchildren and two great-grandchildren.

Jo retired from real estate in 2006, just as the first cracks in the booming real estate market began to portend a major downturn. Her retirement party and the gift of a new car were well-earned rewards for her thirteen years with Pacific Communities Builder. The timing was fortuitous; her dad grew sick, and she was able to be there at his side in Indiana when he passed.

Jo and I went on to travel well over a million miles together with the team, allowing us to see family in Indianapolis, Cleveland, Chicago, Memphis, Oklahoma City, Orlando, and Washington, DC. We exercised our passion for Broadway theater when the team visited New York City twice a year. *Hamilton, Book of Mormon, Phantom of the Opera, The Producers,* and *Wicked* provided joyous nights at the theater. We had our favorite dinner haunts all over the league: Bohanan's in San Antonio, Osteria al Doge in NYC, St. Elmo's in Indianapolis, Prime 112 in Miami, Murray's in Minneapolis, Marble Room in Cleveland,

Gibson's in Chicago, Union Oyster House in Boston, Frank Fats in Sacramento, Bourbon Steak in Washington, DC, Arnaud's French 75 in New Orleans, Ristorante Sotto Sotto in Toronto, Harris's Restaurant in San Francisco, Pat's Steaks in Philadelphia, Itta Bena in Memphis, Elway's in Denver, Kres Chop House in Orlando, Meso Maya Comida y Copas in Dallas, Regina Pizza in Boston, and Giordano's Pizza in Chicago. We pretty much ate our way through the league each year. We had many a happy evening at these spots while on the road, often with members of our Fox Sports TV crew.

Traveling with Jo was absolutely the best. Sometimes our schedule was just: plane, bus, hotel, bus, game, bus, plane to next town, etc. Other times we would make the very most of a day or two off. We did all the touristy things, like exploring Dealey Plaza in Dallas, the Alamo in San Antonio, the Cowboy Museum in Oklahoma, the monuments and the Smithsonian in Washington, Fifth Avenue in NYC, the Loop in Chicago, Estes Park in Colorado, the State Capitol in Sacramento, the steps to the Art Museum in Philly, the Peabody Hotel and Graceland in Memphis, the Tabernacle in Salt Lake City, Bourbon Street in New Orleans, and Beale Street in Memphis, and, of course, riding the Hansom cabs through Central Park.

Our time on the road was easier and less stressful than at home. While traveling, it would typically be a ten-minute bus ride from our hotel to the arena, whereas it took us an hour to get to Staples from our first home together in Laguna Niguel, a frightful two hours when we lived in La Quinta, and a full hour to an hour and a quarter after our return to Marina Del Rey. The move to the desert was foolhardy, in retrospect. I was in my late sixties and anticipating retirement. Still, it was a great spot to be in after fifteen wonderful years in Orange County. I was coming off of my prostate cancer surgery, but family and friends pitched in to help with the move. We were thinking winters in the desert and summers in Oregon. That was the plan, anyway. I figured we could handle that drive for a season, or two at the most before retiring, but it wound up being six or seven years.

We moved to the Marina in 2013 and signed a six-month lease with every intention of retiring at season's end. Jo would walk the beach almost daily. We could walk to good restaurants, the supermarket, our dentist, and even the team doctor, who became our trusted family physician. The Marina was a special place to live, and our lifestyle was extraordinary. We were invited to so many special events, including a night honoring two iconic legends: UCLA's famed basketball coach John Wooden, and the Dodgers' brilliant Vin Scully. Another night, we helped honor two Hall of Fame hoopers from UCLA: Ann Meyers and Bill Walton.

Jo was such an avid fan of the Clippers, and now she had plenty to cheer about. The road games were a little more difficult for her, as she was seated with fans from the opposing team; she had to strive to contain herself during games. But at Staples Center, she could let it all hang out. We would arrive at the arena two or three hours before game time. I would be busy right up until airtime, but Jo and I would share dinner in the media dining room, home and away (we discovered that the Detroit Pistons served the best pre-game meals in the NBA, no contest). I would try to find a minute or two to share with her before I went on the air. She would always ask, "Are we going to win?" It was just comforting to touch bases with her before going live.

As we aged, Jo and I realized more and more that life is all about shared experiences, and we worked hard to find special people and places. NBA travels provided ample opportunities. Jo joined me on our trips to Japan, Russia, China (twice), and Mexico City. We also took full advantage of the off-season to explore new destinations, including a peaceful trip down the Danube through Europe. We've spent many summer days exploring the wonders of Central Oregon. We love Hawaii and have been to all the major islands. How lucky we are to have traveled to the UK, France, Italy, Japan, China, Russia, Spain, Belgium, Australia, New Zealand, the South Pacific, Mexico, Canada, Puerto Rico, and the Caribbean. Wow. What a life!

Epilogue

The Homestretch

WE DID NOT KNOW WHAT TO EXPECT when the basketball season began without us in 2019. I was preparing for some major withdrawals. Jo and I decided that the best means of compensating would be to remain busy when training camps were opening in late September. That month, after my Naismith Memorial Basketball Hall of Fame induction, the family joined us on a trip to Boston together to share one of our favorite NBA towns.

Jo and I went on to travel the Eastern seaboard from Maine to the Florida Keys. We never had time to even think about the Clippers flying off to Hawaii for the opening of training camp without us. Fun and adventure filled the month including stops along the way to visit with family and friends. Our final stop was Chicago where we were to fly home to Bend, Oregon. Bad weather cancelled all late night flights out of O'Hare. We were re-booked on an early morning departure to Oregon. Area hotels coincidently raised their prices to the chagrin of some weary travelers. I was not inclined to pay four hundred dollars for three hours of rest in a hotel room. A trip that began in the bright spotlight of the Naismith Memorial Basketball Hall of Fame in Springfield, Massachusetts, ended with us spending the night stretched out on a rock-hard bench in the terminal at O'Hare International Airport in Chicago. Life does have a way of keeping us humble. We arrived home the next day and that truly marked our first day of retirement.

266 FORTY YEARS IN THE NBA

The NBA had provided us with NBA League Pass, and that helped us keep track of what was going on around the league. We seldom missed a Clipper game; Jo was pleasantly insistent that we watch them. Oddly, I was not missing the job I had loved since 1978. We enjoyed the games on TV. I spent most of my time critiquing the announcers; some were very good and some not very good. I especially enjoyed Marv Albert (TNT), Mike Breen (ESPN), and Kevin Calabro (Portland) on television, as well as Al McCoy (Phoenix), Mark Boyle (Indianapolis), Chuck Swirsky (Chicago), Sean Grande (Boston) and Tom McGinnis (Philadelphia) on radio. Jo would always toss in a "Lawler's Law" reference when appropriate, as well as an occasional "oh me, oh my."

We agreed that what we missed most was our association with the people in the Clipper family. We had been with that group from the opening of training camp in Honolulu through the final game of the post-season. We'd been together after the greatest of wins, as well as the most crushing of defeats. We spent time together on airplanes, buses, and even a few trains between Philadelphia and New York.

The long list included Doc Rivers and his entire coaching staff. The names Mike Woodson, Armond Hill, and Sam Cassell immediately come to mind, along with longtime trainer Jason Powell; chiropractor extraordinaire Dennis Collonello; team physicians Dr. Steve Krems and Dr. Steven Shimoyama and his family; PR head Chris Wallace; basketball boss Lawrence Frank; business president Gillian Zucker; the personable and approachable owner Steve Ballmer; superfans Billy Crystal, James L. Brooks, and James Goldstein; trusted security guys Bob Picker and Hector Ramirez; broadcast partner Brian Sieman; Nick Davis and Sara Takata of Fox; stage managers Donna Moskal and Dean Benson; longtime stat man Norm Peters; sideline reporters Kristina Pink and Jaime Maggio; pre-game host Jeanne Zalasko; TV partners Corey Maggette and Don McLean; and all the ushers and arena security people at Staples and around the league who always made me and Jo extra comfortable. These people were all our friends. The bond of being with a team ties tightly, and we miss every single one of those people. We also miss the fans.

None of this would have been possible without my dear, sweet Jo. We have missed countless birthdays, anniversaries, and holidays because of our basketball travels. No more. I will be there for Jo and our family for the rest of my days, just as they were always there for me through my forty-year run with the Clippers.

We just keep on keeping on.

Afterword

by Doc Rivers

I HAVE KNOWN RALPH for a long time, dating back to my play-ing days in Atlanta in the 1980s. Our relationship reached a new level in 1991, when I was traded to the L.A. Clippers. We always enjoyed sharing our thoughts about basketball, life, and family.

I went from playing to working in television, and worked a few Clipper games as Ralph's analyst. That exposed me not only to his knowledge of the game but also his impressive work ethic. He came prepared each and every night. My career carried me to working games on TNT, and then on to coaching when I got the call to be head coach of the Orlando Magic in 1999. I would see Ralph, in person, twice a year over my seasons with Orlando and then Boston. I would see him much more often on television as I reviewed video tapes. It remained apparent that his willingness to work had not waned over the years. He was not only on top of the action as a play-by-play man, but his infectious enthusiasm consistently made the games fun to watch.

I respected Ralph's understanding of the game. When the Clippers came to Boston to meet the Celtics in the middle of the 2007–2008 season, Ralph and I had our usual pre-game conversation to catch-up on each other's life. We had a very good team, but I was looking to add some depth. It was common knowledge that Sam Cassell of the Clip-pers wanted to finish his career with a contender. I asked Ralph what he thought about Sam at that late stage of the player's career. He gave me a very favorable assessment, and that acted as confirming evidence of what we thought.

Sam was soon bought out of his Clipper contract, and the Celtics jumped on the chance to sign him once he cleared waivers. Cassell gave us the valuable limited minutes we needed at the point guard position and was an important part of our 2008 NBA Championship. He has served me as a trusted assistant coach in Los Angeles and Philadelphia since 2014. Ralph's support earns him an assist.

I spent seven years in Los Angeles as coach of the Clippers, and Ralph was the team's broadcaster for the first six of those years. That's when I spent the most time with him, and learned even more about his character and professionalism. We worked together on a segment for the team's pre-game television show, which was called *The DOCtrine*. It was just Ralph and me for about ten minutes prior to each televised game. We must have done well over 400 of those interviews over the years. It seems we talked about almost everything—yes, basketball, but also life, family, politics, philosophy, and our diverse sports interests.

I do a lot of interviews in my line of work, and they're often redundant and boring. Not with Ralph. He worked hard to find diverse topics for discussion. He never tried to put me on the spot, but he found ways to ease me through some awkward and revealing topics. In a word, it was a pleasure. Ralph has a great sense of the history of the game of basketball and the NBA as a league. We enjoyed talking about the old days, as well as debate the future of the sport. We had a unique situation with the Clippers.

In 2013, Ralph came up to me the day I was announced as head coach of the team. He told me that he was thinking about retiring. He mentioned that his wife, Jo, had been traveling with the team for the past several seasons and wondered if I would be comfortable with that if he returned. I assured him that it would not be a problem. Happily, he stayed around for six more years, and I got to know Ralph and his wife much better. Jo was a fixture with the team; she and Ralph would be there, in the second-to-last row of our charter airplane, each and every day and night. It was always a nice break from watching video and game-planning in the coaches' section to come back and visit with both of them.

We also enjoyed dinners together on the road, including one memorable meal in Cleveland during his final season. The big concern he expressed that night was the identity of his replacement the following season. He and I were both hoping that the team's radio announcer, Brian Sieman, would get the call. Ralph was worried that the delay in making the announcement did not bode well for Brian—another example of Ralph's sense of loyalty to the team and his friend. Brian did get the job after all, and I worked my final season in Los Angeles with him. There will never be another Ralph, but Brian Sieman is doing a great job.

I worked a few years on national TV broadcasts, and it is an entirely different animal from being a team broadcaster. Ralph understood the difference. There was never a question that he was the team's announcer, but viewers could never question his objectivity. He enjoyed great plays and performances by opposing team members, as well as those by the Clipper players. He could handle it when a Clipper player was having a bad night. Ralph never trashed the players, but was there to help the fans put a player's bad night into hopeful perspective. He could adeptly put high and low moments in a historical light, because he had been there through so much of the league's history.

I still stay in touch with Ralph to this day. He remained a loyal supporter after I left his beloved team, and I miss seeing him along the NBA trail. It really seems odd to watch video of Clipper games and not hear his rich baritone voice calling the plays. He was a great part of the fabric of the Clipper franchise for so many years. I was with him the day they placed his star on the Hollywood Walk of Fame in 2016. It was richly deserved. I am thrilled that he was given the ultimate honor by the Naismith Memorial Basketball Hall of Fame in 2019. I hope he enjoys retirement as much as NBA fans enjoyed his career.

Acknowledgments

MY CAREER SPANNED SIXTY YEARS. It involved broadcasting games on radio or television for seven different professional teams and an even larger number of college teams. I broadcast all the major sports, from the NFL and MLB to the NHL and NBA. I called sports as varied as auto racing, boxing, and pro box lacrosse. It was an adventure that took me all over the world.

I always felt that I had a book in me. Frankly, I had no idea how to get it out.

A very special thanks goes to publisher Jeffrey Goldman and Santa Monica Press for having faith in me and my story. Thanks also to co-author Chris Epting, who helped guide me through one chapter and on to the next.

This story would never have been worth writing without the unending love and support of my wife, Jo. She has been with me through my forty years with the Clippers. She was there to keep me on track, and without her, my broadcast career would have ended before the team had even made the move to Los Angeles in 1984.

Irv Kaze was my special angel. His career included front office posts with teams in the National Football League, Major League baseball, the American Basketball Association, and the NBA. He hired me to broadcast games for three different teams in three different leagues. Irv was a great mentor and friend. I am beyond grateful for his vision, guidance, and support.

Hall of Fame basketball player and broadcaster Bill Walton has been a close ally along the way. He opened my eyes and expanded my horizons. He has been as great a friend as any man could ever hope to have.

Professor Henry VanderHeyden at Bradley University in Peoria, Illinois, saw promise in me that I did not know existed. He showed me the path to a career that engulfed parts of seven decades. Hank's imprint on my career is indelible.

My final years with the Clippers were elevated by the inspiration of team owner Steve Ballmer and the support of the team's president

272   BINGO! FORTY YEARS IN THE NBA

of business operations, Gillian Zucker. My only regret when I left in 2019 was that they had not taken over the team ten or fifteen years earlier. The same feelings go to the team's chief communications officer, Chris Wallace.

Thanks to all the believers and even to the doubters I have encountered along the way.

It has been the ride of a lifetime. I am so grateful to be able to share it with you in the pages of this book.

—Ralph Lawler

WHEN I FIRST MOVED to Southern California in the mid-1980s from New York, where I had grown up, one of the first things I wanted to do was go watch some professional basketball. Going to see the Lakers was not an option. Anyone who has been raised a Knicks fan understands what I'm talking about. So I bought myself a ticket, went down to the old Sports Arena, and watched the Clippers take on the Atlanta Hawks. It was a good experience. The arena felt funky and lived in, the sightlines were amazing, and the fans seemed blue-collar and knowledgeable in a way that this East Coast fan could appreciate.

Thus began my relationship with the Los Angeles Clippers. It was certainly tough for many years as they remained the laughingstock throughout the league, but during it all, there was somebody who got us through. Ralph Lawler. His professionalism, knowledge of the game, and performance style were all things I loved from the very beginning.

Over time, the Clippers finally began to steal some thunder in town and it was a joy to listen and watch Ralph finally have the chance to broadcast on the behalf of a winning team. It's been an absolute honor and privilege to work with Ralph on his memoir. He brought the same professionalism and preparation to this project as he always did in the broadcast booth, making this one of the most enjoyable writing experiences of my life. Thank you, Ralph.

Thanks as well to Jeffrey Goldman for thinking of me on this project and for always being a terrific editor, publisher, and most importantly, friend.

—Chris Epting